Other Sports Classics from Fireside Books:

Five Seasons by Roger Angell
My Turn at Bat by Ted Williams with John Underwood
A Handful of Summers by Gordon Forbes
A False Spring by Pat Jordan
A Donald Honig Reader by Donald Honig
Heaven is a Playground by Rick Telander
Dock Ellis in the Country of Baseball by Donald Hall with Dock Ellis
Dollar Sign on the Muscle by Kevin Kerrane
Veeck as in Wreck by Bill Veeck with Ed Linn
The Hustler's Handbook by Bill Veeck with Ed Linn
Run to Daylight! by Vince Lombardi with W. C. Heinz

SUNDAY
DRIVER

BROCK YATES

A Fireside Book ▪ Published by Simon & Schuster Inc.

New York　　London　　Toronto　　Sydney　　Tokyo

Fireside
Simon & Schuster Building
Rockefeller Center
1230 Avenue of the Americas
New York, New York 10020

First Fireside Edition 1990

Published by arrangement with
Farrar, Straus & Giroux

FIRESIDE and colophon are registered trademarks
of Simon & Schuster Inc.

Designed by Barbara Marks Graphic Design
Manufactured in the United States of America

10   9   8   7   6   5   4   3   2   1

Library of Congress Cataloging-in-Publication Data

Yates, Brock W.
    Sunday driver / Brock Yates.—1st Fireside ed.
        p.   cm.—(Fireside sports classic)
    "A Fireside book."
    Reprint. Originally published: New York : Farrar, Straus and Giroux,
1972.
    1. Yates, Brock W.   2. Automobile racing drivers—Biography.
3. Automobile racing—History.   I. Title.   II. Series.
GV1032.Y37A37   1990
796.7'2'092—dc20
[B]   89-39937
                                                                                          CIP

ISBN 0-671-66826-9

TO SALLY

SUNDAY
DRIVER

1

▗▖▗▖▗▖▗▖▗▖▗▖

The helmet bag does it every time. There you are, striding around in public places, holding this black vinyl satchel with BELL HELMETS printed on its flanks in blazing red letters, and people automatically think that you are a very tough stud indeed. A Bell helmet bag is one of those arcane symbols of automotive macho that mean so much to Americans, like the guys who drive around in MG Midgets and Austin Healey Sprite sports cars with the bare spars of their convertible tops elevated to look like roll bars, or who mount surfboards on their panel trucks or ski racks on their Porsches while living in Grand Island, Nebraska. So you fly across the United States and stand around in the open portals of the Ontario, California, airport, in there with the lean, watery-eyed nouveau-hillbillies who increasingly dominate the Golden State's destiny, with your Bell helmet bag, and if you look taciturn enough, people will sure as hell think you are a race driver. The balding young night clerk at the Avis counter finally asked me, "Excuse me, sir, are you a driver? I mean, a *race* driver?"

I should have been ready with some kind of witty but thoroughly ambiguous answer. I wasn't. "Er, ah, you see it's like this..., " I mumbled.

"Well, they're testing over at the Speedway, and I thought possibly..., " he countered, trying to let me off the hook.

"Oh, yeah. No, I'm not testing. But maybe, just maybe, in a couple of days I can answer your question." I thought that might pass as a sufficiently woolly reply and strode into the darkness to find my rental Galaxie, or as they are more commonly called in racing circles, "rent-a-racers," or "U-wreck-ems." It was a stifling, midsummer night in the Ontario desert, and as I moved into traffic with the Ford's air conditioning humming furiously, I mused about the guy back at the Avis counter and his instant recognition of the helmet bag. I felt sorry that I hadn't been able to reply, "Yeah, I'm Jackie Stewart, and I've been in Samoa for a welcome-home party for Amelia Earhart. Everybody was there, Sophia, Jackie and Ari, Princess Grace, Dick and Liz, Hef and Barbie, the President of France, Picasso, the U.N. General Assembly: the same old crowd. These weekends are getting to be a bore. Keep this quiet, but tomorrow I'm going to test a secret race car designed by Howard Hughes for the CIA. The computers say it will lap Ontario at three hundred seventeen miles per hour." I wish I could have said something like that. I wish I could have at least said I was a race driver, *any* race driver, because to people at Avis counters race drivers are very mysterious and romantic people. Their lives are filled with glamour and danger. Unlike conventional jocks, who tend to sell aluminum siding and give canned speeches to parochial-school athletic banquets in the off-season, race drivers never shuck their image when they leave the stadium. They are supposed to be zany, nomadic soldiers of fortune who are involved in wild endeavors during every waking moment. This, of course, is positively subversive to the establishment sports writers, who feverishly nourish the fable that every Major-

Leaguer-All-Pro-Superstar is just like you and me or the kid next door, who made it, thanks to tireless practice, clean living, and rigid devotion to the American way of life. This egalitarian fantasy is natural enough in a culture so firmly opposed to elitism, and the doyens of its sporting press cannot tolerate racing simply because they can't find anybody in the sport who dovetails with their hackneyed stereotypes. After all, how in hell can you explain to American youth why apparently normal guys like A. J. Foyt and Jackie Stewart are always leaving the wife and kids to fly all over the damn world to risk their asses in speeding automobiles? Everybody in the daily press, from Red Smith to the Vatican's *L'Osservatore*, has denounced racing as the domain of death-hungry lunatics. The late John Lardner, son of the great Ring, probably fired the most colorful, if not the most accurate, shot several years ago when he called race drivers "motorized lemmings." I remember as a kid reading that crack in *Newsweek* and being infuriated.

Something had gone wrong with my youth. While I maintained an acceptable level of enthusiasm for conventional games, my first love was automobile racing. My grandfather had taken me to a race at the Niagara County fairgrounds in Lockport, New York, in 1946. I can remember sitting in the cavernous grandstand and looking down on the glistening single-seaters parked on the red clay track. Drivers in white shirts and pants lounged against their machines, smoking cigarettes and joking prior to the race. The strident beat of Sousa's "Stars and Stripes Forever" was pounding out of the loudspeakers. I grew up dreaming of the day when I would tour the country, towing my lacquered and chromed, Kurtis-Kraft, Offenhauser race car behind a big station wagon, wearing white duck pants and smoking Camels while John Philip Sousa marches played forever on the radio.

That never happened, primarily because I buckled to the pressures of "good sense" and "responsibility," which sent me off to places like college and the navy instead of the nation's racetracks. But automobiles stayed glued inside my

head. I haven't the vaguest reason why; what particular psychic need caused that distraction to displace more rational—
or at least more conventional—interests. Especially racing
cars, with all the noise and speed and violence they embodied. There's no sense in attempting to skew the thing into the
realm of normalcy, despite a natural urge on the part of us all
to justify our interests and activities in behalf of decency, reason, and the good of mankind. Ripping around a racetrack is
a nutty thing to do. Responsible men have scorned it for
years, and it might be argued that their denouncements will
rise in intensity as technology sanitizes and protects our
lives. On the other hand, the risk of life has always fascinated
men, and whether you choose to explain it on the basis of
everything from arrested development to regressive genes to
death wishes and screwed-up anal compulsions, it is a part of
our experience and in my opinion, will remain so as long as
we walk the face of the earth. It was inevitable that this flaw
in my senses would somehow meld with my interests in jour-
nalism. If the middle-class magnetism toward career and family was too strong for me, at least I could write about racing
cars. That I did, for a variety of motoring journals, until 1964,
when I became part of a tiny, noisy, iconoclastic collection of
car freaks who were producing *Car and Driver*—a magazine
that, I will unabashedly brag, we turned into one of the
brightest, toughest, most articulate special-interest periodi-
cals ever published.

I managed some sporadic, low-key, amateurish forays into
racing during that time, but more important, *Car and Driver*
permitted me to meet and to know a number of the men who
had been my boyhood heroes. For the first time, they appeared as real people, rather than distant forms strutting on a
starting grid or hunched and helmeted deep inside their
shiny, speeding machines. I found that they were—and are—
an amazingly diverse collection, defying general stereotypes
of social strata and personality, although the European road
racers tend to be slight, intense men from wealthy, upper-
class families, while the Americans are generally husky,

open-faced, John Wayne–types from the farms and small towns of middle America. But they are bound together— French aristocrat and Hoosier jalopy jockey alike—by a pair of common traits: powerful, overwhelming, sometimes oppressive egos and an urge to compete that is so intense, according to a study by a team of Southern California psychologists, that they make pro football players seem like pussycats by comparison.

And there is their pride and sense of independence. I recall sitting in my New York apartment with the late Ken Miles, arguing over his right to die. A skinny, high-strung Englishman in his middle forties, who could discourse in depth on a variety of subjects from opera to watchmaking, Miles had steadfastly maintained that if he wanted to do himself in behind the wheel of a racing car, it was nobody else's damn business. I had argued that such an act was beyond his control, simply because the welfare of the sport demanded that his life be preserved regardless of what he wanted. The stigma of needless death hampered the growth of racing, I had said. While agreeing in principle that driver fatalities hurt racing, he would not budge in his contention that society had no right whatsoever to govern his destiny, provided he did not intrude on the rights of others. He was never refuted. Within two months after that conversation, Ken Miles was killed in a high-speed crash at Riverside, California.

I had been with Mario Andretti as he stood in a high-ceilinged garage outside Le Mans prior to the twenty-four-hour race and had commented on the death of a pair of his friends in a single sprint car smashup. Someone had suggested that they had been veteran drivers, not known for the kind of rash stunts that might cause such an accident. "Before the race, we all talk good sense. Then we go out and do foolish things," Mario had said softly.

Foolish things. No one in racing is immune, despite repeated efforts to housebreak the heroes with strained testimony that they are in reality cautious, gentle fellows with no more brashness or lust for action than your average certified public accountant. The traditional standard-bearer for decency and good sense in racing has been Dan Gurney. Surely no race driver has had a more all-American image than Gurney, whose chiseled good looks and sportsmanship have made him one of the most admired and respected personalities in the history of the sport. At one point, his press was so good, his reputation as a clean liver so unblemished, that a few members of the press began to refer cynically to him as "America's Sweetheart." Men like Gurney are always being quoted in potboiler magazine and newspaper stories to the effect that fast driving is reserved for the racetrack, and only the most prudent, cautious methods dare be used on the public highways. Like the old kids' con that Babe Ruth always ate his spinach, it has been a part of American sports lore that racing drivers use great care on the highway. They are always being credited with earnest inanities such as, "I save my speed for the racetrack," and "I feel safer driving in the Indy 500 than taking a Sunday drive with my family." Sure. And Babe Ruth never drank anything stronger than milk and Mickey Mantle never swung at anything beside a baseball. It might be speculated that approximately 90 percent of all that is written about sports personalities is either outright lies or wild distortion, and this is certainly the case with the way race drivers drive, including gentlemen like Dan Gurney.

It was a rainy day, on a wide, water-shiny side street in Santa Ana, California. We were returning from lunch, headed toward Gurney's All-American Racers shop, where his well-known Eagle racing cars were being built. Gurney was at the wheel of a new Imperial Brougham sedan, owned by Max Muhleman, AAR's general manager. Max and I were lounging in the soft, leathery expanses of the Imperial's backseat. Up front was Swede Savage, Dan's shaggy-blond young protégé.

We were chatting quietly, letting the big car hiss through the drenching rain, when the conversation veered to Curtis Turner, a spectacular, freewheeling Southern stock-car hero. Now Curtis Turner stories concerning his parties, his driving, and his mad flying feats are etched into racing lore. Gurney, the apple-pie hero, and Turner, the boozy hell-raiser, had raced each other once, in a 500-mile stock-car race at Riverside, California, and people are still talking about the way those two masters flung their Ford stock cars around that tricky road course, far outdistancing the competition. Out of their struggle on the track had developed a strong mutual admiration, although their divergent lifestyles and geographic separation prevented anything that could be described as a meaningful friendship. Gurney enjoyed listening to Max and me retell Turner adventures, and as we slipped along in the Imperial, the talk turned to Turner's uncanny skills as a whiskey hauler, including his mastery of the bootleg turn, a high-speed, 180-degree loop intended to elude revenue agents' roadblocks.

"How in hell do you do a bootleg turn?" asked Gurney rather sheepishly, punctuating his question with a nervous chuckle.

Max feigned amazement. "Wait a minute! You mean to tell me, Gurney, that you've been going around acting like one of the top racing drivers in the world and you don't know how to execute a simple thing like a bootleg turn? God, I sure hope Curtis never hears about this!"

Savage and I joined in a chorus of laughter.

"No, I'm not kidding. I never tried one," said Gurney earnestly.

"It's dead simple," said Max, his North Carolina drawl still strong despite his long residence in California. "All you've gotta do is throw the wheel over and hit the hand brake."

"I've seen Curtis put two rows of Coke bottles twelve feet apart and spin a Coupe deVille Caddy between 'em without touching a thing," I said. "In fact, Curtis told me when he was a kid, he could spin a half-ton truck loaded with liquor on a one-lane bridge and never touch the sides." It was more than Gurney could stand. "Dammit, if Curtis can do it, I can do it," he said with an edge on his voice. Dan hunched forward in the Imperial's seat, setting his jaw. "All you've got to do is throw the wheel over and punch the hand brake, you say?"

"If an old Southern boy like Turner can do it, you ought to be able to pull it off," Max said. The needle struck a nerve.

The Imperial was gliding along through the rain, silent except for the muffled thump of its windshield wipers. The road ahead was deserted, and Gurney stabilized the car at 40 mph. "O.K., here goes," he mumbled, spinning the steering wheel to the left. Now a proper bootleg turn requires a snap movement to catapult the rear end around on the car's axis, but Gurney's steering input was slow and hesitant, causing the sedan to merely slew off course and head for the opposite shoulder. It rumbled off the road in an absurd, mud-flinging slide and headed straight at a Cyclone fence. Only frantic, last-second corrections by Gurney arced the car away from the barrier and sent it bucking back onto the highway. The car was filled with laughter. "That's just great, Gurney! Wait till Curtis hears about this. No, in fact, I'd be ashamed to tell him," Max shouted in mock disgust.

Gurney, a kind of little-boy leer on his face, was rising to the occasion. With the gibes of his friends pounding in his ears, he resumed speed with the Imperial and tried again. Once more the monster car refused to change course quickly enough and blundered off onto the shoulder. More laughter. More resolve in Gurney. Four more tries were equally disastrous, and Dan's ire was rising. Now we knew that it might take three days, but we would stay in that car, day and night, until Gurney executed a bootleg turn. Suddenly it dawned on Max that it was *his* car that was absorbing the punishment of Gurney's practice, and he began to make conciliatory sounds. The rest of us understood only too well that Gurney would never quit until he'd mastered the feat, and our needling slowly melted into silent rooting, based on the simple understanding that the sooner Dan solved the problem, the sooner we could get back to what we had been doing before lunch.

Gurney lashed along the back streets of Santa Ana, coming closer to executing a genuine bootleg. Finally, on a broad street bordered by a low yellow-brick factory on one side and the Briggs Cunningham Automotive Museum on the other, Gurney looped the big car perfectly, spinning it in its tracks, pointing it directly back whence it came and into the bulging eyes of a terrified man in a Volvo sedan who'd been following behind.

Both machines stopped well short of a collision, but the unsettling sensation of seeing a sedate maroon Imperial Brougham spin around in the road in front of him prompted the man in the Volvo to lean on his horn with a combined look of horror and outrage on his scarlet face. Gurney, jubilant over his feat, whipped the Imperial back into the proper lane and accelerated away, presenting the poor man in the Volvo with a wide grin and the finger as he sped into the gloom.

Driving from the Ontario airport, headed for the mass-cult comfort of a Holiday Inn, I pondered men like Gurney, certainly a giant not only within his chosen sport, but perhaps a unique example of *Homo sapiens* as well. What is there about this misunderstood sport that attracts and fascinates men? Certainly it is more than shrieking along a stretch of macadam at 200 mph. There may be a nub of truth somewhere in racing, perhaps brighter and harder—but more cleverly concealed—than much of what we find in other phases of life. Its truth may be much too harsh and simple for today, when we seem to find solace in complication, but nonetheless it appears worth searching for, if for no other reason than to determine why strong, essentially happy individuals like Mario Andretti and Dan Gurney bolt themselves into hot and hostile metal containers and race each other, perhaps accidentally, to the death. Tomorrow, if all went according to a rather uncertain plan, I might begin to find out.

"We are men playing little boys' games," the great pro quarterback Fran Tarkenton had once mused to me. That is true of major-league football—all big-time stick-and-ball sports, for that matter—and it makes them easier to write about. Every sportswriter, no matter how paunchy or fumble-footed, can identify, in the context of childhood memories, with the pain and punishment and the moments of triumph on conventional fields of play. Not so with racing, where the environment of a fuming, noise-racked car cockpit is foreign to normal experience. The void between the press box and the racetrack is broader than the imagination. I felt that I had written about motor racing with a certain clarity, that my reporter's role had adequately been filled. But my involvement had been that of an observer, not a participant. In the end, the pitiful question, "How was it out there?" is the only flimsy bridge between the drivers and the writers. It is too weak to be crossed. It became more and more obvious that if I was to make any personal conclusions about driving a racing car, I could not depend on secondary sources. I would have to do it myself.

There were a variety of avenues open. While I wanted to participate in the most difficult and challenging kind of racing available, certain levels of the sport were beyond my immediate capabilities. Indianapolis would take several years of hard racing before it could even be considered as a goal. No one in Grand Prix racing would trust a novice like myself with a car. The same would be true in Can-Am and Grand National stock-car racing, where the ultra-high-speed competition would make me a hazard, both to myself and others. But the Trans-Am seemed reasonable. A series for the so-called American "sporty" cars—Camaros, Mustangs, Javelins, Barracudas, Challengers, etc.—it was a rugged league peopled by such stars as Mark Donohue, George Follmer, and Peter Revson at the wheels of some very rapid automobiles. They would be competing on such famous race circuits as Watkins Glen, Riverside, Michigan International Speedway, and Elkhart Lake. The cars were big boys' machines, with 450–475 horsepower engines and top speeds over 170 mph. But they were safe and strong, and of all the so-called "big-time" racing vehicles, they seemed to be the most feasible for me to drive. I made an arrangement with Warren Agor, a Rochester, New York, driver and car owner who campaigned in the Trans-Am, to race his second-team Camaro at Watkins

Glen and Michigan International. But one does not merely appear at a Trans-Am and hope to compete. I had not been in a race car in four years, and my competitor's license had expired. That would mean requalifying to the satisfaction of the Sports Car Club of America, the organization that sanctions the Trans-Am. The officials determined that a course at Bob Bondurant's high-performance driving school at the Ontario Motor Speedway, plus participation in an amateur, regional SCCA event, would be necessary before I could try the Trans-Am. If I passed those two tests satisfactorily, then my license would be reissued. Therefore, I had traveled to Ontario to begin with Bondurant in the morning. Hopefully, passing grades would open the way for a rush journey back to upstate New York for an SCCA Regional the following weekend. A young Philadelphia driver named Mike Tillson had bravely offered to let me drive his Lancia sedan at the Glen. If I behaved properly, that would open the door to one of Warren Agor's bright orange Camaros at the Watkins Glen Trans-Am two weeks later. And there was talk of another race at Bridge-hampton in a Datsun 240Z, belonging to *Car and Driver*, prior to the Michigan Trans-Am. But that would all have to wait. First must come school.

2

The Ontario Motor Speedway's main grandstand rose out of the hazy California lowlands like a giant, concrete ziggurat. The Speedway was a massive, severely angled structure that stood among the worldwide bench marks in sporting extravagance, having been built, along with its vast racetrack and elaborate grandstands for something like $25,000,000. It was routinely described as the "Indianapolis of the West," and there were strong similarities to be sure. Its track, a 2.5-mile, low-banked rectangle, was a faithful duplicate of the famed Indiana circuit. Its major race was an annual Labor Day 500-mile event for Indianapolis cars that slavishly copied the traditional Memorial Day race that had been run in Hoosierland for half a century. But the opulence of the place, from its lush VIP suites and thick-carpeted restaurants in the ziggurat, to the ultramodern pit facilities, set it apart from any racetrack in the world. It was auto racing's answer to the Astrodome, and as I approached it, driving through the parched expanses of vineyards above which it had been built, I could not help but be overwhelmed by the boldness of the place—an eloquent expression of the California-developer's syndrome, wherein anything, from the tiniest taco stand to the tallest office building, was erected with a certain zany flair that expressed unabashed optimism, if not good taste.

The morning was cool, and the smog had not yet thickened enough to completely obscure the gray slabs of the San Bernardino Mountains that rose from the valley floor to the north. It was this barrier that placed the Ontario Motor Speedway in the funnel that alternately aimed the powerful Santa Ana winds down into Los Angeles or choked the track with smog. God had intended Ontario to be a fuming, deserted place, and it was only through the sheer perversity of man that he was there at all, much less thriving. When I rolled up to the gate, the track was deserted, save for a few parked cars belonging to the permanent staff. They had been placed near a row of transplanted palm trees in preparation for the murderous heat that would envelop them at midday.

A uniformed guard appeared, smiling. "Good morning. Here on business?" he asked.

"Sort of," I replied. "I'm here for the Bondurant driving school."

He handed me a clipboard holding a daily sign-in log, which I filled out, and he pointed me toward a gaping tunnel that led under the track. I rose up out of the earth in the middle of the infield. An army of sprinklers was spinning water onto acres of new grass, but no one was in sight. I drove toward a cluster of low gray steel buildings that were directly across the track from the ziggurat, buildings known simply as the "garage area": Ontario's version of Indy's legendary "Gasoline Alley."

Big speedways like Ontario, Indianapolis, or Daytona are never deserted. They are too important to the sport they serve to ever shut down completely, and every day, even a lazy midweek one such as this, with the next race over a month away, something of interest had to be taking place. I knew this day would be no different as soon as I spotted a shiny blue truck parked near one of the garages. On its side was painted, in dazzling red and yellow letters, PARNELLI JONES' JOHNNY LIGHTNING SPECIAL. Al Unser's Indy car was inside, the same car that had won two consecutive Indianapolis 500-mile races. Another big truck was parked nearby. There was but one mark on its shiny metal flank, the ubiquitous red oval with the garish letters STP painted inside. That race-car transporter had to be Mario Andretti's. It might be an exciting day at Ontario, with Unser's and Andretti's Indy cars on hand.

I was parking the car when I spotted a small, lean figure walking between a complex of garages. The gait was unmistakable: feet a trifle splayed, weight centered forward on the balls. His eyes were covered by a bulbous, expensive pair of sunglasses, but the flat-nosed profile, topped by a thick swatch of black hair, could only be Mario Andretti's. "Hey, Mario," I called. Most race drivers have public and private nicknames, but Mario is known simply as Mario, except for occasional references as "Super Wop," which obviously nobody uses in his presence. He stopped, turned, recognized me, and gave a diffident half-smile of acknowledgment.

Andretti is one of the good guys in motor racing. An Italian immigrant who reached the United States when he was thirteen years old, he had risen to the top of his sport, having gained fame and vast riches without losing his humanity or humility. His brilliance behind the wheel was obvious, although he had had numerous crashes, literally dozens of metal-shredding crackups, from which he had escaped largely unscathed. People tended to worry about Mario for this reason, but the sport had taken its toll on him in other ways. He had developed two close friends among his fellow drivers. Billy Foster, a wisecracking Canadian, had been killed in a stock car at Riverside. Lucien Bianchi, a quiet Italian, had died in a 200-mph crash at Le Mans. In addition, Mario was one of a pair of twins, both of whom had been driving prodigies around their adopted hometown of Nazareth, Pennsylvania. Aldo, his brother, had been every bit as

good as Mario, in the early days, it is said. Then he had a
serious crash and never regained his touch. But he persisted,
perhaps swept along in the spectacular wake of his brother,
and crashed again in a Midwest sprint car race. He was in the
hospital for months, getting among other things a complete
plastic surgery rebuild on his face. Now Mario and Aldo Andretti don't look like twins anymore.

Mario is constructed in the idiom of European race
drivers. He is slight and wiry, like an oversized jockey. Being
perhaps one of the two or three best-paid athletes in the
world has brought him a private airplane, a personal pilot, a
giant new house on Victory Lane in Nazareth, and a Holly-
wood-sized wardrobe. He had on a sharply cut beige Italian
sport shirt, matching flared slacks, and brown Gucci loafers.
His thin left wrist was covered by a giant chronograph that
looked as if it had been stolen from the instrument panel of
an SST. The ring finger on his left hand held a massive dia-
mond ring in the form of a checkered flag: a ring given only to
winners of the Indianapolis 500—a badge of honor second to
none in the sport.

"What are you doing here?" he asked in a relaxed, dispassionate monotone.

"I ought to ask you the same thing," I said. "Are you and
Al going to test?"

"Yeah, Firestone has the track reserved for this week.
We're testing for the California 500 on Labor Day. Like I said,
what are you doing here?" he asked again.

"Me? Oh, I'm going to do the racer thing a little bit. I'm
going to take a couple of days with Bondurant and his
school."

"Oh, yeah?"

"Yeah, it ought to be fun."

"Yeah."

The conversation was about to lapse into complete silence
when I asked him about his car. Race drivers, good guys, bad
guys, smart ones, stupid ones, almost to a man, find relatively
little reward in talking about things outside their own ken.

The ego drive that thrusts them forward precludes involvement in subjects other than those within the scope of their
own self-interest, so conversations can best be sustained by
keeping them talking about themselves. I asked him about the
car he was going to drive in the test. "This is a new chassis,"
he answered. "It's basically the same car as the old one, but
the tub is a lot more rigid and McGee [Jim McGee, his
boyish-faced chief mechanic with whom Mario had been associated for a number of years] has made a whole bunch of
changes in the suspension and the wing. It's got to be better
than that shit-box we've been running."

The past two seasons had been tough on Andretti. He had
signed to drive, amid great fanfare, with Andy Granatelli, a
promotional genius who was widely regarded within the
inner sanctums of the sport as a showoff who concealed repeated bungling with extravagant broadsides of publicity. It
was a widespread embarrassment to many professional racers
that Granatelli, by dint of advertising and promotional power,
had managed to become a spokeman for the sport in the eyes
of the general public. Andretti, as the consummate pro, had
politely concealed his feelings about Granatelli, but there was
no question that his omission of enthusiasm for his boss implied displeasure. Wins had been scarce, primarily because
Granatelli had contracted with Francis McNamara, an American expatriate living in Germany, to build his Indianapolis
cars. McNamara's specialty was manufacturing Volkswagen-
powered Formula Vee racers, a far cry from the 200-mph machines that run at Indy, and while his selection brought
Granatelli a good deal of publicity, he was simply not prepared to construct a competitive car. In two years, Andretti
had managed to win only a few minor races (excepting Indy
in 1969, when Mario ran his own car under Granatelli's
sponsorship but without Andy's direct supervision). As he
stood there in the Ontario garage area, it was clear that he
was far from happy with his arrangement.

We separated, with Andretti walking off toward the pits
and me heading the few paces toward the crisp, glass-fronted

office mounted with a sign that stated BONDURANT'S SCHOOL OF HIGH PERFORMANCE DRIVING. The furnishings were starkly contemporary, with a large freckled brunette sitting behind a Danish-modern reception desk. One wall was covered with a freestanding bookcase piled with trophies—surely collected during Bondurant's long racing career, both here and abroad. "Bob will be in late this morning," said the brunette, "but Bill Shaw will be working with you, and he'll be here in a few minutes."

I had barely sat down to occupy myself with a gray, dull English motoring magazine when a medium-sized young man opened the door. He was wearing a pair of spotless, sharply creased khaki pants, a dark blue Lacoste pullover, tennis shoes, and Steve Canyon air-force-type sunglasses. His thick, curly hair was cut short, and he carried himself with the jaunty, self-sure bearing of a West Point upperclassman. "Hi, I'm Bill Shaw," he said, extending his hand. His voice was sharp and well-timbred, again very military. "I'm going to be your instructor." His sunglasses were off now, and his eyes were among the levelest I'd ever seen, as if tiny gyroscopes were maintaining perfect equilibrium, compensating for all body movements. He sat there, listening to my reply without visible reaction, then said, "Before we do any driving, let's go through a quick refresher in our classroom. I'm sure you're familiar with a lot of the stuff, but it might be good to go over it again."

At the back of the office was a small room, dominated by a set of shelves that held a collection of orange-painted crash helmets, doubtlessly for use by students. I had brought my own gear: fireproof coveralls, underwear, helmet (in the Bell bag), goggles, etc., so use of the school's equipment would not be necessary. The blackboard contained a number of corner layouts, drawings of various kinds of bends that might be encountered in racing: 90-degrees, decreasing radius, where the corner tightens up from beginning to end, or increasing radius, when the exit of the corner is less tight than at the beginning. Picking up a piece of chalk, Shaw began to talk about "line"—that mysterious course that is the fastest way through a corner. Generally, "line" involves entering a corner on the outside, sweeping to the inside verge, touching what is called the "clipping point," and then accelerating back to the outside on the exit. In this way a curve is turned as much into a straight line as possible. It is a standard racing technique, although its use varies, depending on the kind of corner, or series of corners, to be negotiated.

"We teach smoothness here," Shaw said. "Rough driving tends to be slow driving, and we concentrate on smooth transitions, especially in braking and acceleration. You'll hear me use the word "squeeze" an awful lot in the next few days, both in reference to applying the brakes and applying the power. Smoothness is indispensable in any kind of racing." He stood in front of me, across from a small table with a series of curves outlined on its surface. Pushing a model Ferrari Grand Prix car through the miniature bends, he demonstrated various car behavior characteristics, such as oversteer, where the rear wheels break traction before the front, and understeer, where the front wheels skid before the rear. As his hand swept past, I spotted the lettering on a heavy silver identification bracelet on his right wrist. It read, W. WILBUR SHAW, JR.

"Hey, wait a minute," I interrupted, "was your father...?"

He looked at me with those level eyes. "He sure was," he said proudly.

Wilbur Shaw, Jr.! So that's who this cool kid in the Lacoste shirt was: son of the greatest Indianapolis champion of them all—the man who won three 500's, and very nearly a fourth, a brilliant, colorful hero of the thirties who later became the president of the Indianapolis Motor Speedway before dying in a private-airplane crash in 1954. So this was his son! I'd heard that Wilbur Shaw's only boy was moving in Southern California racing circles, but it never dawned on me that this "Bill Shaw" was the same guy.

I stumbled through a few unconnected testimonies of amazement, which he fielded gracefully. While he had been a

mere lad when his father died, there was an obvious sparkle
of pride in his references to his father. "I was raised partly in
Indianapolis and partly in Arizona, and frankly, racing didn't
mean a great deal to me when I was a kid. Mom and Dad
didn't talk much about it around the house. It was all horses
for me. I spent most of my teens jumping, playing polo,
things like that, and motor racing just didn't enter my mind
until I got into my twenties. Now I'm twenty-four and I dig it
so much I can't stand it."

We talked for a while about how sons of great racing
drivers are attracted to the sport, even when their fathers
have been killed. Alberto Ascari, the former World's Champion and son of the superb Antonio Ascari, followed his father. Both died in racing accidents. Gary and Merle
Bettenhausen, sons of American champion Tony Bettenhausen, race professionally despite their father's death at Indianapolis. Bill Vukovich, the dark-eyed, brooding son of Indy
immortal Bill "the Mad Russian" Vukovich, races as a successful pro despite the shadow of his father that seems to
stalk him everywhere. There were many more of these sons,
some good, some bad, some wildly successful, others, like
Bill Shaw, without a regular ride and passing the time in
other jobs, such as teaching in a race-driving school.

The classroom session ended when Shaw said, "I guess
you know most of this basic stuff anyway. Let's go out and do
a little driving. For the first part we won't even need our
uniforms or helmets." We moved into the merciless glint of
the California morning sun and headed for a garage with
eight automobiles parked diagonally in front of its open
doors. All were painted red with yellow trim—the official
colors of the Bondurant school. At the head of the line were
three boxy Datsun 510 sedans, followed by a pair of Porsche
914/6 roadsters, a Datsun 240Z sports car, a Porsche 911
coupe in complete racing trim, and a tiny, tubular Winkle-
man Formula Ford single-seater.

"Let's try one of the Datsun sedans first, just to get the feel
of things," said Shaw. We picked one of the sedans and

climbed inside. Save for its lack of hubcaps and a flat-black-painted dash, it looked stock. As we untangled the seat belts and shoulder harnesses, an eerie, banshee whoop rolled through the garages. It was an engine—the unmistakable song of a turbocharged Indianapolis Ford V–8 engine. "Mario," I said. "He must be getting ready to begin his test." I started the Datsun, and it blared into life. Its muffler had been removed, and its exhaust note was undernourished but nasty: noise without power. It drowned out the shriek of Mario's Ford for the time being.

Shaw directed me out of the garage area, and we headed across the vast infield toward an expanse of macadam between the third and fourth turns of the big speedway. Ahead I spotted a tiny oval track, perhaps an eighth of a mile, outlined by yellow rubber highway-construction cones. I stopped the Datsun on the outside as Mario moved past on the apron of the big speedway, his engine grumbling at the restraint of a few warm-up laps. He was perhaps two hundred yards away, and his car was a bleached white, without numbers. It was obviously unfinished, without the STP harlot's-vermilion paint that would be applied before its first race.

"O.K., just try a few easy laps. Run slowly, working hard to establish the right line and *squeezing* on the power and brakes. Try for smoothness in everything. No harsh movements if possible," said Shaw. I moved off with the Datsun's impudent exhaust blatting in my ears. The little oval was narrow, and its corners were not constant radius. They could be taken in second gear, while the straights were just long enough to upshift to third for an instant before pumping the brakes and downshifting to second again. I motored around slowly for a few laps, then began to increase speed. Driving under another man's scrutiny is difficult. Suddenly things that have seemed automatic become agonizingly hard. I became conscious that my downshifts were jerky, that I was punching the brakes too hard, that I was charging into the corners too deep, then cramming on the throttle too fiercely. I was not smooth. I was perspiring. Shaw sat there beside me. His face was taciturn. His eyes were hidden behind his Steve Canyon glasses, but I was sure he wasn't impressed. As I spurted down one of the ministraights, a foreign sound burst through the open windows. It was that banshee whoop again, only louder, more resolute. I peeked over my shoulder to catch a glimpse of a white dart sweeping past on the banks of the speedway. Mario had his foot in it, as they say. He powered past us and out of sight, running perhaps 180 mph, compared to our 60 mph.

Shaw told me to stop. "That wasn't too bad, but you were trying too hard. The car movements were jerky. By driving too deep into the corners, you're having to jam the brakes on too hard, and you're getting too wide and scrubbing off too much speed. Let's just sit here for a minute and digest what we've done, then we'll try it some more. Remember, the secret is smoothness."

We sat there, in the middle of the Ontario Motor Speedway, with the thunder of Mario's Ford drumming in our ears and the sun beating down, and talked about driving fast. I went again, and it seemed to be better. We drove the oval in the opposite direction, with Shaw watching every movement, sometimes issuing an instruction or nodding approval or disapproval. We kept going long after Mario had entered the pits and the only sound inside the entire track was the nasty exhaust of our Datsun.

By the time we broke for lunch, the temperature had risen above one-hundred degrees. But there was a breeze moving the dry desert air, and the day was bearable. Shaw and I sauntered out onto the pit lane to take a look at the tire tests. Mario's new car was parked along the low concrete pit wall, and he and his crew, along with a cluster of red-shirted Firestone tire technicians, were watching three burly men unload a shiny, customized Yamaha motorcycle from a battered green pickup. Once the bike was on the ground, one of the trio, lanky, sandy-haired, with high cheekbones, pulled on a pair of leather riding pants, a leather shirt, and a helmet with Iron-

man written on each side. He pumped the kick starter a few times, the unmuffled engine ignited, and he thundered away down the pit lane. Somebody said that he was Lee "Ironman" Irons, a California exhibition rider who had been hired for the prerace show at the California 500, and like Andretti and Unser, was practicing for his part in the festivities.

Ironman rode to the end of the pit lane, which is nearly half a mile in length, and turned around, heading back toward his little cluster of witnesses at full speed. Suddenly he reared back on his seat, tilting the bike on its rear wheel. Maintaining his "wheelie" with the front wheel of the Yamaha pointing at the sky, Ironman zoomed past us and went the entire length of the pit lane before stopping. We were impressed. Then one of his cohorts said, "Hell, he's just warmin' up." Ironman rode back to the pickup, where he jumped off the bike and his friends equipped him with a pair of steel toe guards for his boots and what looked like an old metal tractor seat that they belted to his behind. "Now what the hell is he going to do?" Andretti asked nobody in particular.

Ironman accelerated down the pit lane again, then stopped at the end and turned around. He started back toward us, riding conventionally, then suddenly dropped his feet to the pavement and let the bike slip out from under him. Holding on to the seat, he let himself be dragged along behind the Yamaha with clouds of sparks flying off his steel shoes. "Holy Christ! The guy is nuts!" yelled a Firestone man. "Now watch this," announced one of Ironman's friends. At that moment, the rider reached back, found a grab-bar on the rear fender, and dropped onto the pavement, skating along behind the bike on his steel-shod butt. As he scooted past us, with raucous scraping sounds overpowering the noise of the Yamaha, he turned to his little audience and tossed an audacious wave.

Too much! There we were, in the vast, deserted pits of Ontario, with the sun frying our brains, watching some nut sitting on his ass on the pavement behind a speeding motorcycle. "Now I know why they call the son of a bitch Iron-

man," said somebody. "A guy has to have iron between his
ears to pull a stunt like that," said one of Mario's mechanics.
By then Ironman had somehow hoisted himself back on the
bike and brought it to a stop well down the pit lane. After
making a few adjustments, he restarted his engine and rolled
out onto the wide main straightaway and duplicated his act,
first dropping his feet onto the pavement, then sliding his
posterior down until he was being pulled along behind the
riderless bike. Again he sailed past, running perhaps 50 mph,
and gave us a wave. Only this time there was trouble. About
the time he was waving, the bike slanted slightly to the left,
heading on a course toward the stout concrete retaining wall
that lined the track. Ironman tried to get the bike back on
course, although his only means of control was his handgrip
on the rear fender—hardly a point of maximum leverage. He
managed to get it aimed at the inner wall, every bit as unyielding a barrier, then back again toward the outside. Off he
went down the track with the bike yawing dangerously as the
shower of sparks continued to spew off his backside.

"Oh, oh, this isn't part of the act," somebody said. Now
Ironman had lunged forward, trying to get back up on the
bike's seat, but he had slipped and was being dragged along
the pavement on his knees. "I hope that poor bastard has
steel kneeguards," said a voice. "He hasn't, just plain old
leathers," said another, and we stood there, with our own
kneecaps tingling as we watched the bike drag him maybe a
hundred yards before he got aboard.

Lee "Ironman" Irons rode back to the pickup with his body
rigid, as if he were in great pain. We could see that the knees
of his uniform were ripped away, and the white leather was
stained with blood. He stopped, and his crewmen immediately clustered around him. "Well, I guess we oughta survey
the damage," said Andretti, and everybody followed to look
at Ironman's ruined knees. There were too many people
jammed around by the time I got there, and I made no effort
to elbow my way in. Andretti stepped out of the crowd and
looked at me, feigning that he might throw up, and I knew it

was nothing I was interested in seeing. They loaded Ironman into an ambulance and carted him away, and one of his buddies said, "It isn't anything. He'll be back in a few hours. Hell, two weeks ago they had to drag him out of here with a broken collarbone."

Shaw and I left after that, driving a few miles to have lunch at the Holiday Inn where I was staying. As we arrived, Al Unser and his chief mechanic, George Bignotti, and their crew were about to leave for the track. Unser, a heavy-browed young man whose dainty, pretty-boy face had a perpetual look of innocence, was already dressed in his driver's suit, complete with a layer of fireproof underwear and leather driving shoes that resembled those worn by boxers. Bignotti, a hawk-nosed, friendly Californian who is considered to be one of the best chief mechanics in the world, was dressed like the rest of the crew, in a blue and yellow shirt with JOHNNY LIGHTNING embroidered across the back in large letters. In the old days, uniforms like this were only worn on race day at Indianapolis, but now major teams seldom appear on a racetrack out of uniform. They were a hot pair, Bignotti and Unser, who had teamed up with car owner Parnelli Jones to win back-to-back Indy 500's, plus numerous other championship races in the past two seasons. As they left the Holiday Inn, headed for the tire tests, Shaw and I told them about the recent excitement involving Lee "Ironman" Irons. They listened, amused. Unser shook his head, reflecting on the story. "Them bike guys, they're somthin' else," he said in his New Mexico drawl. "It's like they say, 'No brain, no pain.'"

And then he was gone, to drive 180 mph in the California sunshine.

3

The afternoon session was better. Shaw and I took one of the school's Porsche 914's, a rather boxy, angular roadster that reminded me of a portable radio on wheels, and went to the racetrack proper for some serious work. Ontario's infield road circuit is over three miles in length, which is far too long and too challenging for student drivers, so Bondurant uses two small sections of the big track, one perhaps five-eighths of a mile, which is very twisty and slow, and a larger, faster version about 1.5 miles in length. We had worked on the smaller circuit, trying to smooth out my style. A corner in road racing is generally negotiated by lifting one's foot off the throttle, applying the brakes, blipping the throttle, and downshifting to a lower gear, then gently getting back on the power to guide the machine through the turn. This series of simple hand-foot manipulations can be learned by almost anyone, but melding them into a series of perfectly syncopated motions can be most difficult.

Then there was the "line." Every corner had a fast way through, and deviations from that fast way, or "line," are critical in terms of inches. "Remember, missing the line in one corner will compound itself all the way around the track," said Shaw during a break. "For example, if you are too wide in one turn, that means you will probably be off for the next, simply because you exited too wide and too slow."

So we flung the Porsche around and around the constricted little training course, its tires screeching incessantly, its body tilted over in hard slides, and me inside sawing feverishly on the wheel. We were wearing our fireproof coveralls and helmets, and Shaw sat beside me through it all, looking poker-faced as ever behind the sunglasses. We had stopped from time to time at the trackside to cool off, stripping the sweat-drenched coveralls to the waist and standing in the heat to assess my progress. By the end of the day, I had no idea whether I was improving or getting worse, going faster or slower, being competent or incompetent.

The sun was being sucked into the murk over Los Angeles when I got back to the Holiday Inn. Once inside my room, with the air conditioner droning its best to subdue the heat and rumble of heavy truck traffic on the nearby San Bernardino Freeway, it came to me that I was in a racer's home. They are the Bedouins of sport, these racers, and neatly homogenized compartments such as mine, provisioned with perfectly programed allotments of soap, ashtrays, throwaway plastic glasses, Gideon Bibles, writing portfolios, blurry, bolt-down TVs, towels, blankets, and no-steal coat hangers, serve as their tents during odysseys that often carry them all over Europe and North America. Top-rank drivers like Jackie Stewart fly as much as 400,000 miles a year between races, while plodding second-liners may tow race cars between events to the tune of 100,000 rump-busting miles each season. But drive or fly, big-time or small-time, the destination tends to be the same motels by the same roadsides at the same racetracks.

I stood in the middle of the room, pulling off my clothes.

First came the leather sneakers and athletic socks, both of which reeked with perspiration, then the gritty uniform itself. I became aware of a stinging sensation on my right hand. There, looking red and ugly between my thumb and forefinger, was a broken blister, with a flap of bleached, dead skin hanging loose. It had come from the constant friction of my hand against the spoke of the steering wheel. It hurt. I smiled at my tiny badge of honor and headed for the shower.

In the complicated status measurements of racing, a Holiday Inn is a generally safe middle ground. There is a powerful pecking order in the sport, and a great deal can be told about one's overall position based purely on where he stays at the races. If one is constantly hosteled at an "in" place, where the rates are high and the reservation list is tight, he is likely to be important. If he is staying at an obscure motel or tourist home far away from the track, his status is doubtful. A standard greeting among racing people at the track comes in the form of a brace of questions: "When did you get in?" and "Where are you staying?" The answers are critical. If you reply that you have just arrived on a BOAC flight from London or rolled off a transcontinental TWA "red-eye," the implication is that you are a terribly busy shaker and mover. By contrast, driving your own car from home is hardly worth mentioning. If you are at Indianapolis, for example, and can say that you're staying at the Speedway Motel or the Holiday Inn Northwest, you're golden. The Holiday Inn Northwest, which is about three miles from the track, is "in," while an older Holiday that is practically across from the Speedway's main gate has marginal cachet. The same is true at Daytona, where the Holiday Inn outside the gate used to be important, but has given way to a new Howard Johnson's down the street and to the Carnival or Hawaiian Inn a fair distance away on the beach. From the very top-rank spots, like the Glen Motor Court at Watkins Glen, the Holiday Inn or Griswold's at Ontario, the Marriott in Atlanta, the Ramada at Riverside (now that the aged, tradition-laden Mission Inn has closed), Siebken's at Elkhart Lake, or the Pocono Manor at

Pocono, one must carefully select accommodations in consid-
eration of status. Good chains such as Holidays, HoJos, Ra-
madas, Marriotts, etc., are always acceptable, but cannot
always assure top status, whereas independent motels, tourist homes, or God forbid, the rental of a bed in a private
home, can be socially ruinous. The entire motel syndrome is
carried to absurd extremes at places like the Speedway Motel
in Indianapolis, where reservations are held for years in advance, and only the most important personalities or companies are even considered, and for a minimum stay of the full
month of May, at that. Several years ago, a top film crew,
well-known in the sport, with a proud list of credits, received
a late assignment to cover the Indianapolis 500 and found
that none of the acceptable motels had any rooms left. They
ended up staying in the vacant wing of a new nursing home
and were instantly damned to the bottom of the status ladder.

As I stood there in the shower, sluicing the grit of the Ontario infield off my body, I was comforted in the knowledge
that for the moment at least, my motor-sports social-credibil-
ity quotient was secure. In other rooms of the same motel,
men like Unser and Andretti were tucked away from the sun
and the freeway noise. Their autographed pictures, plus
those of other racing heroes that graced the lobby, insured the
importance of this particular Holiday Inn, at least in the tight,
narcissistic world of racing.

Once, a long time ago, a friend had said, while discussing
a selection of cornball stock-car films with titles such as
Thunder Road and *Thunder in Carolina,* "You know if you
wanted to tell the *real* story of racing, you'd call the damn
movie *Thunder in the Holiday Inn!*" This remark was made
in reference to the Southern stock-car circuit, where the frequency and intensity of motel debauches has reached legendary proportions. The Piedmont Plateau is NASCAR (National
Association for Stock Car Auto Racing) country, where stock-
car racing is a way of life, enjoying larger crowds and a
broader base of interest than even Southeastern Conference
football. In addition to spectacular, blindingly fast, but very

safe competition, stock-car racing has also contributed to the culture a regional exercise known as the "NASCAR Party." A friend of mine described one that took place on a race weekend at the Mark Inn, a hostelry in Atlanta, prior to a big 500-miler at the Atlanta International Speedway. "Me and this other ol' boy had just checked into our room when these other guys came in [the other guys included a prominent millionaire race-car owner and his crewmen, the names of whom have been omitted to protect the guilty], and the first thing they did was order twelve fifths of liquor from room service. Then they sent a guy across the street to a little restaurant for twenty-five bucks' worth of chicken livers. Then four hookers arrived. By the time the night was over, there were fourteen drunk guys, four naked hookers, and the booze and chicken livers, all jammed into that one little motel room.

Wherever the racers go, a certain amount of madness is sure to follow. On race weekends, the area's motels vibrate with a lusty, earthy kind of activity. The cocktail lounge is usually jammed with mechanics, still in smudged white uniforms, who will joke loudly, brag endlessly, drink prodigiously, and brawl occasionally. Up and down the tiers of walkways and corridors, noisy parties swirl from room to room, while in the parking lot someone is invariably smoking the tires of a much-abused "rent-a-racer." Much of what has been written about racing implies that its protagonists are somber, brooding people, perpetually distracted with winning and the specter of death. That is nonsense. Racers for the most part are happy wanderers, with an ability to focus their intense competitiveness in brief spurts at the track. When the racing is over, the fun begins—generally centered around such conventional diversions as women, liquor, and automobiles.

They still talk about the night that Augie Pabst, a fresh-faced heir to the brewing fortune, drove a rented Falcon into the swimming pool of the Mark Thomas Inn in Monterey, California. His reviews were so good that he repeated the act at a Howard Johnson's outside Denver. Others have heaped similar abuses on rental cars: enough to make a multitude of collision repairmen comfortable for life and to cause widespread cardiac arrest among Hertz and Avis executives. They have been raced, wrecked, even rolled and scavenged for spare parts in the middle of races. Others, most surely, have been driven into swimming pools. However, it was left to the great Curtis Turner to provide the grandest aquatic gesture of all: once, in Columbia, South Carolina, at the end of a drunken evening, he drove a new Cadillac sedan into a motel pool. It was his own.

But this particular night it was quiet at the Holiday Inn in Ontario. Save for the din of the freeway traffic—much of it caused by the brutal, ripping sound of the immense, diesel-powered tractor-trailers, rigs that huffed and puffed east on Interstate 10 with a roar that washed against the walls and windows of the motel like heavy surf—it could have been any motel room in the nation. But only California can provide that sort of intense, everlasting rumble and racket of traffic. The day had been tiring. I felt a stiffness across my shoulders that had not been there before. My hand still stung. The dining room was nearly empty as I ate dinner, and the barroom, dark-stained and dimly lit, was occupied exclusively by a pair of salesmen huddled in conversation at the bar. I had one draft beer and wandered back to my room. The pool was refracting shimmering, emerald-green light patterns around the courtyard. It was deserted. I climbed into bed and watched a few minutes of partially focused television before falling asleep. No one showed up; no drunken racers on their way to a party, not Augie Pabst, not even an order of chicken livers.

The Datsun 240Z is sort of a Japanese Jaguar. A sleek coupe with a supple six-cylinder engine, it features superb handling, excellent brakes, marvelously comfortable seats, and a wood-rim steering wheel that looks as if it has been carved out of bamboo. It can be modified into a highly competitive racing car, but the one I used at Bondurant's school was essentially showroom stock, save for an unmuffled exhaust. I had been using it since the afternoon of the first day, primarily because Shaw felt that among the cars in their stable, it might best duplicate the feel of a heavy Trans-Am sedan of the type I was hoping to drive later in the season.

It was a tireless ox of a car, having transported me hundreds of laps around the school's circuit without a complaint. I would climb aboard the 240Z, with Shaw observing from trackside, and hurry around and around, trying to solve the imperfections of my style, which was still flawed by occasional jerkiness and a certain overzealousness. The Datsun

tolerated me without complaint, save for its water temperature gauge, which responded to the desert heat and zoomed
to 240 degrees every dozen laps or so. However, a couple of
gentle, low-speed miles would slosh enough cool water
through the engine's innards so that the gauge would return
to normal reading and I'd resume my thrashing.

To the uninitiated, race driving appears to be a mad endeavor, involving about as much discipline and restraint as a
plunge down a bobsled run. The Datsun and I were learning
different. As Shaw had been urging, smoothness was the key.
A series of three consecutive left-hand bends, followed by a
looping right-hander, provided the major challenge on the
longer circuit and therefore represented the core of what I
had to learn. The first two left-handers were taken at full
throttle, with an upshift from third to fourth gear coming just
after I exited from the second. Then, with the pavement blurring under me at perhaps 105 mph, the third and toughest of
the three bends loomed up. It was rather tight, and its apex
was rippled with bumps that tended to throw the car off line.
I wanted to ease my foot off the throttle and take the turn
perhaps a half second under the limit, but I knew the machine was capable of more. Slowly, I worked my way to the
point where I could make it under full power—taking it
"flat" as they say in Europe, or with the throttle "on the
wood," as is often said in American racing. A lightness overcame the car at that speed. It felt as if it wanted to float off the
road to the outside, powering its way into the roughly bull-
dozed earth that bordered the outer edge of the bend. A furious rumble would rise out of the front suspension as the
Datsun's wheels pounded across the rough pavement on the
apex, but I knew that staying wide of the bumps would either
slow me down or send the car spinning off the road. So I
learned to set the car into that fast curve, placing the wheels
exactly at the entrance, so the machine would drift perfectly
from the outside to the inside and back to the outside again
—all the time making no more than a few minor adjustments
with the steering wheel and keeping my foot hard down. The

car seemingly wanted to take off, to repel my urging to get it through that corner that quickly; to somehow unleash itself from its tormentor behind the wheel.

With the Datsun gobbling up space at a rate where the roadway was a serpentine smear of gray, I would barely leave the left-hand bend before I was aimed into the big sweeper to the right. It was a decreasing-radius corner, meaning it had to be entered rather wide in order to clip the apex on the far side. It could be taken in third gear, provided the entry was smooth and clean. The slower corners anybody could take, but this slalom series, with its relatively high speeds, measured all my skill. As I took a couple of laps to cool the engine, I thought of a remark attributed to the great English champion Stirling Moss, who said, "A man can spend a lifetime taking corners a fifth of a second slower than he is capable of. By doing this he can develop something of a reputation, make a living; even win a few races. But he'll never be a race driver." I also thought of another of Stirling's statements relating to fast driving: "To go flat-out through a bend bordered by level grass is an admirable feat, but to do the same thing in a bend with a stone wall on one side and a precipice on the other is an *accomplishment*." Ironically, Moss's career ended when he went off a high-speed bend at Goodwood, England, skidded over a hundred yards across a lawn, and hit an earthen bank. Serious head injuries took away his competitive edge, and he never appeared in big-time racing again. So much for corners bordered by level grass.

An hour before noon and the Ontario infield was beginning to pulse with heat. A gentle wind was blowing the smog across the track, blurring the great ziggurat and the concrete banks of grandstands that guarded the main straightaway like the walls of a fortress. They echoed the whine of Unser's and Andretti's machines as the tire tests wore into the second day.

Shaw and I were taking a breather beside the parked Datsun, in the middle of the Ontario infield, letting the sun bake us for a few moments before I got in to drive again, when Jim

Shane, one of Bondurant's assistants, drove up. Farther down the track, on the smaller practice circuit, another instructor was working with a pair of students. They were circulating in the Porsche 914's, under his watchful eye, nose-to-tail, at modest speeds. Every few laps he would call them in, and I could see him pointing at various corners and gesturing while they listened obediently, cradling their shiny new crash helmets in their arms. Two young men who wanted to be race drivers. They had paid $800 each for a week of intensified training—perhaps the best high-speed instruction available in the world, worth years of self-taught experience. Who were they? Was one of them a nascent Fangio or Nuvolari? Or would they join that vast legion of perhaps fifty thousand Americans who race on weekends at a multitude of stock-car and sports-car events—"hobby racers," as the professionals call them—men who compete to vent certain juices and view racing as a purely personal challenge. Or would they spend their money, take their rides, and never again appear on a race track, knowing in their hearts that they lacked that mysterious combination of physical and mental skills that makes a "racer"? At this moment, on the Ontario desert, they were finding out.

Shane was an open-faced, easy-smiling Californian in his middle twenties. He was endowed with the instant affability generic to the West Coast that often strikes Easterners as superficial. Although it was not necessarily true with Shane, one sometimes got the feeling with many Californians that you could become their closest friend and after ten years understand no more about them than you did after the first hour we met. Shane was loose, gregarious, and given to chattering about a stream of subjects that filtered through his facile mind like cartridges through a machine gun. He yanked off his shirt and stood with us, his slight, wiry body tanned and his hair sun-bleached in authentic California style. Somebody mentioned the heat. "Yeah, man," Shane burbled. "The heat; it's a pig fucker."

We reeled in laughter. Out there in the middle of the fuming desert, with the noxious smog biting at our eyes and the sun frying our flesh and the turbocharged Indy engines buffeting our ears, Shane had made the totally absurd remark, the perfectly obscene statement that seemed to sum up the situation. Yes, the weather, perhaps the endeavor itself, was, if nothing else, "a pig fucker," and Shaw, Shane, and I laughed over that lunatic crack until long after it had ceased to be funny, as if its lack of sense had somehow symbolized the idiocy of what we were doing. After all, while millions of men were at that moment hunched over their desks, doing their part to advance the Gross National Product, the frontiers of knowledge, the very cause of mankind, for God's sake, we were learning how to drive fast. Men were buying and selling, planning and producing, creating and computerizing, moving mountains, spiderwebbing skyscrapers into the heavens, even blasting off for the moon, all of them collectively stitching away at the very fabric of civilization, and what the hell were we doing, besides zooming a Japanese sports car around a deserted racetrack at high noon? If that wasn't a "pig fucker," what was?

5

■.■.■.■.■.■.■.■.■.■

                        There was a kind of vulnerable innocence about Bob Bondurant that made it difficult to picture him as a race driver. His eyes were dark and unblinking, set deeply above high cheekbones and a firm jaw. His wide, soft mouth curled away from a row of perfect teeth as he talked, making it appear as if he said everything with a smile. At first he seemed reticent and self-effacing, but there were moments, as he talked of racing, when his languid eyes would harden and his mouth would firm up, and you knew that the toughness and the ego-strength of a racer were bright and diamond-hard inside his brain.

    Bondurant, Shaw, and I ate lunch in the great ziggurat, seated in a splendid multi-tier restaurant that overlooked the start-finish line. The walls were covered with immense photo-murals of racing cars, and the menu was couched in racing jargon. The place was crowded, primarily with local Ontario businessmen and permanent-pressed tourist families who had dropped in to see the world's most elaborate racetrack. Waitresses in brief white and blue costumes flitted among the tables and booths as we settled back to consume our prelunch 7-Ups. I had thought about a gin and tonic, but decided against it, mainly because my partners were non-drinkers, coupled with a concern that booze might affect my afternoon driving. Out in the glare of midday, beyond the tinted panels of glass that faced the track, Unser's Johnny Lightning Special sat alone and neglected against the pit wall. It crouched there, in shimmering blue and gold, looking like a prop that had been wheeled out to add a racing décor to the otherwise barren stretch of pavement.

We chattered aimlessly about Saint Bernards—Bondurant and I both owned members of that lumbering, beloved breed —before the conversation inevitably turned to racing. The big news around the school had been the appearance of Swede Savage and Dan Gurney a week earlier. Savage, the twenty-three-year-old son of a veterinarian in nearby San Bernardino, was headed for the top of the sport before he had had a serious crash on the Ontario course five months previous. Having been trained under the watchful eye of Dan Gurney, Swede was given access to Gurney's superlative Eagle cars for the big Indy-type races and seemed to have passed that critical period in the young driver's life when second-rate equipment and overzealousness can conspire to destroy him. But Swede was a pure, undistilled racer, having begun competition in miniature cars when he was nine years old. By age thirteen he was a member of a nationally sponsored go-cart team, and by fifteen he was a top-rated motorcycle racer. A gentle, soft-spoken youth with sleepy eyes and a mop of curly blond hair, Swede had burst on the racing scene, proving himself to be nearly the equal of the world's best with no more than a few races to his credit. He lived to race, and there simply weren't enough races in the Gurney cars to sate his appetite. When the Questor Grand Prix was organized at Ontario, Swede couldn't stay away. It was a big-league road race featuring the best European Grand Prix drivers and a strong representation of America's top road-racing and Indy aces.

After Dan Gurney decided not to enter, he released Swede to take a ride in an old Eagle, a car that had knocked around racing for several years with modest success. Two of Swede's close friends at Gurney's shop had made an arrangement with the car's wealthy owner to use the car on a loan basis for the Questor, and Swede, against widespread advice that he should not be sitting in second-rate equipment, eagerly went racing.

I can remember the day, standing in the pressroom high above the Ontario track, watching Jackie Stewart and Mark Donohue battle with the eventual winner, Mario Andretti, when I spotted a puff of dust rise from a faraway turn in the infield. Swede had hit the wall was the word passed among the journalists covering the race. The public-address announcer, his voice struggling against the shriek of the engines, told the crowd that Swede was all right. Then he fell silent about the accident as I watched an ambulance, its red gumball light blinking ominously, speed to the field hospital behind the garage area, pause for a while, and rush away from the track. A bad sign. It is axiomatic in racing that the severity of an accident is usually in inverse proportion to the amount said about it over the public-address system. A minor shunt generally brings a spate of good-natured, upbeat banter, followed by an interview with the driver or drivers involved. Serious injuries normally prompt silence until some sort of condition report is forthcoming from the hospital. Deaths are sometimes never mentioned, at least not until the next of kin are notified, which sometimes comes long after the race is over. The public-address system added nothing about Swede, and I was getting worried. Finally, the word was passed that he had been taken to a nearby hospital for observation, but the announcement was soothing and contained no cause for alarm.

I wandered out of the pressroom and into the Ontario Speedway's hospitality suite, an elegant, glass-fronted room facing the track, with a wide balcony for race watching. The track had developed a certain cachet among the California show-biz crowd, and the place was jammed with tall, thin-lipped women in Bonwit casuals and burnished, intense Hollywood studs uniformed in twenty-dollar sunglasses, flowered shirts, and Gucci loafers. Paul Newman slouched in a corner, intent on the race. James Garner, looking like the prototype movie star, his white teeth glittering, was telling a story to a round, bald man in a safari jacket. Against the rear wall a long, sumptuous buffet was manned by two chefs in white. A vinyl-topped bar was crowded. The place seemed sanitized, unspoiled by the heat and dirt of the race swirling around outside, where men were laboring in the most extreme danger and discomfort. I spotted Monty Roberts, a vice president of the Speedway. As an aggressive young public-relations man for Ford during the company's frantic racing activities of the sixties, Monty had in a sense discovered Swede and encouraged Ford to give him some races on the Southern stock-car circuit. Now his lean, patrician face was lined, and his thick, curly hair was beginning to show gray around the temples. He walked over, looking depressed. His pale blue eyes were dull with worry. "Swede's bad," he said flatly. "His head. He hit his head on the wall in the crash. The neurosurgeons say he's responding only to deep-pain stimuli. There's paralysis."

I reeled out of the place, in part repelled by the brittle, insentient claque from Hollywood, in part by the need to gather my thoughts alone. I knew Swede well, he had spent time with me and my family. He was a household hero to my kids. He was a very likable guy, with a certain brazen innocence about him, and it was difficult to believe that the sport had bitten him so early in the going. Being around racing brings a certain mental hardness about the possible death of men you know, but with Swede it simply didn't seem possible.

They almost lost him. Had he not been young and abundantly strong, the crash, caused by a jammed throttle, would have killed Swede Savage. His car had looped off a sweeping 100-mph bend at Ontario, skidded across fifty yards of sandy

apron, and slammed broadside against a concrete retaining
wall. Much of the impact was absorbed by Swede's special
Bell Star crash helmet, an advanced head protector that is
considered without equal in motor sports. Had he been wearing an inferior product, he would have been struck dead. As
it was, the deep bruising of his cranial cavity left his mind
scrambled for weeks, his memory circuits at first stunned
into silence, then badly confused. He remained amnesiac
about the crash and the Indy car race he had run at Phoenix
the day before. I remember Dan Gurney saying to me some
months later, "Make no mistake about it, Swede was *hurt*."
He said it with such clinical finality that only then did I realize how close to death Swede had come.

Shaw and I had stopped at the scene of the crash during
our morning session. It was perhaps a quarter mile away from
where we had been practicing, but at one point we had
driven past, and compelled by that curious streak of morbid-
ity that lies within all men, we went over to look. The curve
looked innocent enough on that quiet day, five months later.
Yet black blotches from Swede's tires still streaked the pavement, and there were ugly scuff marks on the wall. One could
imagine how Swede had come smoking into that left-hander,
lifted his foot slightly, found the car arrowing ahead, then
frantically sawed at the wheel for a fraction of a second before the barrier rose up and everything went black.

Swede's recovery had recently reached a point where his
doctors said it was all right for him to test himself in a racing
car again. He had come to Bob Bondurant's school just a week
before my arrival to try to determine just how much had been
permanently wrecked inside his brain.

"He was really rough at first," said Bondurant with that
smile breaking away over his teeth. "We started him out on
the little beginner's track, and for the first few hours he really
jerked the car around. Not smooth. Then as the time passed
and he gained confidence, he began to get quicker and
quicker, as if it was all coming back to him. By the end of the
day, he seemed to be in perfect shape.

"The following afternoon Gurney came over and we ran a little test on the full road circuit. We got one of the Porsche 914's, and the three of us really let it all hang out. First Gurney ran some laps, then Swede got in and equaled his time. And if you can run as fast as Gurney, you know goddamn well you're pretty sharp. When it was over, Swede knew he could race again. Hell, nobody had to tell him that, not after running as quick as Gurney."

"Do you think Dan was running as fast as he could?" I asked.

Bondurant's eyes turned dark with mild scorn. "Of course. What would be proved by letting up? We were trying to find out if Swede still had it in him. In a situation like that, there was no sense kidding ourselves: either he was still a racer or he wasn't. Fortunately, it worked out for him." He smiled again, then added, "I'm the only one who got screwed."

"How'd you get screwed?"

"Well, those guys ran ten laps apiece before they got their best time. Then I took the car out for two laps just before the track was closed for a motorcycle test. I was four-tenths of a second slower. I *know* I could have run quicker if I'd taken a couple of more laps, but it kind of pisses me off about that four-tenths. You know what I mean?" He was smiling, but I knew he was dead serious about that four-tenths of a second. A good driver, with nothing at stake except a few meaningless ticks of a stopwatch, would have broken his ass for that four-tenths of a second. Bob Bondurant was an authentic racer.

Talent is the final arbiter of your success on the golf course, tennis court, or football field. Not so in motor racing, where raw bucks can carry you near the top. Most professional drivers agree that the car is perhaps 75 percent of the total combination for success in racing, while the driver contributes 25 percent. Contrast this to most sports, where equipment such as rackets, clubs, shoes, jockstraps, padding, socks, etc., might contribute 5 percent at the outside, and it becomes clear how a routinely talented driver can go far, provided he has a faster machine than his competitors. And generally speaking, ultrafast cars are available to those who have the money.

At the very top, where the Stewarts, Andrettis, Foyts, Unsers, Hulmes, et al, compete, money can never transcend their skill, but a big bankroll can move one through the minor leagues with unbelievable ease. And if Mom and Pop are backing you, all the better. There is a curious mentality among the upper classes whereby parents often finance their children in the purchase of racing cars, seemingly impervious to the brutal fact that these machines can snuff out the lives of their offspring in a wink. The classic example is Papa Rodriguez, a millionaire Mexican who bought monster Ferraris for his two teenage sons, Ricardo and Pedro, and sent them off to race at places like Le Mans and Sebring at an age when most boys were still trading bubble-gum cards. Ricardo died young, trying to outspeed the Grand Prix aces at his home track in Mexico City. Pedro managed to reach the top in Formula One and endurance racing, then was killed himself. Papa outlived them both.

There is a story about the rich young American Sam Posey that perfectly exemplifies this strange syndrome. Posey is a bright Easterner who arrived on the racing scene after graduating cum laude from the Rhode Island School of Design and immediately established himself as a loquacious, brave, and highly talented driver of Can-Am and Trans-Am machines. In the beginning, he generally attended the races in the company of his mother, a cultured upper-class Connecticut lady whose good-natured informality made her an instant personality in the racing community. Sam was well liked, too, but at first many considered him a dilettante. Nevertheless, the Brahmin lady and her son swept across the American competition scene, purchasing exotic racers by the cubic yard and finally underwriting their own car-building operation. Sam tended to crash a great deal, but had moments when he was blindingly fast. Then practice for a race at Riverside brought disaster when he crested a blind hill, found fellow driver Ron

Courtney spun out in his path, and collided with him in a wrenching, flame-scorched smashup. Sam was unhurt, although Courtney was gravely injured and narrowly missed death.

Shortly after the nightmare experience, the Poseys, Sam and his mother—cultured, bright, aware people, sensitive souls seemingly more suited to art collecting than to motor racing—were in the Riverside pits, writing a check for a reported $17,000 for another race car to replace the one he had just wrecked. Within a few hours, while Courtney's life hung in the balance in a nearby intensive-care unit, Sam was back on the track, practicing again as if nothing had happened. This is not unique. Sam was troubled by the crash but felt compelled to get back in another car, lest lengthy reflection on the disaster undermine his resolve. This "eating a bit of the hair of the dog that bit you" embodies the kind of mental toughness that must exist in serious racing, but the improbable sight of Sam and his gentle mother trekking through the Riverside pits in search of another car minutes after the crash is one that is peculiar to racing and its wealthy parent-sponsorship phenomenon.

Race drivers are by nature preoccupied with "rides," the sport's euphemism for steady racing in somebody else's car. Despite the confusion caused by raw dollars obtaining rides for men who might not otherwise deserve them, a reasonably effective farm system operates within the sport, wherein drivers tend to get cars roughly equal to their ability. More often than not, the best drivers get the best cars. Money can carry one just so far, then talent intervenes as the final judge. The grapevine never loses touch with who is paying or being paid what to drive what, and a race driver's stature among his peers is always in question until he proves himself on his own merit with a first-class team. Peter Revson, for example, spent much of his early career falsely accused of being a rich dilettante. He is a member of the wealthy, socially prominent New York family that controls Revlon cosmetics, but he is also a serious race driver. His courage and commitment to the sport became evident when he continued to drive following the death of his brother Doug in a race in Sweden, but his skill was never widely acknowledged until 1971, when he won the pole at Indianapolis and the Can-Am Championship. Until that point, Revson was extremely sensitive to the inference that he was just another frivolous preppie out for kicks. In his case, his money and position operated as a handicap in gaining the much-deserved respect of his fellows. Revson could very probably have afforded to finance his own racing efforts—or at least have gathered strong financial backing—but he realized that his reputation and self-respect as a racer ultimately depended on his proving himself in somebody else's machine, where pure skill was the deciding factor.

The goddamn rides. Always having to kiss some sponsor's or owner's ass to keep your seat; nervously looking over your shoulder for some upstart who might beat you out. Or if you had enough money and tired of the in-fighting and politics, you could go out and buy your own car. Then they'd say you weren't good enough to get asked to drive for anybody else. That kind of dilemma seldom faces other professional athletes. But in automobile racing uncounted men slog around in the mire of the minor leagues for years and never know how good they are. Why? Because for same strange parlay of circumstances, they have never gotten behind the wheel of a good car. That magic 75 percent has never been theirs.

It was in part true with Bob Bondurant, it was entirely true with Shaw. Bill had bought his own Formula Ford and had run well in Southern California club races, but soon realized that that car would take him nowhere, and he had sold it. He managed a couple of rides in some sedan races, but again no major offers were forthcoming. So there he was, possessed of acknowledged talent, equipped with all the bearing, good sense, and instincts that any sponsor could ask, and he was without a ride, keeping his edge by instructing at a driving school.

He had been given the chance to try out for a big-time Trans-Am ride at the beginning of the season. A major tire sponsor was fielding a car that would use their new radial street tires in racing conditions as a promotional tool. Shaw and three other candidates were given a chance to drive the car in tests, with the fastest man presumably to get the job. "I was nearly a second a lap faster than the next quickest guy," he said with a wry smile. "I figured I had it made. The crew who were going to campaign the car for the company recommended me for the job. Then you know what? You know who got the ride? The slowest of the four of us! This guy from back East who was dead slow. He got the ride! I guess he had connections in the ad agency or knew somebody in the company, because he beat us all out, and I swear, he couldn't drive nails."

Bondurant, Shaw, and I agreed that a lot of good men were lounging in the pits while squadrons of balloon-feet were stealing their rides. The inference, if not the outright declaration, was that all of us were members of the former group and not the latter.

"Everybody talks about cubic inches being the key to winning races," said Bondurant. "I'll tell you something, the key is cubic money."

We left the restaurant as Al Unser and his crew trooped in for lunch. Unser was dressed in his driving suit and a red Firestone jacket. His thick, curly hair was rumpled, as if he had just climbed out of his car after a few quick laps. Heads turned in silence as this authentic racing stud strode among the tables. In his van were Bignotti, a couple of mechanics, and a lean, leathery blond lady. As we reached the door, I could see a squadron of waitresses converging on their booth.

Back on the track, behind the wheel of the 240Z, I began to feel that this whole business of driving was coming together; that Shaw's insistence on smoothness and care, on discipline about the line and braking points and gear changing, was beginning to pay dividends. At one point I'd stopped beside the track to let the engine cool and had climbed out to face the level stare of my instructor. As he approached, Shaw gestured toward the Omega Speedmaster chronograph that was strapped to his wrist. "Not bad. Not bad at all. You know how much you've improved? You're running ten seconds a lap quicker. *Ten seconds*, man, and I'll bet anything you're trying about half as hard."

Of course he was right. As the sessions had progressed, I'd found myself using more of the road, but using less brakes and steering. I'd found that by braking earlier but longer as I approached a corner, the entire entry process was tidier and quicker. Instead of rushing up to the turn, waiting until the last particle of a second to brake, then flinging the car around, I had discovered that Shaw's urging to squeeze on the brakes in a gentle, more prolonged process would compress the suspension, squatting the chassis on the springs and shocks, making it more stable throughout the corner. While I had known I was getting smoother, I had not known if my speed had been improving. Shaw's Omega said yes, and it made me feel beautiful.

The Datsun's clutch needed some adjustment, and its gas tank was nearly empty, so we drove back to the garage area. While a mechanic made the car ready to run again, Shaw and I sipped a few cups of cold water in the office, then walked through Bondurant's garages. The area where they tended to the Datsun was a typical high-performance shop. It was considerably neater than normal garages, with its workbenches cleared for work and not acting as random storage for a litter of tools. Against one wall was a shoulder-high, S-K tool chest, mounted on a matching dolly. Its flanks were plastered with hundreds of racing decals. The walls of the shop were hung with posters, one a striking low shot of Dan Gurney in a blue Can-Am car against a yellow background, another of Mario Andretti in a brilliant red Ferrari coupe, slicing through a turn at Sebring. The doors yawned wide open into the bright sunlight, and a radio was tuned to a local rock-and-roll station that rattled compulsively somewhere out of sight, like a bedridden old man bawling for attention.

The garage just adjacent had one door closed, and it was

nearly empty, save for the bare bones of the frame of a small single-seat racing car. Around it were littered shiny castings, pieces of the suspension and steering gear. Sitting on the floor, next to a wooden shipping box, was a compact four-cylinder engine, obviously intended for installation in the car. Shaw explained that the mechanics were setting the machine up for club racing and worked on it during their spare moments, when the school cars did not need attention.

The gray double doors of the end garage in the row were shut tight, but unlocked. Shaw and I, compelled by nothing more than idle curiosity and the need to waste a few minutes, slid one of the doors open, and the dark space was partially splashed with light.

"Good Christ!" I exclaimed when I saw what looked like a bloodstained shirt hanging from a steel girder. As my eyes adjusted to the gloom, I determined that the shirt was in fact the jacket of a two-piece driver's suit. It was cream-color Nomex—the standard fireproof material used in racing uniforms—and its sleeves were decorated with a single red stripe. On the left breast was sewn a Firestone label. The entire front of the garment was most certainly smeared with dried blood. "Some poor bastard really did it to himself," I mumbled as I stood gaping at what had to be the relic of a horrible racing crash. Then, beneath the stains on the right breast, I made out an embroidered name... CLAUDE AURAC.

"Claude Aurac? I never heard of a Claude Aurac," said Shaw, his voice evidencing a rare tone of bafflement.

I gazed around the room, which was empty save for a few large cardboard boxes and a couple of bulky shipping trunks. Stenciled on the trunks was SOLAR PRODUCTIONS, and suddenly the entire scene made sense.

"Of course," I said, relieved. "Solar Productions is Steve McQueen's film company, and this stuff must be left over from Le Mans. Remember, Claude Aurac was the Frenchman who crashed the Ferrari and crawled away from the car just before it exploded."

"Now I remember," Shaw said sheepishly. "Bondurant bought all of the old uniforms left over from the film. That's what all these boxes must be full of."

We flipped open one of the trunks and found it stuffed with a jumble of driving suits and fireproof underwear in a multitude of sizes, all of it dirty and unfolded, as if the wardrobe man had pitched it in on the last day of shooting and sent it off to Bondurant. Somebody must have opened it to make a casual inventory, spotted Aurac's suit with the clever cosmetic replicas of bloodstains, and hung it up as a macabre souvenir of McQueen's film.

"Some racers have funny senses of humor," Shaw commented as we rolled the door shut, leaving the bloody tunic hanging where it was.

With only a few hours of instruction remaining for me, Shaw suggested that he take the Porsche 911 coupe—which was an ex-championship car in Southern California amateur circles—out to the track, where he could run in company with me. I could follow him for a while, watching how he took the corners; then he could follow me, evaluating my style. It sounded like fun, but sooner or later I knew we would end up racing each other. That had to be.

The Porsche was a faster car than the Datsun, but some of its performance had been nullified by the use of Sears radial passenger tires. All of the school cars used the Sears radials: one, they were rugged, long-wearing tires that lasted perhaps five times as long as conventional racing tires, and two, Bondurant had an agreement with the company whereby he was supplied the rubber in exchange for advertising and promotional endorsements. "The radials make the Porsche a ball to drive," said Shaw. "They make it very skittish and sensitive, so you can fling it around with the throttle, hang the tail out, and all that. You've got to try it. It's crazy."

So we went back out on the track, and by the time we got ready to run, the desert glare was gone and the sun was setting in the western sky. Shaw led the way for a few laps, flinging the little Porsche, which reminded me of a manic, red June bug, around in a series of perfectly controlled slides. I stayed close on his tail, losing a few feet here, gaining a few feet there. The Porsche had more speed on the straights and more powerful brakes, but its treacherous, loose-tail behavior in the corners about equalized its performance to my Datsun's. It would lap faster when driven flat-out, but Shaw wasn't interested in running away from me, but merely in leading me around in the fastest possible fashion. I chased him, trying to maintain discipline about my driving in the face of the competitive juices that were beginning to flow. Glued to his back bumper as I was, I had to resist the temptation to do exactly as he did: to brake when he did, to corner as he did, simply because our cars behaved differently. No matter how close he was, no matter how badly I wanted to pass him, I had to force myself to drive my own car and not simply trail along behind him, acting as a caboose in his locomotive.

Then he slowed and waved me past. I was leading now, and I faced the new preoccupation of the rotund form of the Porsche filling my rearview mirror. No matter where I went, how cleanly I cornered or how crisply I accelerated, the shape was still there. I could see Shaw, sitting back in relaxed fashion, away from the wheel, his Steve Canyon glasses making his eyes look as big and dark as hockey pucks. I was driving as hard as I could. I wanted to race away from him, to make that red June bug smaller in my mirror. But it clung there, like the image on a tiny film screen, and the faster I went, the faster he went.

We were racing.

I hammered out of a sweeping right-hander and bore down a short straightaway with Shaw hard on my heels. At the end was a hairpin right, with room for only one car at a time. I moved to the far left verge of the track, giving myself a maximum sweep into the corner. Shaw powered past me, nipped by on the apex of the corner, and took the lead. I resisted a momentary temptation to drive beyond my shut-off point and held my line as his car came alongside, inches apart. I heard the nasal blat of his exhaust for the first time as he squirted ahead, then cranked the Porsche into the turn.

But he was going too fast. As we bore into the corner nose-to-tail, with him holding the lead by a few feet, the rear end of the Porsche lashed around and spun off in a flurry of gravel and sand.

I laughed. I sped past him as he was sitting sideways and helpless on the side of the track. I was delighted that he'd gone off. I had raced him, and for a brief moment, victory had been mine, and there was a strange, almost cruel jubilation that overcame me. It had been a violent little encounter, utterly normal in racing, hardly worth mentioning, but within those fractional seconds of testing one another, with the laws of physics ultimately determining the winner, I had felt, in microcosm, what racing was all about. The man in that red car—Shaw or anybody else—had been the enemy, and for a few foolish moments, both of us had been prepared to face substantial risk to see who would come out of the corner first. The result had been incidental. The important fact was that we had been racing.

I waited for Shaw to restart, then watched in my rearview mirror as he sped up. I saw him raise both hands from the wheel, make an exaggerated shrug of his shoulders, and smile widely. We went on, racing hard again. I held for a few laps; then he found another spot on the track where the superior brakes of his Porsche worked again, and he charged past. I didn't want to let him by, but there was little I could do. And besides, as the teacher in the faster car, it was important that he lead.

I drove the Porsche for a few laps as it got darker and the entire Speedway grew deserted. It was a zappy, responsive little machine, with a vague-feeling gear shifter and a gutted full-race interior, complete with a roll cage and single, wrap-around bucket seat for the driver. It was fun to drive, as Shaw had said, but somehow, with the day about over and our little confrontation complete, it seemed anticlimactic. Our racing

had overheated the Datsun again, forcing Shaw to watch me
from the sidelines, and after a few laps I parked the Porsche.

"I think that about does it," said Shaw with a tone of finality, and we packed up and headed back to the garage. While I
took off my driving suit and stowed my helmet in its Bell
satchel, Shaw went off to fill out the logbook that I had
brought along from the Sports Car Club of America. In order
to obtain a full competition license, I had to receive a positive
evaluation from Bondurant's school. If Shaw's remarks were
negative, I might as well have forgotten the whole thing.

Shaw was standing by his Volkswagen outside the school's
office when we said good-bye. I was sorry to leave in a way,
because I felt that he had taught me a great deal, especially
the kind of restraint and discipline that my driving needed. I
told him I hoped that he found that magic ride he'd been
seeking, and we made a few informal declarations about getting together at the races in the near future.

The school and Shaw and the red cars were behind me as I
headed the Ford for the main gate of the Speedway. It was
dead silent, except for Marty Robbins's "You Got Me Singin'
the Blues," which was pouring out of the radio on KLAC—a
sound that heightened a strange feeling of sadness that came
over me. I couldn't wait any longer. I stopped the car at the
entrance to the infield tunnel and dug my logbook out of my
pocket. Flipping the pages to where Shaw had placed his remarks, I read his precise printing. Beside a category marked
"Judgment" he had written "Very good." My technique he
had described as "Good." My attitude was "Excellent," he'd
said, while he had evaluated my reactions as "Very good."
He'd ranked both my courtesy and comparative lap times as
"Excellent."

In a place for random remarks, Shaw had written, "Brock
does a fine job, very savvy. Excellent performance here."

I read and reread the words in the gathering darkness, a
feeling of elation building within me. I had passed. I nosed
the Ford out of the track and headed for the airport. If the

airlines cooperated, I would be at Watkins Glen tomorrow afternoon, where Mike Tillson and his Lancia would be waiting. Bill Shaw and his stopwatch would not be there. No more brief flurries of competition with an understanding teacher. It would be an authentic motor race at Watkins Glen.

6

Suicide Betts was running hard. His skinny frame was hovering over the steering wheel of his BMW as we arrowed over the Finger Lakes country highways, headed for Watkins Glen. We had called him Suicide since the day he managed to flip an all-terrain vehicle while demonstrating it to his pregnant wife. But his record for nutball deeds was long and checkered. His bespectacled, choir-boy countenance was an outright deception, because Betts was a devotee of such activities as skydiving, ice-boat racing, white-water canoeing, and flying home-built airplanes. He drove his BMW 2002 with a kind of zappy earnestness that made it difficult to sleep. I had flown all night from Los Angeles, but the attempt to nap between the time Betts had picked me up at the Rochester airport and we reached the track was futile. The impending race, plus the bouncing of the BMW, made sound sleep out of the question, and I sat up to witness our rush down the gently curving Route 14A that led through scrubbed villages like Penn Yan and Dundee and across lush farmland before reaching Watkins Glen.

Betts zoomed past a slow-running Porsche and pointed at a red oak tree towering, alone and aloof, in the middle of a pasture. He said that it reminded him of the time this loud-mouthed, know-it-all businessman showed up at a skydiving club he belonged to in Colorado. After a few hours of instruction, which he assiduously ignored, he insisted on taking his first jump.

"The wind was bad that day, and we told this blowhard not to go. But he bailed out anyway and came down in this giant meadow with one big tree in the middle. The silly son of a bitch never even tried to control the chute. You guessed it, he sailed into that tree full-bore. Hit it a ton. Compound fractures all over the place. We never saw him again." Betts chuckled.

"Some guy once told me that skydiving is like cutting your throat and seeing if you can get to the doctor before you bleed to death," I said.

"You're a perfect one to make a crack like that," Suicide retorted.

It was Betts's mention of the tree that triggered a memory of Roger Clouser and his infernal, junker MG, and how we nearly drowned in it on this same road on the way to another, long-past Watkins Glen race. Clouser and I were friends, college drinking pals; he was an usher at my wedding, and we'd been conspirators on a particularly disreputable college humor magazine (for no good reason called Pot—a trifle avant-garde for 1953). He was a brilliant philosophy major who, in the end, didn't give a rat's ass about philosophy and for much of his college career could be found playing shuffleboard in dingy saloons or writing term papers for money. He never cared about cars until school and the army were behind him, and he'd become a junior copywriter in a Rochester advertising agency. At the time, I owned a Triumph TR3 roadster, while Clouser was driving a lumbering Ford station wagon, which he proudly noted to me during a visit to his house was propelled by a 390-cubic-inch Interceptor engine. After numerous beers, a dispute over whether the Triumph or the Ford was faster culminated in a series of drag races on a nearby highway. While our wives fumed and our infant children wailed, Clouser and I squared off for dozens of races, all of which had the same result. The Triumph was decisively quicker. Time after time it blew off the Ford. Clouser was stunned at the performance of a such a tiny car. This trauma had a long-range effect on him, because it helped stimulate a passionate involvement with sports cars. Being a competitive man, it was inevitable that he would be attracted to racing. He bought an ancient MG TD that had been raced extensively during the early 1950's. It was as clapped-out as any car could be and still remain mobile, but Roger was extremely proud of his new acquisition. Because he had not yet qualified for his racing license, and I had just recently obtained mine, he asked me to drive it in a regional race at the Glen: a similar event to the one to which Betts and I were hurrying. Clouser's MG was slow for a road machine, much less a racer. With its aged engine wheezing through a stock exhaust system and its rusty bodywork buttressed by an absurdly heavy roll bar that looked like a girder from the Golden Gate Bridge, the poor thing was a rolling roadblock to normal traffic on the highway, much less the racetrack.

Clouser, the fledgling race-car owner and entrant, and I, his ace driver, drove the MG to Watkins Glen. No trailer or fancy van for us; we just climbed into that crippled red box and motored off to the track. The trip was uneventful—with no trouble from the police, primarily because the car could barely break the speed limit—until we reached this same stretch of Route 14A. A summer rain squall descended on us, and because we had ripped out the convertible top as a crafty weight-saving device, we were instantly drenched. There being no effective windshield wipers, we had to stop, finally finding refuge under a massive elm that bordered the road.

There we sat, with the rain filling up the inside of the MG, while Clouser extracted a couple of cans of Budweiser from the jumble of tools behind the seat, and we drank to the impending victory.

The race was a total disaster. Very few slower cars have ever appeared on a racetrack of any kind. On the gentle uphill slope beyond the start-finish line at the Glen—a place where my competitors were shifting into fourth at a solid 80–90mph—the MG was droning along at perhaps 60 mph in third. The winner of the race, a friend in a black Alfa Romeo spider, lapped me something like nine times, and I will never forget the urge to hide down under the cowling so that somehow no one would recognize me driving the car. Through some miracle, I had managed to pass a single car on the first lap, but he had quickly darted past and left me to complete my agony in isolation, watching my rearview mirror for the periodic appearance of the black Alfa, which seemed to be rocket-propelled.

But my ordeal was not over. Just before the end of the race, when I could have quietly slunk into the pits and tried to sublimate the entire affair, the goddamn MG broke. It clattered to a halt on that same slope that had acted as such an impediment to its feeble engine for the entire race, and there I was, in full view of everybody, stuck at trackside. One of the most humiliating moments of my life came when a tow truck arrived and dragged me and my broken stove of a car all around the track to the pits, accompanied the entire way by the hoots of the crowd. A look under the MG indicated that all of the bolts holding the transmission to the engine housing had fallen out. Looking disappointed, at the dismal showing of both his car and his driver, Clouser and another friend scrambled under the car to make repairs. My only urge was to flee. Using the rationale that big-time drivers seldom worked on their own cars, I said a few brief good-byes and left with Sally, my wife, who'd driven our car to the race, her skeptical female mind convinced that I'd need transportation home.

That incident soured the friendship between Roger and me for years. It was a foolish moment, hardly worth any lingering anger, but both our egos had been bruised in such curious ways that many seasons passed until our relationship regained a firm footing. In the meantime, Clouser became an active amateur racer and a stalwart member of the Finger Lakes Region of the Sports Car Club of America. Much of this activity was carried on without the sanction of his wife, Ellen, a sweet Irish gal, reared by a genteel family and a Catholic convent education. At the beginning, Ellen was dead-set against Roger's racing, and a major domestic crisis took place one weekend at Watkins Glen, when he flipped his new Sprite racer upside down in a ditch. He was unhurt, and the car not seriously bent, but Ellen lost her Gaelic temper in spectacular fashion. As they led poor Clouser, muddy and dazed, off for a routine medical examination, Ellen, her eyes blazing, shoulders hunched in fury, trailed him like a lioness. Periodically she would leap in front of him, and pointing back at the rumpled machine, would shout, "There, you damn fool, there's your trophy!"

Somehow Roger survived both Ellen's fury and the considerable expense of repairing the Sprite, and went on to become an accomplished club racer and a ranking power in SCCA racing affairs. In fact, the chief steward and the man who would be watching me closely on the track the very day of my return to the Glen would be Roger Clouser. For a while I tried to find that elm tree where we'd parked the MG long ago, but gave up in favor of one final attempt at sleep before the racing began.

The race to which Betts and I were hurrying was an SCCA Regional event—purely minor league and completely amateur. If I was to win or place well, the best I could expect was a pewter mug or a silver tray. Races of this kind were the beginning: a small-time training ground for young drivers and a low-key outlet for hobbyists who desired to race casually only a few times a year. While the SCCA ama-

teur driver has been the subject of ridicule by other segments of the sport who somehow consider themselves
ballsier because they race for money, the fact is dozens of
great drivers such as Dan Gurney, Phil Hill, Walt Hansgen,
Peter Revson, and Mark Donohue began their careers racing
their own cars in events exactly like the one I was heading for.

We took a back road into Watkins Glen, a route that used
part of the original road circuit that had meandered over a
6.6-mile patchwork of public highways. We entered a long,
downhill curve to the right, where men like Phil Walters and
John Fitch once drifted through in their giant Chrysler-pow-
ered Cunninghams at 140 mph. Then the turn straightened
out and plunged at a terrifying incline into a sharp left-
hander at the edge of the business section. A hundred yards
more and the track snaked past the local bank and headed up
Main Street itself, on this day an undistinguished vista of
supermarkets, restaurants, drugstores, and auto agencies, virtually like any one of a thousand small towns from coast to
coast. We passed a souvenir shop at the entrance of the Glen
State Park, where seven-year-old Frank Fazzary had been
watching the races in 1952. He had been sitting on the curb
amid multitudes of people who had apparently never considered the possibility of a car's going out of control. Fred
Wacker, a member of the prominent Chicago family, moved
wide as he approached the turn at the end of Main Street, and
the rear wheel of his Cadillac-Allard sliced into the wall of
people lining the roadway. It struck little Frank, killing him
instantly. Before Wacker regained control, the tail of his car
had clouted twelve other spectators, injuring some of them
seriously. That accident ended racing on the streets and roads
of Watkins Glen forever. In retrospect, it is a miracle that
scores didn't die, considering the vulnerability of the audience.

We stopped at a ramshackle landmark called the Seneca
Lodge. A large, low-roofed, log house surrounded by a clutter
of run-down cottages, the lodge is a favorite hangout for the

amateur sports-car types who form the foot soldiers of all road racing. During the big professional events like the Trans-Am, Can-Am, and United States Grand Prix, they act as registrars, timers, and scorers, paddock marshals, gate attendants, course communications, and emergency workers. For the most part they labor without pay, save the reward of being on the "inside" of the sport. Because everything is done on a volunteer basis, Parkinsonian inefficiency is standard, and generally three people do the job of one (the rationale being that all those willing to work are given jobs whether they are needed or not, simply because their services might someday be necessary).

A few sports cars were parked in the gravel lot outside the lodge when Betts and I arrived, but since it was midmorning and the bar was still closed, the place was unusually quiet. Race registration was being held in the basement, where a group of women from the Finger Lakes Region of the Sports Car Club of America manned a long table cluttered with manila envelopes. They expedited the myriad form-signing and paper-shuffling required to enter formally and told us Tillson and my family were waiting at the track.

We drove a few miles farther on the old Glen circuit, passing a low stone marker on the inside of a sweeping right-hand bend. That monument was to Sam Collier, the first driver to die at Watkins Glen. A wealthy Florida sportsman and ex– naval officer, Collier and his brother Miles were prime movers in the early road-racing movement in the United States. Sam was cool and elegant; well liked and respected among the gentlemen competitors as a fine driver. During the Grand Prix of 1950, Collier was driving a tiny Ferrari entered by Briggs Cunningham, who was to become America's greatest gentleman auto racer. Collier lost control on that narrow curve and flipped into a field. It was a stunning moment for the fledgling racers, who had never seriously considered that men could die driving race cars. To this day, during the major races at Watkins Glen, a small wreath is placed on the monument to Sam Collier. As we headed into the gate of the new and elaborate racetrack that replaced the patchwork of public roads upon which Collier and little Frank Fazzary had died, I mused that somehow, with all of the safety advances that have been made since those deaths, men still go to the races with the same childlike naïveté. And men still die.

Because amateur sports-car racing hardly ranks as a spectacle, crowds are difficult to attract. Therefore, these events are generally run solely for the participants, with the gates closed to the public. This reduces overhead in terms of personnel, advertising, concessions, etc., and most important, drastically cuts spectator liability insurance costs to a point where entry fees ranging between $40 and $50 for each of the 250 race cars realizes a modest profit for the sponsoring region.

The vast infield was empty, save for a cluster of vehicles around a large, blue-gray steel building mounted with a sign announcing KENDALL TECH CENTER. There were trucks, vans, and station wagons, many of them with low trailers attached. Mingled among them were brightly painted Triumphs, MGs, Sprites, and Porsches, all sporting numbers on their flanks and thick roll bars that sprouted from their cockpits. Men, for the most part young and healthy looking, hovered over the racers. With them were numerous lank-haired girls, clad in low-hanging bell-bottoms, who busied themselves with polishing goggle lenses, sorting tools, checking tire pressures, or merely eyeing the competition. The air was filled with the snotty sound of small engines revving up. Occasionally, one of the racers would spurt out of the crowd, its driver ritualistically blipping his throttle to keep the plugs from fouling, while trying to maintain an expression of clear-eyed, lethal competence.

Suddenly my older son Brock was standing in the dusty road, flagging us down. He had been assigned to watch for us in the jumble of activity and direct us to a parking spot next to a small, lumpy red coupe. Although I had never seen the car before, I knew it would be my ride for the weekend.

Standing nearby was Sally, looking relieved that we'd made it, my son Dan, and my daughter, Claire. A thin, shaggy-haired young man in air-force sunglasses was working on the automobile, and I knew that had to be its owner, Mike Tillson.

He was a soft-spoken Nebraskan who'd come east to make his way in racing. A fine driver in his own right, Mike was working as a mechanic in the shops of Kirk F. White in Philadelphia, one of the best-known dealers in thoroughbred automobiles in the United States. The public imagines a race-car "wrench" as a slack-jawed dunce in filthy coveralls and a baseball hat with the brim turned up, Huntz Hall style. Nothing could be further from the truth, at least in the more serious segments of racing. In fact, maintaining modern racing cars, with their complicated suspensions and engines, requires tremendous intelligence, and mechanics like Mike Tillson have become the rule rather than the exception. He had towed his car from Philadelphia behind a Ford sedan and had quietly guided it through technical inspection, where it had been checked for proper safety components before being allowed on the track. Now he was making a few minor adjustments before running. Except for getting my helmet and coveralls passed by the inspectors (to insure that they conformed with the stringent SCCA fire-safety regulations), there was little else for me to do.

The Lancia was a rare bird. Very few of them have been imported into the United States, and this particular model, a Fulvia HF (which Mike explained stood for "high fidelity," as a testimony not to its harmonic qualities but to owner loyalty), was a curiosity even among the sports-car set. Its small, high-efficiency V-4 engine powered its front wheels rather than the rear. For such a relatively undersized machine, the Lancia was expensive, which was the prime reason it never caught on in the United States market. But it had a reputation for excellent handling and reliability, and the tiny cadre of Lancia owners in the country were wildly loyal. But Mike's car had never been used for mundane transport. It was an ex-factory racer, having been built with the lightness and strength reserved for competition machines. Before coming to the United States, it had run in such major European events as the Targa Florio, the daring open-road race in the mountains of Sicily, and the great Monte Carlo Rally. It had raced at the Sebring 12-Hour Endurance Race in 1967 and 1968, and at the Daytona Continental twenty-four-hour event in '68. Mike, who'd worked as a mechanic on the car in 1967 and had driven a similar machine at Sebring the next year, bought the car and had competed with it in nearly two dozen SCCA races since then, winning his class nine times. Their last event had been a five-hour endurance race in Monterey, Mexico, where they had run third overall and first in class.

"The little thing is unbelievably reliable," said Mike as we stood there and reflected on the machine. "In fact, I didn't even change the spark plugs. It has the same plugs we ran at Monterey."

It was almost time to drive, and something was stirring inside me. It wasn't outright nervousness, because there was no palpitating or heart-thumping or faltering salivary glands. I examined the Lancia, peering under the hood specifically to check the throttle linkage—because that is the Achilles' heel that can cause instant disaster if it jams wide open. But I forgot to make a thorough check—my mind probing ahead to the moment when I would roll onto the track for the first time.

"We better get out for some practice. There's only one more session left for this class, and you've got to have a minimum of five laps of practice to race," Mike said. I picked up my Bell helmet bag, dug my uniform out of a suitcase, and went off to find a place to change. Racetracks are for the most part devoid of amenities like dressing or locker rooms, and I had to settle for a neglected shower stall in the dank men's room of the Tech building. I stood in there, wrestling with my clothing, trying to keep it out of contact with the filthy floor, while a string of drivers, mechanics, and race officials strode

in to arch their bodies against the single, acid-smelling ur-
inal.

Once dressed, I stepped into the sunlight feeling transformed. It was part of that weird aura of a uniform—any uniform that sets one apart from the crowd. No man is
invulnerable to this weakness, from unadorned Maoists to
seedy university professors, because nonuniforms ultimately
provide just as strong an ego trip as that of an insanely decorated Ethiopian field marshal. The tight-fitting coveralls felt
great, and I knew that they had instantly boosted me to the
top of the pecking order at Watkins Glen that day. Rocket-fast
or stone-slow, I was a driver—or at least dressed as a driver
—and I walked with a jauntiness reserved only for those who
know deep inside that their appearance has set them apart
and above their peers.

I climbed inside the Lancia. Its interior was an empty expanse of flat-black metal. There were no floor mats or upholstery of any kind (all had been removed to save weight and to
reduce the fire hazard). A large roll bar was mounted behind
my seat, a tiny leather-covered shell that tucked around my
ribs like a corset. Mike helped to adjust my seat belt and
shoulder harness, while young Brock handed me my helmet,
gloves, and Nomex hood that was intended as further protection against fire—in the end the major fear of all competition
drivers.

We were ready. Mike climbed in the passenger's door
while I turned the key. The crackle of the Lancia's exhaust
filled the inside of the car. While the rest of the crew—Sally,
Betts, my children, and Mike's girl—left to station themselves on the inside of the first turn, Mike and I chugged off
through the paddock area to the pits. The clutch felt light and
forgiving, and the steering seemed precise. As we idled
along, Mike shouted above the engine noise, pointing out
various switches. Ahead, a small army of marshals in white
coveralls waved us through a series of gates that cut the pits
off from the regular spectator area. I noticed that the telltale
needle on the tachometer pointed at 6,000 rpm's. A telltale is

exactly that: a needle that records the highest rpm reached by the driver. If he goes over the rev limit, the telltale indicts him, with no recourse. As I pulled into a line of cars also awaiting practice, I stopped the engine and asked Mike what kind of rev limit I should use.

"The car will run forever at 7,500 rpm. It's practically bulletproof. And don't pay any attention to the telltale. It's been unreliable for years." I thought about how some drivers flog engines and bear no shame. When Parnelli Jones was the star driver for the Ford Mustang Trans-Am team, he gained a reputation for being hard on equipment and seemed openly proud of it. At one point, an engine builder, a meticulous craftsman, had completed a new power plant for Parnelli. He had spent days precision-fitting the engine, and before its first practice, Parnelli looked at him defiantly and warned, "That thing better be an anvil. Otherwise I'll break the son of a bitch."

I had no intention of testing Mike's Lancia at its absolute limit. "Just to be safe, I'll run it at 7,000. That's give us 500 rpm's margin," I said.

"Oh, you can take it to 7,500," Mike countered unconvincingly. I could tell by the tone of his voice that he'd be happier if I kept it at 7,000.

A marshal was waving his arms, and the line of cars ahead of me was beginning to bellow with sound. My practice session was about to begin, and a hodgepodge of machines, from massive, wide-bottomed Corvettes to tiny Mini-Coopers, were going to run. I was unhappy to see the faster machines like the Corvettes in line. This would mean I'd have to keep my eye on the rearview mirror more than normal, which would cut my concentration on learning the car and the track. With a top speed perhaps 40 mph greater than the Lancia's, the Corvettes would overtake at a rapid rate, and with my novice rating, I didn't want to get in anybody's way. One complaint to the stewards that I was blocking faster cars, and my license could be in jeopardy.

Mike was out of the car now and around on my side, peering into the window to take one final look at the gauges. My helmet was on, and as I pulled on my gloves, the car ahead, a red MG, accelerated down the pit lane. I shouted at Mike, "I'll take five easy laps and then come in." But with the Bell Star helmet covering my face, I couldn't be sure he heard me. He waved casually, his thin face showing no expression, and turned away.

I was alone. It was a beautiful moment of uncertainty, of knowing something was going to happen. A great percentage of adventure, it turns out, is the exquisite anticipation. I turned the car out of the pit lane, and suddenly I was on the racetrack, the legendary surface of Watkins Glen that had absorbed the bite of the best racing cars, driven by many of the greatest drivers of the past two decades. The car spurted ahead, its plucky little engine feeling and sounding more powerful than its modest 1,300-cc size might indicate. As I accelerated past the start-finish line, I spotted the starter, a longtime friend, Bill Moran, standing at trackside holding a green flag. I felt like waving, then realized he couldn't possibly recognize who I was. Behind him were a jumble of officials, including, I presumed, my old pal Clouser. The track curved to the right and up the hill where the TD had crapped out so many seasons before, then darted left and right through a pair of hair-raising S-bends before heading up a long straightaway to a blind, downhill right-hander called the Loop. From there, the track ran straight and level through a grove of trees, then cut sharp left and, following a short straight, right again. This led onto a broad straight that passed a new, partially constructed pit area and into a slow, treacherous 90-degree right-hander just before the start-finish line. It was 2.4 miles in length. The track was in the midst of a multimillion-dollar remodeling program, in which the circuit had been rerouted and lined with a high row of steel barriers on each side. For no apparent reason, the steel fencing had been painted an insipid blue, which looked particularly ugly against the green fields and wooded surroundings of the Glen countryside.

Some of the drivers had complained about the fence, saying that it gave them the impression of driving through a drainpipe, and that the effect of all that close-in steel was claustrophobic. I hardly noticed it. I was too interested in making an acquaintance with the Lancia, which burst out of the esses and bustled up the front straight with surprising alacrity. I braked and downshifted early for the Loop and applied a bit of power as I entered the corner. Front-wheel-drive cars like the Lancia have to be driven slightly differently in that they operate best when their front wheels "tow" them through a corner. The best way to negotiate a corner with a front-wheel-drive car is to steadily increase power as one proceeds through the turn, whereas a conventionally driven automobile will tolerate varying applications of throttle.

As I clipped the apex of the Loop, where the track seemed too narrow because the corner tightened at the bottom of the hill, I saw another friend standing in one of the flag stations. Again I subdued the urge to wave. "Pay attention, Yates," I said out loud.

Upshifting to fourth gear past the pits, I saw Mike standing against the steel rail and gave him a thumbs-up gesture to indicate things were fine. With the start-finish line in sight, I decided to run the Lancia to its rev limit. I saw 7,000 on the tach and slipped into third gear. The little car whined through the esses, and I thrust in the clutch and yanked the shift lever back down toward fourth. The clutch engaged, and the engine made an insane, agonizing shriek. *Holy Christ, I'd hit second gear! Shit!* I punched the clutch again and quickly jammed the shifter into the proper slot. The poor engine quieted down, and I proceeded up the straight, cursing loudly to myself. The oil pressure and temperature gauges—early indicators for a broken engine—read normally. The engine seemed to be humming along as if nothing had happened, so I proceeded. Finally, just before braking for the Loop, I worked up nerve to look at the telltale. It read 8,400 rpm. That son of a bitch isn't *all that* unreliable, I thought to myself. I completed the rest of my five laps without trouble, trying to operate with the kind of smoothness Bill Shaw had taught me and most of all not to hurt Mike's car.

I pulled into the pits and stopped. The day was cool, but I was soaked with sweat. Mike approached the car, looking relieved that his car was unmarred. I smiled widely as I pulled off my helmet to reinforce the impression that everything was all right. "This little shit-box really runs," I said.

"You shouldn't have any trouble winning your class," Mike said. "Everything O.K.?" he asked.

"Perfect. No problems." I almost blurted the confession about the missed shift. For a second it seemed right and decent to confess my mistake. But then it came to me at the last second that the Lancia was apparently uninjured by my error, and such a revelation would only unsettle Mike. I didn't expect that it would happen again, so why worry him over nothing?

"That goddamn telltale; it's gone wonky, I guess," I said, pointing to the stool-pigeon needle.

"Sometimes the vibration bounces it up there," Mike answered. "But then those kinds of revs wouldn't hurt the engine anyway," he added, eyeing me squarely from behind his sunglasses. Old Mike, he knew. He knew the needle didn't bounce up there with any vibrations, it was thrust up there by the dim-bulb driver, but he wasn't sweating it. It would take more than a few extra rpm's to rattle Mike Tillson.

There's a place for practically every racer in SCCA competition. A complicated class system has been established that permits a multitude of cars to compete with each other, some on the basis of comparable performance, others in relation to their engine displacements. Its multiplicity is one reason why paying spectators stay away in droves, but it does offer plenty of opportunity for men with weirdo machines—Abarth Simcas, Griffith 200's, Daimler SP250's, Turner Climaxes, Rene Bonnet CRBs even Lancia Fulvia HFs—to put them on the racetrack for low-cost competition.

The Finger Lakes racing program, referred to as the "Fun One," because of its emphasis on giving the participants as much racing as possible during the course of the two-day weekend, was rather typical of the hundreds of SCCA regionals that are run each season. Once we'd completed practice, a series of six races were scheduled for later in the afternoon. They were to be fifteen minutes in length, and finishing position in those events would determine the starting spot in Sunday's twenty-five-minute races.

Most of the fields were a jumble of classes. My race included everything from BMW 2002 and Datsun 510 sedans to Volvo P1800 coupes and MG Midgets. While I was theoretically competing against everyone on the track, my direct rivals numbered only three: a trio of Mini-Cooper sedans. Those cars, plus mine, composed the "C-Sedan" class—the smallest and slowest of three SCCA sedan classes. "A-Sedan" included such domestic sporty cars as Camaros, Mustangs, and Javelins, while "B-Sedan" was set aside for the Datsuns, BMWs, and Alfas.

The Mini-Coopers, despite their ludicrous, breadbox-on-wheels appearance, were quick. I had seen one of the cars run before; it belonged to a Rochester kid named Miller, the son of a man who managed the Gannett newspaper empire, and I knew that the automobile had all the "goodies," as they say. It could be fast. The other Minis I did not know, but Mike kept assuring me they were no competition.

It had clouded over when the time arrived to drive the Lancia to the false grid behind the pits. There a platoon of marshals parked the cars in the exact position from which they would start. We'd merely roll onto the track, take a warm-up lap, and begin the race when the green flag waved, presumably still lined up in the same order. Our practice laps had been timed by the officials, and the order of start would be based on the fastest times; with the quickest car starting on the pole, and working backward to the slowest. According to the sheet posted by the timers, I would start fifth out of eigh-

teen cars. I was delighted. Maybe I could win overall, I dared
to dream. Mike and I parked the Lancia back down the pit
lane, well away from the false grid, and got out to survey our
competition. Out on the track a mob of Porsches and
Triumphs was churning past, filling the air with a feeble buzz
that sounded like we were being strafed by a squadron of
Piper Cubs.

Slowly our rivals rumbled past and took their places on
the grid. We had plenty of time, but my tensions were accelerating. I couldn't wait any longer. I jumped into the
Lancia, and it came awake, growling. I drove it between the
parked race cars and amid much waving and gesturing from
the marshals, parked it in the vacant fifth position on the
starting line. A girl, dressed in white slacks and jacket and
holding a clipboard, came by, looked at me and my car,
checked her list, and made a mark with her pencil. Five
minutes remained until the race, so I got out once more
and paced around. On the pole was a gray, neatly turned-
out BMW 2002. Too fast for me. Beside him was an aged
Volvo sedan, a bulging old lady that I thought I could beat.
Directly in front of me was another Volvo, a P1800 coupe
driven by a swarthy kid with a broad smile. Parked to my
left was an MG Midget, a squarish English roadster painted
red and sporting shiny wire wheels. The driver was seated
behind the wheel, swathed in his helmet and a Nomex
scarf that covered his face like a train robber's. A network
of roll bar tubes rose high above his head, giving the car a
top-heavy look. Behind me, parked two-by-two, sat the rest
of the field, eleven more small sedans and sports cars that
suddenly looked vulnerable and easily beatable. I was beginning to feel bullish about my chances when a gravelly,
familiar voice sounded at my back. "Jesus Christ, don't you
know this is a young man's sport?"

I turned to face a smiling, blue-eyed man with a hawk nose
and sandy hair. "Bauer, you bastard! What are you doing
here?" I exclaimed. Dick Bauer was a longtime racing friend.
He had worked for Ford as a public-relations man during the

company's great burst of racing fervor in the midsixties and was still involved in the business, operating his own PR firm in New Jersey. He was a friendly, thoughtful, feisty guy who did everything with an intensity that seldom overwhelmed his sense of humor. On that day he was wearing a driver's suit. I stepped back to examine his outfit. "Bauer, you're not in this race, too?" I asked.

He explained that he and a friend were competing with a BMW sedan, and that some mechanical troubles had kept them from posting at qualifying time. He was going to start at the back of the grid. He said that four B-Sedans, including his own, plus a Cortina, a very fast Datsun 510, and another BMW had not officially qualified and would start from the rear. "Watch your ass when we come through, Yates," he kidded. "You should be so lucky," I retorted as he waved and returned to his car. I scanned the other cars at the back of the grid and spotted two of the Minis. The Miller car—the fast one—wasn't to be seen. Mike came over and reported that it wouldn't be in the race. It was sitting alone and ignored on a trailer in the paddock. Something had broken at the last minute.

"If I was a sportsman, I'd say it was too bad he can't run, but let's face it, it's one more we don't have to beat," I said.

Mike smiled and motioned me into the car. The other race was completed. It was silent on the track now. We would be starting soon. I climbed aboard and pulled on my helmet. People trooped past the car and peeked in. Some smiled. I tried to smile back, until I remembered that the Bell Star and the hood covered my face. A marshal at the head of the line started waving his arms, signaling that we were to start our engines. Exhausts began to blat around me. I pressed the Lancia's starter button and felt the little machine vibrate. We all stuck our hands into the air to signal we were ready to roll, simply because in the din the officials couldn't tell which engine was running and which was not.

Another sweeping motion of the official's arm and we jerked ahead, a two-by-two van of multicolored racers snaking out of the pits and onto the track. We lumbered around on the pace lap, nose-to-tail, moving perhaps 60 mph. I tried my steering, veering the Lancia from side to side, then pumped the brakes a few times on the long straights. The noise, blowing in the open window and hammering off the hard metal surfaces of the interior, was deafening. I had intended to wear earplugs but had forgotten them at the last minute. I adjusted the rearview mirror and noticed that the yellow MGA directly behind was jammed against my rear bumper. A certain detached feeling of excitement was coming over me; there was no lightness in my stomach or those strange fibrillations that pass through one's body prior to giving a speech or facing a microphone. I felt as if my sensory organs were operating at their peak, and a total aliveness—that sweetly ominous sense of imminent combat—was filling my brain. "Smoothness, Yates, smoothness," I kept repeating to myself as we wheeled in formation toward the start, lest my urges for competition overwhelm my desire to drive quickly and cleanly.

Bill Moran appeared ahead on the edge of the track, peering at the field from beneath a wide Stetson. He held a green flag in his right hand. The Lancia was in second gear, straining at high revs. Moran lashed out with the flag, and I jammed down the accelerator. Motion and sound became one as I rushed forward, trying to nose the car inside the Volvo in front of me. I caught third gear up the hill, and the red MG was still beside me, challenging for the line through the esses. For a moment I thought we might brush fenders, but we burst free onto the straight in a mad jumble. Ahead I could see the gray BMW had shot into the lead, and the old crock Volvo sedan was hard on his heels. It was fast, and I realized the Lancia didn't have a prayer of catching up. The MGs were falling back, while the Volvo coupe and I struggled briefly for fourth place.

There was little impression of speed. While the surrounding landscape whizzed by at an impressive rate, the cars around me seemed to be mired in place, a few yards ahead and at scattered distances behind. It was as if we were mounted on a roller coaster, all sailing over the landscape at relatively equal speeds. Films about racing suggest that a racing driver's view of the track is a zany pastiche of cars and curves zapping in and out of view like a Keystone Cops chase scene. But it was all strangely stable and in focus. Up ahead I could clearly see the lead BMW. He looked close, as if I would be able to catch him easily by going just a mite faster. It was, of course, the illusion of relative speed. While at trackside the cars appear to be streaking past on the edge of control, the driver's view is broad and stable, much as if one is motoring down a public highway.

A new pair of cars appeared in the rearview mirror. One was the Cortina, its reflected image making it look tall and narrow; the other the blockish form of a BMW; both growing larger in the mirror. They had started at the back of the pack and were catching up at a furious rate. They zapped past me, their exhausts droning beside me for an instant, their drivers peering straight ahead. I had lost two more places, and I mused about my idiotic notion that I might have had a chance to win the race overall. But the Minis were nowhere to be seen, meaning I had a long lead in my class. What's more, Bauer had not appeared.

Mike was manning the pit wall with a sign that said I was in seventh place overall and first in class. I waved to indicate the car was running perfectly, then set myself to take the slow but treacherous 90-degree right-hander at the end of the pit straight. It was a tight, downhill swoop, and the track was bumpy at the entrance, making the car bounce and dip under braking. I tried hard to make the entry with care, applying the brakes a trifle early to reduce the danger of a wheel locking up. The corner could be negotiated at perhaps 50 mph, and because of its modest speed, it inspired overdriving. Poor race drivers tend to drive too fast in the slow corners and too slow in the fast corners.

The Lancia took power and towed itself through the turn without effort. I accelerated down the short straight, past the cluster of officials, including Clouser and Moran, who stood impassively at the finish line. On my left was a high, nearly empty concrete grandstand. Cantilevered out over the track was a platform used by the officials during the major Glen races. As I rushed under the platform, I shifted up to third gear. Nothing happened. The engine revved up, but the shifter stayed in neutral. At first I thought I'd missed another shift, but a second attempt at engagement brought only more helpless sounds from the exhaust. I was rolling up a shallow hill, and the Lancia was losing speed rapidly. Frantically I tried to thrust the transmission into third gear, but it was futile. It seemed as if the clutch had blown. Ahead were the narrow esses, and it occurred to me that at the rate I was coasting, the car would stop in the middle of those bends— where it would very likely be crunched by another car. I had no choice but to punch the brakes and pull the Lancia over to the trackside, snubbing it as close as possible to the steel guard raid.

I stopped the engine and set the parking brake. It was silent for a moment. "Fuck!" I shouted to no one, sitting helplessly inside the car. Then an MG, a Sunbeam, and an Alfa howled past, scrambling up the hill with their suspensions leaned over and looking as if they were going very fast. Occupying a stricken car on the edge of a racetrack is not recommended by safety experts, so I unbuckled my harness and climbed out. As I stepped onto the track, another cluster of cars went by. One of them was a red BMW, and I spotted Bauer, smiling widely and waving. "Fuck you, Bauer," I said, perfunctorily returning his wave and watching him sail away over the crest of the hill, free as a bird.

I walked around to the front of the car, bent down to see if any puddles of oil were gathering underneath, saw nothing unusual, and stood up to remove my helmet. My hair was soaked with perspiration. The cars were streaming by again. Bareheaded, they seemed much louder and more ominous. I stepped behind the guardrail and looked around. There is something totally embarrassing about getting out of

a disabled race car in the middle of a racetrack. I felt as if
every eye in the place were glued on me, and people were
saying, "Look at that dumb bastard, he broke his car." I
suppose it is natural human egocentricity that causes one to
presume that his personal triumphs and disasters are of
equal significance to others—especially in a forsaken
corner of a semideserted track, but I felt chagrined and
frustrated beyond all proportion to the importance of the
moment. The two Minis, my direct competition, buzzed by.
I smiled and shook my head as they disappeared in the
esses. One of them would win now that I was stopped, and
the idea infuriated me.

I thought of Sally on the other side of the track, who would
now be conscious that I had not come by and would be bom-
barded with nightmare images of me being extracted from the
rumpled, smoking ruin of the Lancia. And Mike. He would be
convinced that another missed shift had exploded his poor
little engine like a land mine, sending him into early bank-
ruptcy. I looked at the Lancia once more, inert at the edge of
the track, inches from the skidding bulk of its onetime rivals,
and another awful thought came through my head. The
worst! Years ago, on that miserable day with Clouser's MG, I
had staggered to a halt on this *same* hill. The Lancia was
stopped within yards of the place the MG had chugged its
last, veneering the present disaster with a layer of ironic absurdity.

A youth in white coveralls and a red baseball cap came
puffing up. "You all right?" he yelled over the din.

"Do I look hurt, for Chrissake?" I snapped with unneces-
sary irritation. He was a member of the emergency crew that
manned the communication and flagging network around the
track, and he was only trying to help. It was hardly fair to
punish him for my frustration. "Listen, call the pits on your
phone and tell my crew I think the clutch is blown." He
started to return to his station, then drew up, turned, and
called, "Will you need a truck to bring the car in after the
race?" With the noise I only caught snatches of his question,

but after a few seconds my brain deciphered the message, and
I answered, "Don't I *always* need a tow truck when I stop on
this goddamn hill?"

He looked at me blankly, as if trying to conceal his realization that I was a raving madman, then sprinted back to
his station with his report. Two more forms appeared running across the vacant acreage that separated me from the
pits. My sons, Brock and Daniel, appeared, and I shouted,
"Go and tell your mother everything is all right. I think I
blew the clutch." They jogged away as Mike came up. He
looked passive, even serene. I had expected his face to be
strained with worry, but he approached in a relaxed stroll,
as if nothing had happened. That Mike Tillson, he is a cool
one, I thought.

I reported to him what had happened, and we walked over
to the car. He lifted the hood, ignoring the race cars that
thundered past at his elbow. In the meantime, an MG had
shuddered to a stop on the hill behind the Lancia. Its youthful driver got out and discovered the entire supply of oil from
his crankcase sluicing onto the gravel beneath the car. He'd
"lunched" his engine, as they say, and as he caught my eye,
he smiled meekly. Understanding, I smiled back and
shrugged my shoulders.

The race was over, and the noise went away. Mike got in
and pumped the clutch. He looked puzzled. He snapped on
the engine and gently eased the Lancia into first gear. It
scrambled ahead, its clutch biting firmly. "The clutch feels
fine," he said. We drove onward, with me sitting on the bare
floor, holding my gloves and helmet. Mike explained that he
presumed a small tensioner spring on the shifting mechanism
had fallen off—a minor failure but one that made gear-chang-
ing practically impossible. It had been good, in a way, that
nothing more had happened. But I was still disappointed
about the result.

Mike cruised around the entire track, and I peered out the
window to stare back at the knots of stone-faced spectators
and flagmen who watched our progress. We were heading for

the pits, where I knew I would explain my troubles a dozen times, using each, I suppose, as an opportunity to absolve myself of blame. In the meantime, Mike would replace the spring, and tomorrow—beautiful, perfect, feverishly anticipated tomorrow—we would race again. Tomorrow we couldn't lose.

7

Sunday rose warm and cloudy over the Finger Lakes. A thick haze blanketed the great trough that contained Lake Seneca to the north. I had not slept particularly well, having run and rerun the race of the day before, always to have it end in helpless immobility on the edge of the track. But the dawn had brought renewed hope, as always, and by the time the racing program began again, I was convinced the day would be better.

I went down to the starting line and stood against the fence, chatting with Clouser. We laughed again about the old days and watched in alternate shock and amusement as a series of Formula Vee racers (inexpensive, unstable, open-wheel cars based on Volkswagen components that are popular among amateur competitors) careened off the track, some merely spinning amid billowing clouds of dust, others clouting the fence and sending wheels and shredded bodywork skittering across the track. No one was hurt in the bashes, so our conversation turned to other things. "Your friend Bauer is raising hell," Clouser said.

"Oh, yeah, what about?" I asked.

"He says he's going to protest the whole goddamn mess of BMWs in your race. He claims they are all underweight." Most classes of racing cars have a minimum weight regulation of some kind. This is to equalize the competition, obviously, and to prevent builders from making cars so light and flimsy that safety and structural integrity will be affected. "Bauer says most of the BMWs he raced against yesterday were under the legal weight limit. Now he says he wants them weighed, under his protest, before they can race again."

"Hell, there's about half a dozen of those cars here. Are you going to weigh all of them before they race?" I asked.

"We'll wait until afterward. Who knows, maybe Bauer will win and forget the whole thing."

"He'll have to run a helluva lot faster than he did yesterday," I said.

Because I had not finished the preliminary race, I had to start at the back of the field in the twenty-five minute feature event. Two other cars, a pair of BMWs—one known to be among the fastest in area racing circles—were to start behind me simply because they hadn't been able even to run the day before. I knew the quick one, a neat white model driven by a University of Rochester graduate student and part-time mechanic named Mike Noble, would be far faster than I. The other guy I wasn't so sure about. Mike Tillson came up smiling. "The Mini drivers have a plan," he said, obviously amused. "I just overheard them talking. The guy in the red number eleven is going to block you at the start, so that the other guy, the one driving the green car, can get the lead."

"Jesus, that sounds like something out of an Elvis Presley movie," I said.

Bauer came up. He was in street clothes. He explained that his partner was going to drive. I asked him about the protests. "Those bastards are all too light, and goddamnit, it just isn't fair. Guys like us try to observe the rules, and these guys come here with cheater cars. Well, it's their ass if they aren't legal."

The start was beautiful. Tagging along at the end of the seventeen-car field, with Noble hugged behind, I hit the starting line on the end of a long, mechanical crack-the-whip. Noble's superior acceleration got him past me in an instant, but he was blocked by slower cars, and we sailed through the esses nose-to-tail. We roared onto the long front straight with the BMW running interference like a big guard clearing the way for a halfback (except in this case the lineman could outrun the ballcarrier). I was barging past slower cars, gobbling them up in twos and threes. It was an exquisite orgasm of power. I easily passed the two Minis and thought about their abortive blocking tactic. So long, dead-ass, I thought giddily as they fell behind. I was taken with the urge to stick my arm out the window and fling them the finger, but I was burrowing into the Loop amid a collection of other cars, and there was no time. The Volvo coupe that I had run with briefly the day before rose up on my left. I braked hard and nosed inside him at the entrance of the corner, stealing his line. He fell back. I had him. In that opening flurry I had passed eight cars, placing me roughly where I had been at the start of yesterday's race. The Volvo was only slightly faster, and I managed to hold him off for a few laps. Its driver, the grinning kid, had enough power to pull alongside at the end of the straight, but the Lancia's stronger brakes got me deeper into the turns, and I ran ahead briefly. In the end, his superior speed prevailed, and he lunged by and slowly pulled out a big lead.

The red MG challenged for a few laps, then gave up for some unknown reason, and lost ground. I was alone. The track ahead and behind me was empty. The faster cars had outdistanced me, while I was well ahead of perhaps eight others.

Then two cars showed up in my rearview mirror. At first they were specks darting among the guardrails, then they loomed larger and larger. I was taken with a certain panic. Had I slowed down? Had somebody at the back of the field found a secret reservoir of power? I bustled along, distracted by my new pursuers. Soon they came close enough so that I could identify them. They were the vanguard of the bigger B-Sedans. Holy Christ, I thought, they are coming like the hammers of hell. Those early fantasies about beating them took on a new level of absurdity as they powered by me: first a faded yellow Datsun 510, then Noble, followed closely by another BMW. It was a shattering experience. Blowing off those stragglers on the opening lap had puffed my confidence to a point where I thought I was capable of running with anybody on the track, and there I was, being mercilessly lapped by the leaders.

My concentration was broken briefly, and I noticed Bauer's red BMW appear on the horizon. Now even the slow guys were catching up. I tried to drive faster. Swooping off the loop at the south end of the track, I overtook the Cortina. He was in trouble, limping toward the pits. I passed him, then noticed that he had speeded up, and the mass of his bigger car filled my mirror. We hustled down the straight with him glued to my bumper. For a moment I thought he might be trying to bash me in the rear. Go ahead and hit me, you dumb bastard, I thought defiantly. Then he fell back, slowing down to his original crippled pace. I wondered what the point of his burst of power had been, other than possibly to demonstrate to me that I had passed him only because he was having trouble. People sure do silly things on racetracks, I mused.

The goddamn red BMW was gaining. Within two laps he was hovering around my tail, inching closer all the time. Several corner workers began to show me a blue flag—a signal to notify the driver of a slower car that he is being overtaken and should give way. The flagmen at the Glen are notorious for excessive use of the blue flag, being inclined to wave it whenever two cars get in sight of each other. Screw you, flag-wavers, I said to myself. If that son of a bitch back there wants to get by me, he'll have to drive past. We hurried on, nose-to-tail, for several more laps. More blue flags. I was furious. This was an equal race between equal cars, and I was damned if I'd politely move over. As I passed the pits, somebody hung over the wall and waved the blue flag at me and pointed angrily. I gave him the finger, shoving my gloved hand up against the windshield, and tossing the bird at him for the entire world to see.

The BMW and I were hard at it. I didn't know the guy in the car, Bauer's partner, from a row of soldiers, but I hated him. I wanted to see him disappear, to hit the wall, to lunch his engine, to spin out, to flip upside down through a wood lot; I didn't give a damn how he did it, but I didn't want him back there anymore. We came past the pits again, aiming for the 90-degree sweeper. He came alongside, on my right, obviously planning to outbrake me and steal my line. I went as deep as I thought I could before punching my brakes, but he went deeper. He had passed me, but somehow I felt I could repass him at will, and I savored the thought of revenge. Then, as I accelerated past Bill Moran, I saw him standing at the edge of the track with the checkered flag in his hand. The race was over! The BMW had passed me on the last corner!

Rationalizing that the loss to the BMW had meant nothing because he had been in a faster class, I headed for the pits. I'd won C-Sedan decisively, even if my only competition had been two rather slow Minis. However, I'd finished seventh overall, having beaten a number of presumably faster machines. That was ample compensation for yesterday's debacle and for my last-minute loss to Bauer and his friend. When I climbed out of the car in the pit area, Mike was there, his face spread with a broad smile, prompted in part, I'm sure, by the realization that his Lancia had survived the ordeal without apparent damage. My sons showed up, leading a small van of rooters including Sally, my nine-year-old daughter, Claire, plus Betts and his wife. I drank a Coke and leaned against the car, absorbing those glowing moments of postvictory. How I had won, whom I had beaten, my competence or lack of it, were of no consequence. Postmortems would come later, but that time was reserved for unabashed elation and the simplistic gratification of ego.

There might be less denunciation of mankind's primitive distraction with victory if the world permitted more winning. Everybody experiences such moments of glory, be it in a game of cribbage or a pie-baking contest, and to deny that they are an endemic human need is to misunderstand the very spirit of man. We hear more and more complaining about sports and their "dehumanizing emphasis on victory at all costs." What a pitiful bleat. To remove man's urge to compete and to triumph, especially on an individual basis, is to carve up his soul. While much of man's savagery can be traced to his competitive urges, *all* of his laudable feats, from politics to religion, have somehow accrued from his motivations to doubt, to struggle, to innovate, to compete against the existing state. The essence of competition is the questioning of the status quo; the perverse refusal to accept the premise that a given system, government, ideology, team, or individual cannot be bettered. Being a primitive animal, man often translates this competitive zeal into nasty spates of bloodshed (which, as Lord Kenneth Clark observes, invariably accompanies the rise of all advanced civilizations), but for better or worse, these restless compulsions to prove one's worth against another have served man from the time that he, furless, skinny, and short-toothed, began to challenge nature itself. To dispense with them in behalf of a utopian state of undistilled pacifism, to destroy the hawk for the sake of the dove, would bring about the end of mankind as surely as the ultimate nuclear competition.

I enjoyed my triumph, limited and forgettable as it was, as a simple, slightly savage human being. The race had been for a small prize, and the compensation was simple joy.

When the racing was over and a suggestion of evening was

looming over the track, they tapped a keg of beer at the base of the timing tower. Everybody was invited, and they stood in line, chattering about the events of the day, clutching paper cups, while volunteers manned the tap, feeding rations of foam-clogged brew to each celebrant. It was a time for reflection and relaxation, and I had to admit to myself that it was pure pride that had prevented me from changing out of my driver's suit. I drained off a few ounces of warm beer from beneath the foam and knew deep down that I still wore that uniform because it was a pure macho symbol that placed me within the elite of the assemblage. If I had lost, if my car had once more stumbled to a halt on that devilish hill, I no doubt would have leaped into my street clothes quicker than a coal miner fresh out of the portal.

Clouser came up, looking weary. He said that he had just returned from a stormy inspection session, where, in accordance with Bauer's protest, the BMWs had been weighed. Three of them, he said, had been disqualified for being too light. One of the cars had been four hundred pounds underweight.

"*Four hundred pounds!*" I exclaimed. "Good God, how can you possibly miss by that much?" Cheating by building a car under the weight limit is not common, simply because the ploy is so easily detectable. Most expert stock-car builders will carve vast amounts of weight off the standard shell, then reballast the machine to the proper level, with the weight located nearer the center of gravity to enhance handling, but simply removing gobs of illegal pounds is rare. Taking off four hundred extra pounds is madness.

Clouser chuckled. "You would not believe this kid. He modified the car himself, see, and said he guessed at the weight when it was finished. Then he took it down to the local coalyard and put it on their scales. To save time, he weighed it on his trailer, then subtracted the weight. So I asked the kid, 'How much did the trailer weigh?' He said a guy had sold him a very lightweight trailer, and it only weighed three hundred pounds. *Three hundred goddamn pounds* for a steel trailer designed to haul a 2,500-pound car, can you believe that poor schmuck? The thing probably weighed closer to a thousand pounds, and of course when he got through with his calculations, the weight of his car was a helluva lot less than he thought it was. He figured his car was legal."

"So what did you do?"

"What could I do? I threw his ass out."

They set out a portable PA system near the beer keg, and a tall, scholarly lawyer in horn-rimmed glasses, who'd been active in amateur racing for years, began to announce the winners. Each class, twenty-one in all, was recognized. Trophies were awarded to the first four finishers in each category, meaning that an endless line of drivers trooped forward to receive offical recognition for their efforts. Such was the compensation for amateur racing: this collection of bowls, mugs, plates, and plaques. I was doubly compensated. For winning I received a handsome silver-plated serving plate engraved, THE FUN ONE, CLASS WINNER. I was also given a sheet of paper that stated I had set an offical lap record for the C-Sedan class at 82.383 mph. While this looked good, my elation was tempered by the knowledge that this was the first time amateur sports cars of any kind had run on the remodeled Glen course, and therefore, my record, while fastest for that particular weekend, would likely fall to more serious C-Sedan competitors.

It was nearing darkness by the time I gathered up the family and headed home. A few hangers-on still clustered around the beer keg, and the empty track echoed to the raucous buzz of a small motorcyle bounding over its infield. Station wagons and tired sedans moved away, towing the race cars toward a hundred destinations, their owners dreaming for the most part of better days. So it was with me, cruising easily over the low, wooded hills toward home. In two weeks there would be another race at Watkins Glen, only this time my car would not be a friendly, indestructible, forgiving little Lancia, but Warren Agor's nasty, overpowered Camaro. And my competition would not be weekend racers in underpowered Minis, but the likes of Mark Donohue, Peter Revson, George Follmer, and some of the fastest race cars in the world.

8

Agor was late. I had paced around the Watkins Glen Tech building for two hours awaiting his arrival, and as each minute passed, I became more concerned that the whole thing might have involved serious misunderstanding; that perhaps he and his team weren't arriving until tomorrow. Two weeks had passed since my small triumph in the Lancia, and the scene at the Glen was vastly different. It was only Friday, but the place was clogged with cars and people. It was to be a major weekend of racing, with a series of National Championship amateur sports-car events on Saturday and two Trans-American Championship contests: one for small sedans, the other for the "big cars," Camaros, Mustangs, Javelins, and the like, on Sunday. Dust rose from the roads as a constant stream of traffic crisscrossed the infield. Large transporters and semitrailers were parked everywhere, each emblazoned with the logo of a racing team, while mobs of perspiring mechanics labored with racing machines in the late-morning sun.

Inside the Tech building, away from the heat, it was wall-to-wall automobiles. Stalls along the outer perimeter and in the center of the large, dim room were occupied by gleaming Trans-Am machines, most of them on jack stands with their hoods yawning open like ducklings waiting to be fed. A pair of aisles were jammed with more cars undergoing technical inspection. On one side were the amateur cars, a similar but larger collection to that which had appeared two weeks earlier. On the other was a line of Trans-Am machines, for the most part Camaros and Mustangs. Inspectors in white coveralls hovered over them, interrupting their intent gaze on the mechanical innards only to consult their ever-present clipboards. The entire technical inspection was being supervised by a gaunt man with a trimmed Vandyke named John Timanus. A California veteran of sports-car competition, both as a driver and builder, for much of his adult life, it was Timanus's job to make final judgment on whether or not a car was qualified for competition. Some of his decisions had to be based on considerations of safety: if a roll bar was welded properly or a seat belt mounted so that it would stay secure in a series of flips, etc. But it was the other part of Timanus's job that had given him the early crow's feet and a permanent look of weariness. Racers are persistent, ingenious cheaters, and it was his assignment to insure that every competitor was operating within the rules. The deck was stacked against him like a customs inspector in Marseilles. On pure racing cars, such as the ones used at Indy or on the Grand Prix circuit, rules are simple and therefore outright cheating is rare. But whenever production cars are converted for competition, such as in Grand National stock-car racing or the Trans-Am series, the rules can be stretched to absurd limits. Engines and front suspensions are often moved to improve handling; bodies are lightened by dipping the fenders, hood, etc., into tanks of acid; windshields and hoods are pared down to improve streamlining; specially built, nonproduction parts are substituted for pieces the rules specify must remain stock; *ad infinitum*. It is a never-ending game of deception and detection, the competitors generally staying a step or two ahead of the inspectors—even as capable and conscientious a man as John Timanus. But he was plugging. At Watkins Glen he was checking the engine displacements of all the Trans-Am cars. The big machines had an engine limit of 305 cubic inches, and each crew was required to let Timanus personally measure the size of their powerplant. He stood over each car holding a polished aluminum tube, called a P&G meter, which he placed in one of the spark-plug holes. He impassively watched a gauge as the engine was turned over. The result was irreconcilable; either the displacement was within legal limits or it was not. There was no arguing with John Timanus's aluminum tube.

He caught one. A ranking SCCA national champion, no less, was detected trying to enter a Camaro with a 350-cubic-inch engine—45 cubic inches oversize. Timanus quietly threw him out of the race and went on with his business, looking for more violators.

The building was full of the sound of blatting engines, clanging tools, and urgent voices trying to overcome the noise. That distinct smell of automobiles, a mysterious amalgam of paint, oil, gasoline, rubber, and plastics, which pervades all garages, was overwhelming. In a corner the Goodyear racing crew had stacked fat, oversized competition tires in teetering tiers that rose nearly to the ceiling. People milled everywhere: journalists snapping cameras and scribbling notes, curious couples strolling hand-in-hand, and the harried mechanics trying to work in the noisy, crowded semi-darkness. It was a typical opening scene for a major weekend of racing, as confusing and disorganized as the sport itself, but somehow contributing to that magic crescendo when the field of Trans-Am cars would be rolled into the sunlight and onto the track for two hundred miles of racing. If all went according to plan—which at that moment seemed increasingly doubtful—I would be in that race on Sunday, two days hence. *If* Warren Agor showed up with his two cars.

Agor had been a Trans-Am regular for two years. He had

burst on the racing scene in one furious season, winning the SCCA Rookie of the Year award and proving himself to be both a fine mechanic and driver. He'd become interested in racing while serving a routine army tour in Germany, then returned home to work as a mechanic for several seasons with the crackerjack racing team of Roger Penske and Mark Donohue. Having gained invaluable training with that organization, he'd quit and returned home to Rochester, New York, where he'd built a Camaro Trans-Am machine as close to the exacting Penski/Donohue specifications as he had known how.

Not enjoying direct sponsorship from General Motors, Ford, American Motors, or Chrysler, all of whom underwrote big-buck racing enterprises in the Trans-Am at one time or another, Agor was known as a fast, capable, independent driver—a man whose equipment was not as rapid as the complicated, handcrafted machines run by Donohue and Follmer, but whose skills were above average. No one would ever know how good he was until he got his chance in a first-class car, so he labored diligently, racing mightily for his fifth- and sixth-place finishes, hoping that he would be recognized by a major sponsor.

He came into Watkins Glen at the head of an impressive caravan. In the lead was a two-ton Chevy closed truck with WARREN AGOR RACING ENTERPRISES written along its stainless steel flanks. Behind it, toggled to a dual-axle trailer, was an orange Camaro Trans-Am car bearing number 13, Agor's personal race car. At the rear was an ungainly motor home, looking about as agile and road-worthy as a four-wheeled split-level. The caravan eased to a halt outside the Tech building, and Agor himself slipped from behind the wheel of the Chevy truck. He was a thick-shouldered blond who somehow looked taller than his six feet. In his midtwenties, he was given to a fullness around his midsection, which was accentuated by his Prussian, chin-out, arched-back stride. He exuded confidence, if not cockiness, primarily because of his manner of movement. His outthrust chin and arrogant mouth, which tended to curl rather than smile, served to buttress the impression of self-assurance. Only his eyes, which were wide and soft around the edges and were sometimes positively doelike in their transmission of sensitivity, gave his appearance a saving balance of humility. He was a junior stockbroker by day and a full-time racer in the evenings and on weekends, and as he climbed out of the truck, dressed in a pair of rumpled slacks and an oil-stained button-down shirt, squinting against the dust and sunlight, it was difficult to imagine him bound up in a gray suit and wired to a telephone, hustling odd lots of Continental Can to retired pharmacists. He wasted no time, greeted me as he snapped open the rear doors of the truck and reached for a wrench to unbolt the Camaro from its perch on the trailer. With him was a sad-eyed, muscular youth who looked exhausted. Agor introduced him as Jerry Breon, and they set to work freeing the race car.

"Your car isn't here yet," Agor said, flipping a length of chain into the rear of the truck. "The rest of the crew is still back at the shop trying to get it finished up. The poor bastards have been working on the thing for two days straight."

My car, the sister machine to the orange Camaro sitting in front of me, was supposed to have been completed weeks ago, but racing cars are seldom finished on schedule. It is the endemic optimism of racing that prevents everybody from making hard, dispassionate appraisals of how long it will take to build something, and people always err on the side of blind faith. It is known that building a Trans-Am car like the Camaro takes upward of a thousand man-hours of hard labor, but everybody is convinced it can be done in half the time, and schedules are set accordingly. Foolish perhaps, but then a vast percentage of the world is convinced that crafting a racing automobile that can be smashed into a ball of bent steel in an instant is the embodiment of folly anyway, so what difference does it make? Except to the builders, victims of their own optimism, and to me, who was hoping that I would have plenty of time on the track to practice with the new car.

After all, it had never rolled a wheel, and God only knew what multitudes of problems might arise. What's more, this was no weekend regional. I would be out there trying to maintain control of a 475-horsepower monster. I wanted very badly to get a feel of the new machine before trying to go quickly.

"When do you think they'll get my car here?" I asked, fearing the answer.

"It won't be long. They had it about finished when we left. Just hooking up a few wires and minor stuff like that. They'll be rolling in anytime now," Agor answered confidently.

"How's it look? Will it be a competitive car?" I asked, seeking reassurance that it hadn't been cobbled together at the last minute.

"No problem," Warren said firmly. "The car is identical to mine. We built it exactly the same way. It's going to be a good car, I'll guarantee you. In fact, your engine is brand-new. Really fresh. It's probably stronger than mine. We just bought it from Bartz and stuck it in. I was tempted to steal it and put it in my car, but we didn't have time," he said, smiling.

Al Bartz is a Southern California race-engine builder who specialized in modifying Chevrolet power plants for competition. Ready to go, they cost in the neighborhood of $5,000 —a reasonable cost when it is recalled that the engines used in Indy and Grand Prix competition have over-the-counter price tags six times that expensive. This Agor operation was no cheap romance. While they had no major sponsors, i.e., one of the tire or auto manufacturers, they used a sensible mixture of available funds and hard work to build and run very presentable machines indeed. I took a closer look at Agor's Camaro as it was rolled into the line for technical inspection. The interior was empty except for a black vinyl bucket seat and a spiderweb of thick tubes that formed the roll cage. Rather than being a simple hoop of metal like that used on the Lancia, the Camaro's cage was a trussed steel frame that not only protected the driver in the event of a crash, but added immense structural integrity to the chassis of the car. By stiffening the frame, the handling was improved. All the interior metal surfaces were painted naval gray. The dash panel had been ripped out and replaced with a bare sheet of stainless steel that contained a cluster of efficient-looking circular instruments and toggle switches. Bolted to the floor beside the seat was a small fire extinguisher. The engine compartment was stark and polished with a neat collection of hoses and wires cocooned around the 305-cubic-inch Bartz Chevy—an instrument capable of producing about 475 horsepower at 8,500 rpm and propelling the 3,000-pound vehicle in which it resided at speeds up to 185 mph. The car's external appearance had a bare, brutal quality about it. Aside from large number 13's on its doors and hood, its orange surface was empty of markings and the pockmarks of decals that smear the surface of most racing cars. The fenders had been flared to accommodate the immense racing tires, giving the machine a bulging, musclebound look. The headlights had been removed and their openings used as air intakes for cooling the front brakes. With the chassis lowered to give the Camaro an angled, droop-nose attitude, the gutted headlights helped to make the front view of the car seem downright vicious. From beneath each door protruded a gaping exhaust pipe the diameter of a large flagpole. In all, the Camaro had that squat, sparse, purposeful appearance common to all first-class racing machines, and I could only hope my car was half as good.

Warren, Jerry Breon, and I had just rolled the Camaro into the noisy murk of the Tech building when a spare, worried-looking man walked up. With him was a rather pretty-taciturn girl in her late twenties. He was introduced to me as Dave Hoselton, the man I knew was bankrolling a substantial part of the Agor racing effort. He was the third-generation owner of a prosperous Chevrolet and Toyota automobile agency in suburban Rochester and was known as a quiet, close-mouthed, astute businessman. His large eyes, unblinking behind a pair of *au courant* steel-rimmed glasses, dominated his face. His wiry, medium-sized frame carried outsized appendages. His hands and feet seemed too large for his body, as did his nose and mouth, giving him a kind of overburdened look, as if an extra gravitational force was trying to suck him into the earth. He said little to me, other than to force a cordial smile and introduce his wife, Coralei, who was one of those limber, capable, slightly aloof, upper-middle-class *hausfraus* who didn't look particularly at home among the clutter and confusion of the Tech building, but made it evident that, by God, she stood at her husband's side.

David Hoselton was going to drive. On Saturday, the day before the Trans-Am, he planned to take my car (more correctly, *his* car that I was supposed to drive) and compete in the SCCA National Amateur events. In fact, Warren had entered that race as well, primarily to gain enough points to qualify for the prestigious American Road Race of Champions, a runoff for the top SCCA amateurs held annually in Atlanta. Therefore, Hoselton and I were to share the same machine, a prospect that hardly seemed encouraging, considering the fact that it hadn't even arrived at the track.

The great ark motor home, which Hoselton and his wife had driven to the track, had been stationed near the pits, within a short walking distance of another partially finished garage. It was a gargantuan structure, nearly one thousand feet in length, designed to house the competitors' cars and equipment during the races. Its roof and walls were finished, but a network of scaffolding still scarred the outside, and workmen in hard hats scrambled busily, trying to complete the project. Jerry Breon, who had turned out to be Coralei Hoselton's younger brother and Purdue freshman spending his summer vacation with the racing team, had backed the truck up to a loading bay in the new building while Warren had driven the Camaro down the pit lane. After quickly changing into his driving suit and checking the engine's timing, he made ready to run in the Trans-Am practice session that was already under way. Because of the nearly four hundred cars that were entered at the Glen that weekend — over three hundred amateurs plus approximately eighty large and small cars for the Trans-Am—the practice periods were carefully scheduled to permit everyone to get some familiarization laps. The big Trans-Am cars were already running by the time Agor accelerated out of the pits, the Camaro's engine making ferocious ripping sounds as the car disappeared toward the first turn. Hoselton, Jerry, and I took station along the pit wall. A cluster of cars thundered past. I didn't recognize any of them. Then a red, white, and blue Javelin, its wide snout practically dragging along the pavement, sailed off the turn at the head of the straight and arrowed toward us. It had to be Donohue. The car streaked past, revealing a large number 6 on its doors, and confirming the fact that it was Mark Donohue in the Roger Penske Javelin. With full American Motors backing, rumored to total over half a million dollars per year, Donohue and Penske were dominating the Trans-Am. Their only serious rivals were a pair of orange Boss 302 Mustangs entered by a wily South Carolina stockcar expert named Bud Moore and driven by George Follmer and Peter Gregg. Two of Penske's year-old Javelins were also present, owned by a wealthy young Californian named Roy Wood. Wood himself had raced until earlier that season when he'd crashed off the first turn at Riverside, California, and badly broken his leg. Now he'd come to Watkins Glen, gimping along at the head of a lavishly equipped organization, including a dozen mechanics, two canary-yellow Javelins, and a pair of excellent drivers, the versatile Englishman Vic Elford and Peter Revson, fresh from winning the pole position at Indianapolis and victories in several Can-Am events.

Agor made one lap, then came into the pits with a soft rear tire. That corrected, he took to the track again only to have the practice session end. He rumbled off the track, blipping the Chevy engine to keep the plugs clear, and drove straight into the big garage where Jerry had staked out two spaces. "We've got another practice later in the afternoon," he said, climbing out of the car. "Just in case, you better get your uniform on and get ready. If the car feels good, I'll take a few laps and then you can try it out." I ducked into the motor home to change, trying to scramble as quickly as possible out of my street clothes and into my fireproof socks, underwear, and coveralls in the cramped bedroom space at the back. Up front, Coralei Hoselton was efficiently bustling around the tiny kitchen, preparing the place as a combination command post and hospitality suite for the Agor team. As I was about to leave, carrying my helmet under my arm like an oversized football, she said, "Good luck, and I hope you like the car, Mr. Yates."

"Thanks. But forget the 'mister' stuff. Just call me Brock," I said.

Coralei Hoselton looked at me with level brown eyes, her face serious. "That isn't all I'll call you if you break our car," she said evenly.

She wasn't kidding. She was telling me in no uncertain terms that she didn't want some flake walking in there and busting the family racer. Mildly stunned, I groped for a face-saving rejoinder and finally stammered, "Call me anything you want; just don't call me late for din-din." Then I stepped out of the motor home and walked to the garage, wondering if Coralei Hoselton's warning meant that the team was a good deal more uptight than it appeared on the surface.

Agor's Camaro wasn't stopping well, having a tendency to yank itself to the right under hard braking, so Warren and Jerry had the car on jack stands by the time I got changed. It wouldn't be running for a while, so I wandered off down the pits. Dozens of Trans-Am cars lined the pit lane, and I noticed that the cars and the people around me were covered with labels. The sides of the automobiles were plastered with decals: GOODYEAR, FIRESTONE, CHAMPION, AUTOLITE, KONI, STP, the names of sponsoring dealers and lists of people associated with the machines, including a few notations on some cars that said PAINT BY ... Many of the people looked as if they'd been dipped in badges: cloth emblems of car marques, racetracks, and product brand names covered every available square inch of material, even on the sleeves. It seemed as if everybody had either a stopwatch or a camera strung around

his or her neck. Even I, ambling through the crowd, was so
marked. My jacket carried a *Car and Driver* emblem, and my
driving suit was embroidered fore and aft with FIRESTONE.
Something would have to be done about that, I noted, because Agor had a deal for racing tires with Goodyear, and
they would hardly be pleased to have me driving around
shrouded in a suit supplied by their archrival. I mused about
this compulsion to be identified and wondered if it was
stronger in the United States than elsewhere. It was not, I
decided, recalling that the European tracks I had attended
had been even more extravagantly decorated with logos,
brand names, and commercial identification than in the
buck-hungry old United States. The personal badge-wearing
was more complicated. A vast majority of those present had
nothing whatsoever to do with the products whose names
they bore. While a driver or car owner might wear a badge
because it involved certain commercial benefits (at least free
tires, spark plugs, lubricants, etc., or at best lucrative, long-
range contracts), those among the general fans and spectators
who put STP decals in the back windows of their Pontiacs or
walked around the pits in Watkins Glen wearing blue and
white Goodyear jackets, for which they had paid good money,
were operating as free mini-sandwich men. Why? While
some psychologists might conclude that it involved some va-
cancy of the id, an identity gap of some mysterious sort, it
seemed to me nothing more than a normal fan reaction to the
sport they loved. While football crowds buy banners and
blankets to associate themselves with their favorite teams,
racing nuts wear jackets laden with badges and load their
cars with decals simply to make a personal statement about
their devotion to racing: to be part of the action.

I wandered back to the garage where Warren thought he
had solved the brake problem and was getting ready to make
the final qualifying session of the day. While it was apparent
that my car wouldn't get a chance to run, I still held out a
slight hope that I might get a few laps in his, simply to get the
feel of the machine. Agor jumped in and fired up the engine

as Breon let the car off the jack. The sound was deafening, and as he was backing out of the stall, a uniformed "rent-a-cop" hired for the weekend came running up, waving his arms. He wanted the engine shut off. Agor obliged. "What's the matter?" Warren asked.

"You can't run any engines in the building," said the cop, a wispy, slack-featured man whose hat hung on his ears.

"Who says?" asked Agor sharply.

"The steward."

"What kind of shit is that? I'm trying to get out of here for practice."

"Don't make any difference, that's the rule. And by the way, don't try to use any of these side entrances or exits. Everybody coming in and out of the building has to use the door at the far end."

We looked down the great gallery and saw the door in the distance. There were numerous openings along the sides, but some idiot within the Parkinsonian maze of volunteers that run SCCA races had decided that only one entrance could be used. Shrugging our shoulders, Hoselton, Breon, and I began pushing Agor and his Camaro down the long aisle. As we got nearer the end, the congestion worsened. Cars from the previous practice session were arriving, and soon the entrance was blocked in both directions. I watched Agor in the cockpit, and his eyes glazed over with rage and impatience. "Fuck this action," he growled, and started his engine. The Bartz exhaust sound hammered menacingly off the steel walls. Shocked heads turned as Agor crammed the car into reverse and barged backward away from the jam, disregarding anything that might be behind. I managed to leap aside, with the rear fender clearing me by inches, and Agor screeched along in reverse until he found an open side door. The rent-a-cop stood in inert helplessness as Agor punched the car into first gear and roared out of the building. He was being paid, the cop no doubt reasoned, to keep order in the building, but that did not require him to do combat with a runaway race car.

Agor roared off to qualify. I was becoming more and more

depressed by the minute. Even if my car rolled through the gate at that very moment, technical inspection and other details would consume so much time that the session would be over before it would be ready to run. Warren was still having troubles, and there appeared to be little chance that I'd get the opportunity to drive his car either. When the qualifying period was over, we returned to the garage to discover that Agor Racing Enterprises had been ejected for breaking the rules. Furious, Agor charged off in the direction of the official who'd issued the ban, while Hoselton and I walked back to the motor home. On the surface he seemed like a brooding, humorless guy who carried his burdens with visible strain. But this impression was largely attributable to physical appearance and a natural reticence, and he in fact possessed a substantial sense of humor.

He opened a beer for me while his wife puttered silently in the kitchen, and we sat down, he at the small table and I in the swivel-type copilot's seat up front. He commented that Mark Donohue would be dropping by shortly. "Mark really gets bugged by all the people," said Hoselton. "He kind of hides out in here sometimes. He's known Warren for a long time, I guess, and he feels at home with us. At least he can get away from the autograph hunters."

"I suppose he's been quite a bit of help, giving Warren technical advice on how to set up the cars and stuff like that," I said.

Hoselton produced an ironic smile. "He tells us just enough. But not too much." The implication was that Mark Donohue, perhaps the most capable chassis tuner and development engineer among all big-time racers, wasn't telling Agor everything; that he was holding in reserve some critical information on making a Camaro go fast. It was natural. He hadn't reached the pinnacle of the sport by sharing his secrets, even with longtime associates.

He bounced into the motor home, his round, cherubic face spread wide with a smile, but his eyes looked weary. He swung easily into the cramped eating booth and accepted a

Coke from Coralei Hoselton. I had first met Mark Donohue six years earlier when he was a struggling weekend race driver, scratching out a living in a shoestring auto manufacturing concern on Long Island. He had been out of Brown University only a few years then, but had long since shed any intention of pursuing his vocation as an engineer. Operating as the firm's designer, shop manager, research and development director, and test driver, his prospects of success in racing seemed nil. His close friend and mentor in the sport had been Walt Hansgen, a fellow New Jerseyite who was among the greatest road-racing drivers America ever produced. Hansgen, a gentle man who'd first gained fame with the racing team sponsored by the famous sportsman Briggs Cunningham, had gone on to the very pinnacle of the sport and near the end convinced the Ford Motor Company that a squeaky-voiced, crew-cut kid in Bass Weejuns named Mark Donohue was good enough to drive their cars at places like Daytona, Sebring, and Le Mans. This old pro and his young pal were great at Daytona and Sebring, but they never made Le Mans. Hansgen went to France early to test a powerful 7-liter Ford prototype and crashed at the end of the pit straight. He lived a few days, comatose from massive head injuries, then died. I will not forget that day. When I read the news in the old New York *Herald Tribune* that morning, over breakfast coffee, my two little sons began to cry. They had never met Walter Hansgen, but they had considered him one of their heroes, simply because he had been a topic of conversation in their house. I sat there, watching them sob, and wondered what in hell I was doing involved in a sport that killed my sons' heroes. With Walt Hansgen's death, Mark Donohue lost his ride with Ford and fell into limbo until Roger Penske, himself a retired race driver and a button-down entrepreneur of the first rank, was able to promote a racing program with some prime sponsors and field a car. His driver was Donohue. It makes an interesting footnote on the intensity of motor racing that Penske first mentioned the possibility of teaming with Mark at the funeral of Walt Hansgen.

Some people had trouble taking Mark Donohue seriously at the start. His pie-faced, good nature, coupled with a toe-scuffing bashfulness and a disposition for saying "Gosh" and "Gee" in moments of extreme stress, labeled him as a Boy Scout among the big studs. While some who had watched his career from the beginning—including such men as Hansgen, Penske, and Stirling Moss—realized he was a talent of the first magnitude, other less astute observers, clinging to their stereotyped images of how racing drivers should look and act, decided he was a candy-ass. Parnelli Jones, a brash pro-totype of the American racing driver, a man with the build and courage of a middleweight fighter, was one who mis-judged Donohue. In the early years of the Trans-Am, with Jones heading the official Ford Mustang team and Donohue driving a Chevrolet-backed, Penske-owned Camaro, Parnelli repeatedly tried to intimidate Mark by "laying a little metal on him," the stock-car racing euphemism for bashing into a competitor to move him out of the way. The bullying was a failure, and Donohue quickly proved that he was just as tough and aggressive as Jones and in fact, bunted Parnelli off the track on a number of occasions. From there on, very few insiders in racing doubted Donohue's grit, and while some journalists persisted in referring to him as "Captain Nice," the fact was that, man-for-man, he was probably as tough a racing driver as there was in the world.

As he sat in Dave Hoselton's motor home, it was apparent that some things had changed. He had let his hair grow, not long, but to a considerable length beyond his long-familiar brush cut. Still in his early thirties, he looked like an under-graduate. His face was refusing to age, although it now seemed to evidence a certain puffiness, and his eyes, which used to shimmer with an enthusiasm for life, now seemed dull and bored by comparison. Mark Donohue was a reluc-tant hero. While many sports celebrities respond to public exposure with as much brio as the most extroverted enter-tainers and politicians, others are consumed by their craft and find the fact that their excellence has attracted an adoring public almost uncomfortable. In motor racing, men such as Stirling Moss, Graham Hill, Jackie Stewart, and Mario Andretti are basically gregarious, and they love the crowds. On the other hand, many great drivers, including the late Jim Clark and Donohue, were and are essentially private men. Having established himself as among the four or five best drivers in the world, Mark Donohue still considered himself more a development engineer than a pure race driver. "I think there are a lot of guys who are pure racers: guys like the Unser brothers, A. J. Foyt, and Parnelli. That's all they know how to do. But with me, I'm pretty good at setting up a car for racing, adjusting the chassis, etc., and that helps me to go fast. But sometimes I wonder if that makes me a racer," he had said to me a number of years ago, and there was reason to believe the question still remained in his head.

Dressed in a gold-colored fireproof suit with black stripes down the sleeves, Donohue slumped in the breakfast nook and chatted easily. We talked about the day's practice, mainly as a formality, then the subject changed to boats. "I just got this unbelievable thing," he said enthusiastically. "It's a Donzi ocean racer with a turbocharged Chevy engine. I bought it from Mecom [John Mecom, Jr., the oilman and owner of the New Orleans Saints football team, who has had a long-standing involvement with racing] after he only used it a couple of times. It's unbelievable. It makes over 600 horsepower, and when I start that thing up, the whole marina goes crazy." He was animated, chattering happily about his new toy, marveling over its speed, chuckling over his troubles in getting the overpowered, cumbersome monster moored. Like most drivers, he was fascinated with any means of rapid transit, be it boat, plane, or car, and it was obviously a moment of unabashed joy when he could break away from the clutch of the crowds and onto the waters of Delaware Bay and the Atlantic, savoring that beautiful moment when the Donzi was pounding over the swells.

Agor climbed through the door, shaking his head. He went directly to the refrigerator and pulled out a Coke. Swigging it,

he plunked into the driver's seat and mumbled, "Those goddamn SCCA officials are unreal."

"Did you talk your way back into the garage?" asked Hoselton.

"Yeah, we're back in. I got two stalls, one for each car, but
all the bullshit I had to go through. This so-called garage
steward was the one who threw us out, so I went down to see
him. I told him how important it was for me to get out for that
last practice session, and that's why I couldn't wait for the
jam-up of cars to get untangled. Then it turned out that he
wasn't so upset about us using the wrong door, but he was
sore because we started the engine in the building. That's a
no-no. And you know why? You know why that son of a
bitch won't let anybody run their engines in that building?
Not for safety, not to reduce fire hazard or anything like that.
He admitted it to me; he won't let anybody run their engines
in there because *the noise hurts his ears!* How's that for logic?
Honest to God, these bush-league officials will be the death of
me yet."

9

Burdette "Birdie" Martin had a voice like Andy Devine's and a taste for outlandish clothes that left him looking as if he'd been decorated by Andy Warhol. But he was the boss of the Trans-Am, and a good one at that. A longtime SCCA leader from Chicago, Birdie operated as the professional steward of the Trans-Am series, traveling with the racers and making sure the rules were applied with consistent fairness from track to track. It was a difficult, worrisome job, but Birdie somehow managed to maintain his good nature, and when I found him early Saturday morning, he was lounging on an observation platform along pit lane, chatting easily on a telephone. He was wearing a pair of plum-colored slacks, white shoes, and a vermilion sport coat that might have been tailored from the draperies of a Miami Beach hotel. He had a round, open face and friendly eyes that faced the world from behind large glasses. Birdie was known to be fair, earnest, and a consistent advocate of the racer's best interests. He was a rarity, because a good measure of all sports officialdom operate as pawns of the management and generally place the welfare of the participants in a subordinate position. Not so with Birdie, probably because he had raced for many years and had stumbled too many times through various mud bogs of the sport's bureaucracy himself.

Theoretically, I was screwed. My car was still absent, although Warren continued to buoy me with bulletins about its imminent arrival. But the final Trans-Am practice session was coming up, and if I did not make that, I was presumably not eligible to attempt qualification later in the afternoon. However, Warren had assured me that I would get several laps in his machine, and that would be perfectly acceptable with the stewards. When qualifying opened later in the day, I could merely jump into my machine and make official entry into the race. It sounded simple, but I wanted to confirm the situation with Birdie, especially in view of the added complication that Dave Hoselton was planning to drive the car in the amateur race as well. Birdie was great. He listened to my problem, then agreed that I could attempt qualifications if I was able to get a few laps of prior practice, either in Warren's car or my own. "We qualify five cars at a time," Birdie said, "and try to group them in terms of relative performance. We put the fast guys like Donohue, Follmer, and Revson out together, and the medium-fast guys together. Because you're new, we'll put you out with a slower group. Then you can run at your own pace. Don't sweat it, though, we'll work it out."

"I sure appreciate that. I was afraid we'd get all wound up in red tape and never get a chance to run," I said.

"That's one of the reasons I'm here: to try to cut down on some of the bullshit and make life easier for the racers," Birdie said. "Sometimes everybody forgets all the guys who are out there risking their asses and unbelievable amounts of money, just to enforce some idiotic rule. I'm game to try anything as long as it doesn't interfere with anybody else's rights or isn't safe."

To footnote his protest against red tape, I told Birdie about

Warren's adventure with the steward in the garage and how
he'd been tossed out for irritating the official's eardrums. Birdie shook his head in disgusted agreement. "That's so typical.
You give some guys a little authority, and they go nuts. See
that telephone pole over there? It's just another pole, but say
you gave some SCCA member the job of 'guarding' that pole
at each Glen race. Hell, within two years he'd have a whole
damn committee of guys to guard that pole, and they'd be
holding planning meetings and grinding out rules and
bylaws, and they'd have it so complicated that not even the
power company could get within fifty feet without a notar-
ized pass. That's what we face in racing. We're so overorgan-
ized it's a miracle anything gets done."

I left Birdie to carry on his struggle with the incompetents
and started back toward the garage, where Warren and his
crew, which had increased appreciably in numbers, were at
work on his car. Up ahead there was a new, unfamiliar Camaro parked behind the pits. There was something mean and
efficient about its appearance that was difficult to pinpoint.
Perhaps it was lower than the others of its genre, but there
was an intangible quality about the machine that said it was
something to be reckoned with. A lean, dark-haired man in a
black sombrero was kneeling by its left rear wheel, tinkering
with the brake caliper. He was instantly recognizable. With
that black hat and the slogan BEST DAMN GARAGE IN TOWN emblazoned on the back of his white work shirt, it had to be
Smokey Yunick, the legendary stock-car builder and mechanic. Smokey was a genius; a man who'd gained racing
fame in the early sixties by building a series of powerful,
all-winning Pontiac stock cars and had gone on to establish
himself as one of the best engine tuners in the business. A
morose Ukrainian who lived in Daytona Beach, Florida,
blocks from the famed Daytona Speedway, Smokey was a
longtime sub-rosa lieutenant of auto magnate Semon
"Bunky" Knudsen. Smokey had built the Pontiac stock cars
when Bunky was general manager of the Pontiac division of
GM. When Bunky moved to Chevrolet, Smokey began ap-

pearing at the tracks with Chevy cars, although Chevrolet officially eschewed participation in racing. After Knudsen moved to Ford, Smokey built Ford racers for a time. Finally, after Bunky's spectacular firing by Henry II and his subsequent entrance into truck manufacturing, Yunick went back to building Chevys, primarily because they were easist to work on without factory sponsorship and had the broadest public demand. It had been rumored that Smokey was bringing a car to Watkins Glen, although it was known that he considered the SCCA technical people to be unreasonable and shied away from the Trans-Am for that reason. This stemmed in part from his background in Grand National racing, where the rubbery rules could be stretched to absurd dimensions, depending on the box-office demands of the moment, and in part from his first attempt to enter a Trans-Am race at Riverside several years previous. There, Smokey's car had been ejected for fourteen major rule violations, including illegally raking the windshield for better streamlining, altering the engine position and the wheelbase for better handling, etc. Therefore, he had come to the Glen through a back door, having a wealthy Canadian business associate enter the car in his behalf. This time his car had been built with a certain faithfulness to the rules and had passed inspection without difficulty. Initially it was thought that A. J. Foyt would drive the Camaro, and in fact one of the few markings on the car stated A. J. FOYT CHEVROLET, HOUSTON, TEXAS. But A. J. was nowhere to be found, and instead Smokey's driver would be Swede Savage, making his first start since his crash at Ontario.

I had met Smokey once, when Curtis Turner had been driving his black and gold number 13 Chevelle so successfully in Grand National competition, but he was intent on his work with the brake caliper, and it didn't seem the proper moment to try to renew acquaintances. Then Swede came up, a big crooked smile covering his face.

I was wearing my racing uniform when we greeted each other, which prompted a short interlude of banter. Then I said, "Swede, you look great. Do you feel good? Are you ready to race?"

"I feel perfect. The neurologists have given me a clean bill of health. They say I'm completely ready to go. Actually I've felt great for three or four months now, except for my memory. For a long while I couldn't remember names or anything. That made me crazy. Guys would come up to me and I'd know that I'd known them for a long time, guys I considered good friends. And I couldn't think of their names. Man, that was terrible."

"I know what you mean. I saw you at Indy, and I knew right away that you couldn't remember who I was," I said.

"I knew who you were, but I couldn't remember your name."

"That's all over with now, you say?"

"My memory is one hundred percent. Except for one thing: I can't recall a thing about the day of the crash or the race the day before at Phoenix. That's a blank, but the sawbones say it'll come back in due time."

"Has Smokey got a good car?" I asked, motioning toward the nearby Camaro.

"It's boss! Smokey has got horsepower like you wouldn't believe. That thing is *strong!* What's more, it's number is 79. That's the number I carried on my first quarter midget when I was nine. Isn't that superbitchin'?"

"Hey, I've got to ask you something," I said, changing the subject. "I notice a lot of the big shoes like Mark and Follmer are wearing regular helmets. Not the Bell Star full-face type. It must be because they're in a closed car, and they don't feel they need that extra protection or something. How about you? Are you using a Bell Star?"

"Are you kidding? I wouldn't get in a car without one. That thing saved my life at Ontario. In fact, when my neurologist saw the kind of protection it gave me, he went out and bought one to use while riding his motorcycle on the street. Man, you've *got* to use one," he said, obviously considering it a matter of life and death.

"I'm using one, too," I said. "The only thing is that with the Star, I can't get a regular pair of goggles to work, and with the full visor, I don't think I'll get enough air to breathe inside the closed cockpit," I said. (Most race drivers use some kind of eye covering, even in a sedan. This offers protection if the glass windshield is shattered by a stone or a crash and keeps dust, etc., from hampering vision.)

"Bubble goggles, that's what you need. The stock-car guys use 'em. They're just little clear plastic jobbies, but they work perfectly. I've got an extra pair in the truck. C'mon, you can have 'em."

We walked to a nearby Chevy truck. It was unmarked, although the Florida license plates indicated that it belonged to Smokey. Swede opened the cab and rummaged through the glove compartment. Finding a small cardboard box, he pulled it out and handed it to me. "Take awful good care of them. They scratch real easy," he warned.

Stuffing them in my jacket pocket, I described my troubles over the late arrival of my car and expressed concern over not having enough practice time. "There's a lot at stake tomorrow, like with Follmer and Donohue fighting it out for the championship, and I don't want to get out there and screw up. You know, if I got in one of the fast guys' way and caused him to crash or blocked him so he lost the race or something, I'd feel terrible."

"Just remember, concentration is the key," Swede said. "Every second that you don't concentrate completely, you are losing time. Or you are going to get into deep shit. You can't afford to let your mind wander, even for a particle of a second. Gurney has hammered that into my head over and over. Concentration. If you've got a car that's only eighty percent as good as the best, but you drive it to ninety percent of its potential, you'll be ahead of the guy in the car that's ninety percent, but only being driven at eighty percent of its capability. Just pay attention out there. Never let your mind wander, not even for *one instant*, and you'll be O.K."

It being Saturday morning, the Glen paddock and pits

were swarming with cars. The amateur races had already begun, and the entire place was enveloped in engine sounds, some at raucous, lumpy idle while being tuned, others protesting at low-speed transport around the pits, and others at their frantic, ear-busting limit on the track. I walked through the swirls of people to Agor's garage, where his number 13 was off the jack stands and appeared ready. "We just got word. Your car will be here before noon. But you better take a few laps in mine, just to get acquainted with the track," Warren said.

It was time. After all the pacing and waiting, it was time to get on the track in one of these strange beasts called Trans-Am cars. Bruce Johnson, a close friend of Warren's who served the team as the chassis expert, had arrived the night before. Mike Fitzgerald, a freckled, open-faced Irishman who worked as a General Motors district manager had overall supervision of the team. Several other volunteers hovered around the car, all seeming to work in relative harmony. For a semipro organization, there was an air of efficiency about the Agor team that was impressive. Wrenches clanged against the concrete floor after some final nuts were tightened on the Camaro, and I climbed aboard to adjust the seat belts and shoulder harnesses.

There were no frills. Aside from a small collection of gauges, the instrument panel contained only four switches: one for the master ignition, a pair to activate the twin fuel pumps, and one to start the engine. I flipped them all to the "on" position, and the engine started instantly. It was much like sliding onto the back of a Brahma bull in the starting chute. The entire car vibrated beneath me. There was nothing dainty about the Camaro. The steering, operating through the immense front tires, was sluggish and heavy, as if the entire unit was lubricated with cold molasses. The gearshift, a massive chrome bar that nudged my right knee, was trucklike in its lack of ease and precision. With no insulation or sound-deadening material, the engine exhaust echoed and resonated off the flat metal surfaces and harmonically vibrated every

last bolt and screw in the entire chassis, so that the machine
operated like a giant, cacophonous amplifier. The smell of
hot oil and near-boiling coolant mixed with the sour fumes of
gasoline. It was barren and purposeful, designed for one
thing: to run fast; and as I rolled down the pit lane and
punched the throttle, it rocketed ahead, forcing my body
deep into the tiny bucket seat. At speed, the car transformed
itself. The steering became lighter and nearly effortless, and
the gear shifting, when done at high rpm's, was easy and positive. While not running too quickly, I was beginning to establish a rapport with the car. It seemed to handle well
enough, and while powerful, it certainly didn't have enough
surplus of horses to fling itself off the track with an impru-
dent poke of the throttle. Yet, somehow, the Camaro acted as
if it weighed about three tons. There was nothing about it that
suggested élan or nimbleness. It seemed glued to the earth by
its bulk. While the steering and shifting became lighter as the
speed increased, the effort necessary to activate the clutch
was something you might associate with a tractor. Its brakes
were firm and efficient, although I came nowhere near using
them at their maximum. Warren had talked at length about
how you could fling the Camaro through corners, its tail hung
out in spectacular power slides. I could also remember Mark
Donohue remarking several years earlier that in order to go
fast in something as primitive as a Trans-Am car, you had to
drive it around the track like an unbroken horse, using more
willpower than style. Parnelli Jones had been more explicit:
"If you're under control, you're not going fast enough," he
had cracked.

I was not going fast enough. Trying to acclimate myself to
Warren's car, I cruised around the track for several laps, braking early, applying the throttle gently, and negotiating the
corners well below the limit. The giant tires seemed to stick
so solidly that they gave the impression that once they came
unglued and lost adhesion, the car would skate off the track
without a prayer of saving it. That wasn't the case, but that's
the message that was being transmitted to the seat of my

pants, and I drove accordingly. Then I went and did something stupid. Accelerating away from the esses, I changed up from third gear to fourth—and missed the shift. The lever crunched to a stop somewhere short of fourth, and the engine, responding to my increase in the throttle, whooped a sound of agonized, free-winding rpm's. I watched in mild terror as the tachometer needle whisked up to 8,700 rpms—1,200 over the limit I'd been using. I immediately slowed and managed to jam the car back into third. I accelerated up the straightaway, feeling sheepish. I passed a flag station, where a clutch of white-garbed flagmen and course workers peered at me from behind a low guardrail. They looked like a hostile jury. I wondered if any of them had been manning the post two weeks earlier, when I had missed a shift in the Lancia and almost exactly at the same spot.

That was enough. Thankful that the engine seemed to be performing normally despite its overrevving, I stopped at the pits. Warren, obviously proud of his machine, asked me how I liked the ride. "Great," I said unconvincingly. "She really handles, but it's going to take me a little while to get used to the whole thing." The rest of the crew had clustered around, listening to our conversation. "You'll have plenty of time to get used to your car," Warren said smiling confidently.

"When?" I asked unwittingly.

"Tomorrow, in the race," he answered quickly. Everybody laughed. We all laughed. They laughed harder than I laughed.

My car, the younger sister to Warren Agor's number 13, was finally towed into the Glen late that morning, trailered inertly behind a Chevy pickup with a tall aluminum camper unit teetering on its stern. I met the rig near the Tech building, where a burly, long-haired youth with deep-set, red-rimmed eyes staggered out of the pickup to greet me. He was Rich Dilcher, Agor's only full-time, paid mechanic. Dilcher worked for Agor during the racing season, then studied for his mechanical engineering degree at the University of Buffalo in the winter. Sporting a day's stubble of beard and caked with dirt, Rich was hardly at his best. Deadpan and mildly sardonic by nature, exhaustion had drained most of his remaining sense of humor, and he greeted me by gesturing toward the race car and grumbling, "There it is. 'The two-week wonder.' It's a miracle we even got the son of a bitch near a racetrack."

Dilcher was part of a special breed: half medieval artisan, half chief boatswain's mate. Racing mechanics—"wrenches" —have seen it all. They have experienced every possible emotion in racing, from the giddiness of victory to the stifling depression of death. They have spent days spread-eagled beneath broken automobiles or hunched over turret lathes, have crisscrossed the country at the wheel of heavy, slow-moving transporters and burned their hands and bent their bodies during the brutal ballet of a fast pit stop. Such experiences have left them with a good-natured fatalism that in the end their labors will be nullified by a combination of driver butchery and owner incompetence. It is the same attitude that makes sergeants and petty officers so sure that they run the armed services despite the bungling of the office corps.

There was still work to be done. While it was complete enough to get through inspection, the entire crew set upon my car to finish up a multitude of details that had been left to the last minute. Number 12 had been painted on its bodywork, but the scoring officials, for obscure reasons, had assigned it number 42 for the race. This meant that we had to change the number before the car could run. Hoselton and I, using rolls of tape and a razor blade, redid the numbers until the original 12 was transformed into a 42. Time was ticking toward the qualifying session, and for the first time it looked as if I might actually get to drive in the race.

"We've got to bed the brakes before he runs the car hard," Dilcher announced to Warren. Racing brake linings are made of an extremely hard compound, to resist the high temperatures of competition. They must be warmed up slowly, otherwise the linings will glaze with a slippery exterior surface and barely work at all. Linings are generally bedded-in during the opening warm-up laps, when a driver can cruise along, applying the brakes every few yards. That opportunity would not be mine, so I was sent off with my "two-week wonder" to cruise up and down the roadway behind the pits, punching and repunching the brakes. This afforded the first opportunity for me to drive "my" car. As Warren had promised, this was an exact replica of his, except for details. The ignition and fuel-pump switches had been mounted on a special console box inches away from my right hand. I liked that, because if the throttle jammed open, I might have a chance to shut the engine off by merely brushing my hand against the collection of switches, hopefully killing the ignition in the process. Also, in the event of a crash, I would—again hopefully—have an easier time shutting off the fuel pumps and diminishing the fire hazard. The only other difference between "mine" and "his" involved the front suspension. Warren's had been lowered. Mine was not. To accomplish such a thing required that a section be sliced out of the front coil springs, thereby reducing the height of the automobile. Lowering the front end would ostensibly improve the handling and slightly increase the aerodynamic efficiency. Aesthetically, I thought it would be nicer, too, if the front of my car drooped menacingly like the others, instead of yawning upward like a begging puppy. Rich and Warren had assured me that the springs would be shortened that evening, after I had qualified.

Chugging along behind the pits, I noticed that my right leg was beginning to get numb. It was the rake of the seat that bothered me. My right thigh had almost no support, and suspending the weight of the upper portion of that leg was exceedingly uncomfortable and fatiguing. To try it for two hours in a race would leave the leg dead as a stump. "I've got to have some padding in the seat," I complained to Rich when I got back to the garage. As I was pointing out the location of the problem and where I thought the addition of padding might help most, I spotted what looked like white sand deposited in the base of the seat. "What the hell is that?" I asked.

"Sand," said Dilcher.

"Sand?"

"Yeah, sand. We sandblasted the body of this thing, inside and out, to lighten it. Sandblasting ain't as fancy as acid-dipping, but it does help get off some spare metal. We swept most of it out, but there's probably still some left in the nooks and crannies."

Warren came up and stared at my uniform. "Hey, unless we want to get the Goodyear guys really pissed off at us, we better cover up the Brand X label on your uniform." Both Goodyear and Firestone personnel refer to each other as "Brand X." Warren went to the back of his truck, which was elaborately equipped with built-in cabinets and tool chests, and found a roll of silver tape, an all-purpose air-conditioning and heating-duct tape that is known variously as "racer's tape" or "200-mph tape," because of its extraordinary versatility. Practically everything has been held together at one point or another by racer's tape, including loose fenders, broken windshields, and engine parts that have ruptured in the middle of races. It will stick to everything, including Nomex, because Agor plastered all of the Firestone identification on my suit with long swatches of tape. "There, you're still not on the right team, but at least you're not on the wrong one," he said, eyeing his work with satisfaction.

Somebody checked the schedule of events that had been stuck to the side of the truck and said, "Yates's qualifying session is in ten minutes. We better get the car in line." I was to qualify with four other cars, all of them ragged campaigners in the Trans-Am wars. I knew nothing about the machines or their drivers, except that they were now rivals. We would not race together. Each car would be flagged off at thirty-second intervals, be given one warm-up lap, then three laps under official clocking, of which the fastest would count for qualifying. The uncertainty of my situation bordered on the absurd. Here I was, about to drive Warren Agor's number 42 Camaro for the first time in its young life—its initial introduction to the racetrack, for God's sake—and trying to qualify for a major professional race at the same time. Ideally, "sorting" a new race car would consume two or three days of careful, trial-and-error testing. As I sat in the car, waiting to be flagged away, I took an extra cinch in the seat belt, adding the last bit of insurance in the event the machine was unmanageable. It might do any number of bizarre things: its brakes could be so badly balanced that the front or the rear pair might lock up at high speed, or the throttle might stick wide open, or the suspension might be so untuned that it would be impossible to handle at racing speeds. Anything could happen. However, if I did not qualify in this session, I was out of the race. This was my final opportunity, and as I accelerated out of the pits, I was hoping for only one thing: a reasonably honorable showing. At the very least I did not want to qualify last on the grid. There was something about being the last dog in the pack that distressed me, and I wanted very badly to record a time that was at least faster than *somebody*. I didn't harbor much hope of running as quickly as Warren, who had qualified at 1.23.5, averaging 104.6 mph. That was a very presentable time indeed, considering that George Follmer had recorded the fastest time in his Mustang at 1.18.4, 111.5 mph. If my own car ran properly, I was hoping to run under 1.30—a modest aspiration, considering that was twelve seconds off the pace, but there were others who were considerably slower than that, and a 1.30 qualifying time would relieve me of the embarrassment of starting last.

The grandstands were spotted with fans, and the start-finish line had its usual cluster of officials as I accelerated past and headed up the hill toward the esses. The car seemed to be behaving acceptably. In fact, had it not been for the cramped, rather uncomfortable seat, it might as well have been Warren's car. I bustled along, quickly gaining confidence. Heading onto the front straight, I gave it full throttle, and the Camaro seemed to crouch closer to the pavement as the engine passed the threshold from low-speed running to high revs, where the power is hidden. There is a point of demarcation with a racing engine—with my Camaro it was about 5,500 rpm's—where the power comes on with the suddenness of a trapdoor bursting open. At lower rpm's, the engine burbles along with a kind of ragged disinterest, acting as if it's firing on half its cylinders. But once the pivotal rpm is reached, and the camshaft and carburetion begin to harmonize for the sake of real power production, the engine is transformed into a marvelously syncopated mechanical being. Passenger-car engines, with their docile timing, have no such "on-off" characteristics, and they produce power smoothly and efficiently at all rpm's. But when a racing engine "gets up on the cam" (that is, when the radical, high-rpm camshaft begins to operate at full efficiency), it is akin to lighting the afterburner in a jet plane. My Camaro was making power. I watched its tachometer needle sweep quickly toward 7,500 rpm and snapped it into fourth gear. The car was running perhaps 130 mph when suddenly I was enveloped in a strange dust storm. For a moment I was baffled. If I'd been a cartoon character, the balloon over my head would have read, "What the...???" as this mysterious cloud swirled through the cockpit. Fortunately, I'd been wearing Swede's bubble goggles, and my vision wasn't affected, but I zoomed along for a considerable distance before I realized what was happening. Dilcher's sand! At high speed, with the air eddying through the car, hidden deposits of sand were being sucked loose and were flying around inside the car. For a while it was like being inside one of those snowflake paperweights that, when shaken, unleash a blinding shower of snowy white particles throughout the container, virtually obscuring the little snowman or ice-laden cottage inside. I was the snowman for an instant, until the suction of the airstream cleared the view.

That minor ordeal having been overcome, I drove onward for the required timed laps, marveling that the machine was working like a race-proved veteran. My time trial completed, I drove into the pits and was greeted by Agor. He was smiling. "Not bad, Coralei got you at 1.29. That's O.K. for a start."

I was secretly ecstatic. I had *bettered* my personal goal of
1.30, meaning that I was far from the slowest in the field. I
was, however, eleven seconds slower than Follmer, and five
to six seconds slower than guys like Agor, so I could hardly
be considered a major threat to anyone.

The crew hurried the car back to the garage, where it was
made ready for the amateur event, a half-hour affair in which
both Hoselton and Agor would compete. I tried to translate as
much information to Dave as I could about the way the car
handled, etc., and he listened passively, his large eyes looking almost morose. He, too, would get his first crack at the
machine in the heat of competition, and I had to admire his
pluckiness. A year before, Dave Hoselton had never been
within a short walk of a racing car. Then he'd met Warren and
had become interested in motor sport merely as a promotional tool for his dealership. He had told me that the first
time Warren had given him a ride in the Camaro, during a
victory lap at an Eastern track, he'd been unbashedly terrified. But he had viewed racing as a challenge to be faced, and
earlier that same season he'd attended a drivers' school and
obtained his amateur license. He didn't seem to be particularly excited about his driving, but then again Dave Hoselton
was undemonstrative about most things, and it was difficult
to tell in what context he considered racing. Except for one
thing: he was a competitive man, and I knew that I had established the initial bench mark of performance for the car he
was going to drive. He would do his best to run faster than
1.29. While nothing was said, we, as sharers of the wheel of
number 42, were rivals.

Warren briefly contested for the lead in the amateur race,
then coasted silently into the pits. He got out, his face
strained, and told Rich the engine had blown. He and the rest
of the crew immediately pushed the car toward the garage,
knowing that a great portion of the night would be consumed
in installing a fresh engine. I stood at the pits, watching Hoselton. He was running well, holding a solid fourth place in
his class. But his times, which his wife was recording on her

split-action stopwatch, were slower than mine. He was clocking 1.31's—about two seconds slower than my time, and I
felt a selfish pleasure coupled with a certain guilt. I liked
Hoselton. He was a man of worth, showing a lot of guts simply to get out there with as little experience as he had, and I
told myself that it was hardly fair to absorb pleasure or satisfaction from those few seconds on the watch. But I did anyway.

Long banks of fluorescent lights kept the warm night at bay
inside the vast garage. For the full length of the place, dozens
of men bent toward the innards of inert, helpless racing cars.
Agor's entire crew buzzed around his stricken machine, engaged in the complicated, exacting job of replacing the engine. The track itself was dark and empty, but the infield was
speckled with car lights and campfires. Music, some the raucous, electronic bleating of transistor radios, some the casual
strumming of guitars, mingled with the murmur of traffic and
laughter. The greasy odor of cooking hot dogs merged with
the fumes of the garage. The admission gates would be open
for the entire night, giving entrance to thousands of enthusiasts who'd driven from all over the Northeast to see tomorrow's race. Many of them had brought tents and trailers and
were camped in the humid darkness, lounged around campfires, drinking beer, and exchanging stories about their adventures with cars. Racing is a highly personal sport, and
while heroes like Donohue and Revson entered their conversations, a vast percentage of the talk centered on themselves
and their own machines: about the new set of radial tires
they'd bought, how they dreamed of owning a prewar Jaguar,
or how they'd talked themselves out of a speeding ticket on
the New York Thruway. They were out there, the heart and
soul of racing, shadows in the night, while the racers themselves sweated over the balky machines and dreamed of sharing a beer and a sleeping bag with a soft girl under the stars.

Paul Nichter was a pure racer. His friends and the IRS
knew him as a successful contractor, but he was a racer. In
his middle thirties, he was a rangy, loose-jointed man with

powerful, sloping shoulders, a prominent pointed nose, and small, hard eyes. Nichter had been racing only a few years, simply because the demands of his business had not permitted such pastimes. But now he was rich enough and free enough to race, and during this, his second season in the Trans-Am, he'd established himself as a flat-out competitor. His Camaro, an older model, wasn't as quick as the factory machines, but when Nichter was on his game, there were very few independents, including Warren, who could pass him. He good-naturedly admitted to making mistakes on the racetrack. Sometimes he'd overdriven and had crashed. On other occasions, his concentration had lapsed—racers call it "brain fade"—and he'd crashed some more. But he always came back, driving as hard as he knew how. He and Warren were good friends, and he had come by to commiserate over the loss of the engine and to offer what moral support he could during the labor.

"I love to race," he said. "I only wish I'd started sooner. But I was like all those other guys, I figured there wasn't much to it. I owned a couple of 'Vettes, fast cars, see, and I'd take 'em out on the road, and bust up and down, and get my kicks that way. Guys would say, why don't you race? and I'm saying, shit, what's the difference between what I'm doing with my 'Vette and racing? Then I tried it. I went racing, and holy shit, I couldn't believe it. It was another world. I couldn't have imagined how hard you had to drive, how demanding it was. After that I started to say to my friends, 'All right, you assholes, you can drive your 'Vettes and your GTOs up and down and get your rocks off, but that isn't remotely related to racing. They thought I was fulla shit. I wanted so bad to *show* 'em. One day I took one of them around a Canadian track during practice. The son of a bitch was scared shitless. I mean shitless! He'd never believed a car could run that hard. I didn't either until I'd tried it. If we could only tell people what it's like out there." He looked at the sprawl of campfires. "Like those fans. There they are, sittin' around, bullshitting each other that they know what it's all about.

Tomorrow they'll watch us breakin' our asses out there and think they understand. If only they did. If only we could give each one of 'em a ride so they'd understand." Paul Nichter lit a cigarette and smiled into the night. He didn't say anything for a while. We were both thinking about tomorrow, wondering ourselves what it would be like.

10

I am not sure that I had ever felt more isolated. When Jerry Breon reached into the cockpit of the Camaro, shook my gloved hand, then mumbled, "Good luck," and walked away, I was completely alone. Thirty-five cars and drivers lined up, two by two, on the starting grid at Watkins Glen, ready to begin two hundred miles of racing. Follmer and Donohue were up front. Swede was directly behind them. Warren was barely visible up ahead, sitting in thirteenth spot. I was twenty-fourth. Behind me were a collection of slower machines, plus Peter Revson, of all people. After my fretting about starting last, it was Revson, one of the fasted drivers in the business, who ended up there. His car had developed trouble during time trials, and therefore he was forced to begin at the back. I knew when the flag dropped he'd be forcing his yellow and black Javelin through the field like a runaway torpedo, and I made a mental note to stay out of his way.

It was trying to rain. A few drops of moisture speckled my

windshield, and I smiled as I recalled the frantic search for wiper blades that had gone on prior to moving the car to the grid. My car had been built with the wiper motor and linkages in place, but no blades had been installed. With the weather threatening, Mike Fitzgerald had sent one of the crew to find some blades—one of the precious few spare items that hadn't been wedged into the back of the truck. He had returned with a pair scavenged from a Jaguar XK-E that had been parked in the paddock. If all went well, the blades would be returned after the race without the Jag's owner having the vaguest notion that his windshield blades had taken a two-hundred-mile extracurricular ride. I tried the wipers, mainly to give myself something to do. They whined obediently across the glass, and I chuckled out loud over the poor guy and his Jaguar, *if* the rain came harder and he decided to leave the racetrack early.

I had not smiled much up until then. I was feeling the pressure, although not in any definable fashion. Men react to prerace jitters in many ways. Some great drivers, including Phil Hill, the first (and only) American World Champion, tend to vomit. Others become testy and distant. Many yawn, a reaction that is often mistaken for devil-may-care bravado. It is, in fact, a common symptom of nervousness. My own reaction to the upcoming race had been more subdued, manifesting itself by an inability to stay in one place and with ragged lapses in my span of concentration. I had found myself losing contact in the midst of conversations. My mind had kept wandering off to something else, generally to a detail that had to be checked prior to the race. A young man and his girl had walked up and greeted me like old friends. I had feigned recognition. He had chatted about his racing, assuming I understood, and had even mentioned the time he had visited my home. At that particular moment, I hadn't known him from a grilled-cheese sandwich. I had tried to keep my mind off the race, feeling that it was impossible to prepare mentally for all the eventualities and that it was therefore better to leave my mind unencumbered by plans and tactics that would never be usable. I had encountered the same problem the previous night. Sleep had been difficult, despite a long and relaxing meal with my family, a hot shower, and a brace of aspirin before retiring. I had awakened in the pre-dawn hours, thoughts of the race accelerating through my head. I had felt the familiar, pliant form of Sally beside me in deep and relaxed sleep. The steady breathing of our daughter, Claire, had issued from the other bed. The room had been half lit by the night lights of the motel courtyard, giving me a first impression that dawn had come. Try as I might, I could not resist the magnetic thoughts of the race, and for a long time I had wrestled with my own brain in an attempt to divert it away from that central distraction. Finally after a trip to the bathroom for two more aspirin, I had been able to cram the gnawing concern over the race into my subconscious and had managed a few more hours of fitful rest.

I had gotten into my uniform in the Hoseltons' motor home. It had been deserted at the time, and a certain sense of the impending drama had come over me. It had entered my mind that I might be dressing for the last time, a thought that I immediately tried to suppress as the height of soap-opera bathos. Actually, that sort of preoccupation with myself had disappeared only twice in the intervening hours before the race. One occasion had been at the drivers' meeting: a session where Birdie Martin had used a bullhorn to outline the rules by which the race would be run—details concerning how the ambulances and fire trucks would operate during the race, the victory lane ceremony, etc. I had spent that session talking with George Follmer, the only man with a clear-cut chance of beating Donohue. The other moment of distraction had come on the track, during the brief prerace warm-up. That incident had involved Donohue himself.

Follmer was a swarthy, scowling man who always looked angry. A former West Coast insurance man who'd won the United States Road Racing Championship in 1964 and turned professional, he was a driver of the first rank. Because he tended to be a private, somewhat moody person, he had not enjoyed the adoration, both from the press and the public, afforded other racing heroes. But George had proved himself on the track in a variety of cars, and as we had stood together, half listening to Birdie's electronically propelled messages, there was no question that Follmer was a devoted professional. "I love racing. It's the only thing I've really enjoyed doing in my life, but the money is getting tough," he said. "The purses aren't too bad in some places, like Indy, but the expenses are so high that most guys still lose money. Hell, did you see where Al Unser's team won nearly $500,000 last season and still *lost* money? Something's wrong somewhere. Take this Trans-Am series—it's a helluva program. You won't see better competition anywhere. But the bucks aren't here. If I win this thing today, I'll get about $7,500. Now a lot of people might think that's big money—just for going out and driving a car for two hours. But they forget I split the purse with the car owner—Bud Moore, in this case—and all of my living expenses, etc., have to be paid. So if I netted three grand at the end, I'd be in good shape. Now you know you're not going to win 'em all, so with some high finishes—and you've got to have a number one, front-line car to do that— you might make twenty grand for the season. If your luck is bad, it could be half that. Hell, I made a lot more than that selling insurance."

They called him "Fumbler" in the business, but the nickname contained no intended slurs on his skill or his general competence. He knew his trade. He had the supreme confidence of a race driver: the sureness in his soul that he was as good as any man. And he had the combativeness to prove it. Yet his pragmatic nature was telling him that at the age of thirty-seven, time was coming for him to make a move. He had flirted with the big-time, having driven at Indianapolis and other major events, but it had not gone together for him in totality. The major teams were not pounding down his door. He didn't need an agent to sort through piles of endorsement offers that would boost his income to six figures.

He had a way to go, and at his age it was obvious that a moment of decision was coming. I had left him, still slouching at the drivers' meeting, still frowning, still seeming to eye the world with a measure of anger, knowing that he was hooked; that like most of the men in that group standing under the leaden skies of Watkins Glen, motor racing would be a part of his life until the very end. Outwardly, he had remained calm, but the grinding pressures for him to win (for himself, for Bud Moore, and for Ford and Firestone, his major backers) in the face of Mark Donohue made my foggy concerns over doing a workmanlike job seem trivial by comparison.

My other prerace distraction had come during practice when the entrants had been permitted to take a brief warmup primarily to bed our brakes. We had all climbed into our machines and rumbled out onto the track, where we had proceeded to jerk along, alternately accelerating and applying the brakes. I had been watching a line of cars in front of me, snaking along with their brake lights winking and their noses dipping toward the pavement, when a vivid red, white, and blue Javelin had burst up alongside me. I had looked over to find Donohue with a comic leer spread across his face. I had tried to mug an appropriate reply, but had recalled that my full-face helmet concealed my expressions. I had nodded an agreement and lifted my hands off the wheel in a mock shrug of futility. Donohue had laughed some more, obviously enjoying himself, apparently oblivious to the tensions of the imminent race, and then charged by, tossing a little wave as his brake lights flashed in the deepening gloom.

Those brief encounters with Follmer and Donohue, the men who would most seriously contest that particular race, had been good for me, both as distractions from my own fretting and as insights into the way professionals mentally prepare for combat. They hardly viewed the whole thing as a date with destiny, but rather as part of their job, motivated by unvarnished enjoyment of driving fast and the simple hunger

to compete, coating all of the garbled mystique and lugu-
brious psychoanalysis that has been presumed to explain
why men race.

I turned in my seat, feeling the firm tendons of the
shoulder harness restricting my movements, and looked at
my pit crew, now standing motionless behind the high steel
fencing. With their matching orange, lettered shirts, they
seemed appropriately major league, at least in appearance.
Seated above them, at a small table mounted on a collection
of oil drums, were Coralei Hoselton and Lynn Wilson, Warren's pert, pretty fiancée, overlooking the scene. They would
act as timers and scorers, keeping elaborate lap charts that
would determine Warren's and my positions in the race.
More rain dappled the windshield, and I found comfort in
the knowledge that four specially treaded rain tires were
piled in the pits in case the storm worsened. Once a racetrack
becomes coated with water, the wide, smooth tires of the type
all the starters were using—"dry" tires, as they are called—
were as useless as leather soles on an ice rink. If it were to
rain heavily, everyone would have to stop for tire changes.

On my left was the crowd. They were young and boister-
ous. Some were wrapped in old army blankets. Many were
bearded and beery, leaning against the sagging wire fence,
shouting taunts and cheers in the general direction of the assembled race cars. Others were piled atop parked cars and
seated in a partially finished steel grandstand. Still more
were occupying hand-built platforms, some put together from
construction rigging, others hammered from scavenged
wood. In the distance I could see several hearty souls who
had climbed high into a stand of trees for a long-range, wide-
angle look. Smoke from campfires was smudging the gloomy
sky, giving the place an aura of a medieval battle scene with a
mob of ragtag soldiers manning a crude network of ramparts.

I knew none of them, I recognized not a face, but I liked
them. They had come for an afternoon of action. They had
not, as the hackneyed indictment goes, come to see men die. I
knew that because I had been part of similar crowds, watch-

ing desperate adventures unfold before me on the racetrack, and thrilling at the skill and bravery of the men who had faced those heroic moments. A simple bit of reasoning explained why they had not come to see death. All spectators are part of the event. They are vicarious participants. At a motor race, the crowd spiritually rides with the drivers. It is critical to them that their representatives on the track overcome the challenges they face. A crowd is perfectly willing to watch their alter egos encounter the most strenuous difficulties, including awful crashes, provided they survive. If they do not, the death is symbolic for all witnesses. For a driver to face challenges and to overcome them is the key to the emotional involvement of a racing crowd. If the driver fails, the crowd fails. If the driver dies, the crowd dies. Anyone who has ever attended a race that involved a fatality knows this phenomenon. The awareness of death passes through the assemblage like a killer fog, numbing voices and movement. Great mobs of people stare silently ahead, as if meditating in a church, while others mumble morosely with their neighbors. Still more leave. Yes, it is clever to chatter about how people (other people, of course) dig carnage and how racing crowds are the reincarnations of the Roman gladiatorial aficionados, but when someone makes such a foolish statement, you may be sure of one thing: he has never seen a man die at a racetrack.

Again immersed in a heightened sense of my own drama, I recalled that as the crew had pushed my car from the pits to its place on the starting grid, I had trailed along a few steps behind, somehow feeling like a torero in the grand procession. That was nonsense, of course, because very few of the spectators had been paying the slightest bit of attention. The action is diffused at a motor race, and it is difficult for the crowd to concentrate on any one element. The noise generally pounds the public-address system into incoherence, so very few people know what is going on, including the officials. To most of the fans, the race is quickly reduced to a swirl of noisy cars. They may know the leaders, but on the road course, even that can be uncertain, simply because pit stops can be made without their knowledge, and the man they think is ahead might be many laps in arrears. I had thought to myself, as I strolled in front of them, how nice it would have been if I had been able to explain to each of them about the newness of my car and the general uncertainty of my situation, in an attempt, I suppose, to counter any later observations about how slow I might be going. And then I had thought, hell, not one in fifty of them even knows who's driving the cars—or really cares—so what difference does it make? But then, as Paul Nichter had lamented, if they only had some idea of what it was like...

My nose itched. Right on the tip. I dug around with my gloved hand, trying to probe a finger inside the helmet and the Nomex mask, but it was no use. What's more, my right thigh was beginning to lose feeling, and my left shoulder, wedged as it was against the unyielding fiberglass back of the bucket seat, was turning sore. Then up ahead I saw a marshal trotting between the lines of race cars, waving his arms in a circular motion. "*Start your engines!*" I bolted into life, as if a shot of voltage had jolted every nerve ending in my body. Engines hammered around me, ripping and rattling the placid, muggy air. I flipped on my switches, attempting to start my engine, and felt a faint vibration, but the surrounding welter of sound was so great I could not hear my own power plant. I looked at the tachometer, which was indicating 2,500 rpm's. The oil-pressure gauge was registering poundage. Otherwise I wouldn't have known if my own engine was running or not. The noise that surrounded me like a thick wool muffler reminded me of a last-minute oversight. I had planned to stuff cotton in my ears to help preserve my hearing, but the tension had caused me to forget. I would have to bear the sound. It was too late to turn back.

We started to roll ahead. The field shuddered away, with engines blatting and clutches slipping. We would make a pace lap, then take the green flag. I busied myself with tightening my harness, checking gauges, and making sure the steering and brakes felt proper on that one revolution of the track. People lined the fences everywhere. Clusters of flagmen and emergency workers seemed poised for action, looking more intent on their job than at the Regional a few weeks earlier. We sailed past pits, picking up speed, and rolled through the tight 90-degree corner, heading toward the starting line like a runaway freight train. Then I saw a green flag flapping in the billowing cloud of dust that was being sucked from the track by the leading cars. Throttles yawned open, and we surged ahead as one, some cars brushing each other while winding through the esses. Once on the straight, the god-awful sound reached an almost unbearable crescendo. I found an inside lane open and managed to sneak past a few cars. Then came a yellow and black one past me. Revson! Past me already, going like a rocket. Stunned at his speed, I swept over the blind hillcrest leading to the Loop, and suddenly the sandstorm was back. More sand! Only this time it was getting in my eyes. *My goggles!* They weren't on! In the stress of the start, I'd forgotten to pull them down, and now the sand was swirling around inside the car, threatening to blind me. My first instinct was to snatch them over my eyes, but by then I was sawing through the middle of the Loop with the car feeling light and twitchy on the downhill sweeper. Once on the straightaway again, I pulled the goggles in place and rushed ahead, feeling sheepish at the oversight.

We were running hard, myself and a knot of about five cars. The track was rushing past at a furious rate, perhaps faster than I could have imagined. A pair of cars was immediately ahead, while two others clung to my rear bumper. I was trying to drive conservatively, doing my best to brake early and corner smoothly, but I couldn't seem to break the status quo. I couldn't pass my rivals ahead. My rivals in back couldn't pass me. As we shot up the straight toward the Loop, I spotted the cruel glimmer of a red light flashing on the track. The flagmen were hanging over the steel fence, waving yellow and white flags. An accident ahead. The white flags warned that an emergency vehicle was on the track—

surely the source of the red light. Since it was a blind hill
leading to one of the most dangerous corners on the track, I
slowed. The two cars behind me, a pair of Camaros, shot past,
barely nipping by a giant fire truck that loomed up in front of
us. "You dumb bastards!" I shouted in the wind. I squeezed
by the truck and entered the turn. There was a car wedged
against the inner wall with smoke pouring from its hood. I
could see its driver frantically clawing at the heated metal,
trying to yank it open so that fire extinguishers could be
poked at the fire inside.

By the time I picked up speed again, my two friends had
pulled far ahead, and for a moment a feeling of futility came
over me. It seemed useless to try to catch them. Then I spotted Revson's car parked at the side of the track, abandoned.
Somehow, that gave me heart, and I pressed on. The next
time around the Loop, the track was covered with absurd
white suds of fire-fighting foam, making the area look as if it
had been the scene of some ridiculous pastry fight, leaving
behind a vast residue of meringue. The poor car, as the target
of the foam blast, was standing up to its fenders in the goo,
adding to the comedy of the scene.

As I accelerated down the pit straight, I spotted an orange
car spurting out of the pits. It was Warren. He had made an
unscheduled stop, obviously. He entered the race immediately in front of me, and we went nose-to-tail. Then he began
to open a lead, and I knew that he was running harder and
faster than I. We nearly made the Loop when a shower of
sparks tumbled from beneath his car. At first I thought they
signaled a fire, but in an instant they were gone. Warren was
dragging something, something was rubbing the track surface
under hard braking. He was in serious trouble, and sure
enough, as we swept past the pits again, he reentered.

Then came Donohue and Follmer, running side by side.
They powered by me on a straightaway, moving as if they
were welded together. Both were traveling perhaps thirty
miles an hour faster, and they shot by so fast I barely had a
chance to determine who they were. The harsh, ripping

sound of Follmer's Ford engine shot through the window like a spear, inflicting physical pain on my ears. I winced, in a sense mentally intimidated by their massive show of power. I watched them hurry onward, and the thought came to me that maybe half the male spectators crowding the fence thought they might be able to drive just as quickly as the guys on the track. If only they had the opportunity to rub fenders with a pair of masters like Mark and George; to be traveling at what they thought was a dazzling speed and to be blown into the weeds by a twosome like that. They were, as they disappeared from sight, carrying the art of driving to a level that I wondered if most men could even comprehend existed, much less attain.

Then my watch fell off. I was arcing through a wide corner when the clasp came loose on my metal band, and it dropped from my wrist to my forearm like a loose bracelet. I reached over with my left hand to fix it, then suddenly realized I was running perhaps 110 mph, and I was worrying about my watch falling off. "You goddamn fool! Pay attention!" I yelled at myself, deciding to let the watch hang loose for the rest of the race, rather than risk a crash. Maybe I was losing touch with reality. The race had stabilized somewhat, with the cars spread around the track, lapped and relapped. Many had stopped at the pits to further jumble the order. I didn't have the vaguest idea where I was, and Jerry Breon's pit board didn't help. He had obediently displayed it for me on every lap since the start, but the board was covered with such a patchwork of numbers—intended to give me a capsule of information about laps completed, lap time, how far I was ahead and behind my immediate rivals, etc.—that I couldn't decipher any of it. However, each time I hurried past, I gave him a knowing wave of acknowledgment, as if I understood everything.

Swede Savage had just lapped me when his engine exploded. At first I didn't understand what was happening. All I could see was a cloud of gray smoke spreading across the track like a fog bank. Small dark specks began to appear in the mist, bouncing toward me as if in slow motion. My mind finally deciphered what was going on: Swede's engine had blown up like a Fourth of July rocket, belching out a thick cloud of steam and boiling oil. I watched in dumbstruck fascination as I plummeted into the smoke. The mysterious specks were ominously growing larger. They were taking great, elastic bounces off the track, giving the impression that they were pieces of rubber. Then I saw one of them skitter past me, emitting a shiny, metallic glint. *Engine pieces!* Shards of pistons, connecting rods, bearings, crankcases, etc. That could saw through one of my tires like a scapel. I tried to dodge a few, but one simply doesn't make many evasive course changes at 120 mph. Then an immense piece, looking like an asteroid sailing through space, appeared dead ahead. I saw it drop to the pavement, then carom like a hard-hit grounder straight at my windshield. I braced myself for the impact, then realized it would clear the top of my car. I ducked. Sitting inside my roll cage, covered with layers of protective helmet, etc., I still bowed to reflex and ducked. In another wink I was through the cloud, and as my vision cleared, I could see Swede's car shuddering to a stop at the side of the track. It was trailing oil and steam like the spoor of a wounded animal. I drove on, my mind dulled to the moment just passed. The noise, the speed, the rising heat inside the car conspired to drain my emotions to a point where I had driven through Swede's debris as if it had been a wind-tossed newspaper on a freeway. I was not experiencing fear, nor was I exhibiting courage. In the accelerated milieu of a racetrack, events occur with such rapidity that it is impossible to isolate reaction to any one of them, any more than it would be possible to respond to a single machine-gun bullet at the expense of the rest.

My engine started to act up. It first revealed itself as a miss—a stumble in its power—as I swung the car through a fast right-hander. It worsened with each lap, finally reaching a point where the engine nearly stalled, and I was forced to shift down to third in order to keep running. I decided to stop. I would have to make a regular stop for gas in a few laps anyway, so I made for the pits, catching my crew off guard as I sailed down the lane. Warren was in front of me, still in his driver's uniform, guiding me to a spot next to the wall. Orange shirts surrounded the car. Mike, Rich, and Bruce were at the back, draining a pair of eleven-gallon containers of gasoline into my tank. Warren leaned inside the car and shouted over the deafening roar of my engine, "You're early."

"What?" I shouted back, my voice further muted by the helmet.

"You came in too early!"

"I know, I know, the engine is missing!"

Warren looked at me blankly. I repeated my message. He seemed to understand. He leaped to the hood of the car, lifted it, and peered inside. Rich joined him. Dave Hoselton appeared at the window and handed me a Coke. I grabbed it, then realized that I couldn't drink it without removing my helmet, and handed it back. I pointed at my covered mouth and shook my head. He nodded and disappeared. Warren slammed the hood down and scuttled back to my window. "Everything looks O.K., keep going!"

I looked in the rearview mirror and saw the refueling operation was complete, then stuffed the car into first and sped away. The entire length of the pit wall was lined with people whose faces were smeared by the increasing speed. Several cars, obviously broken, sat unattended. Back on the track, I drove on, as if in orbit, not having the slightest notion what position I was in, how fast I was going, who was ahead, and who was behind. Cars rose up from tiny dots in my rearview mirror and passed me. Donohue and Follmer sailed past for what seemed like the umpteenth time. Revson, who had apparently restarted, went by, as did his teammate, Elford. Nichter surged alongside, flipped a quick wave, and disappeared. My shoulder was beginning to pain, and my nose itched. My watch still drooped on my wrist.

My concentration was going away. Several times I found that I had not depressed the throttle the full distance, that I

was cruising along at something less than maximum power. I
began to talk to myself, commanding my right foot to keep
hard on the gas. Christ, this race must be about over, I
thought. If I could only get a glimpse of the scoreboard on a
hill overlooking the esses. That would tell how many of the
eighty laps had been completed. There was a chance to peek
at the board just past the start-finish line, where the track
angled up the infernal hill on which the MG and Lancia had
stalled. I focused my eyes on the scoreboard for no more than
a particle of a second and felt the car take a nasty jolt. I jerked
my attention back to the track to find I'd driven over the
curbing on the inside of the turn, then managed to yank the
car back on course before it yawed out of control. *Concentrate, concentrate,* you idiot, I thought to myself, remember-
ing Swede's warning.

But the engine was beginning to miss again. It started in
the same place and continued to get worse, until it was sputtering halfway up the straight before resuming proper operation. I had decided it was something in the fuel feed. It
seemed to run acceptably with a full tank, but as the level
lowered, it began to misfire. I stopped twice more to fill up,
both times carrying on a crazy, deaf-and-dumb pantomime
with Warren in an attempt to explain the problem. I went
through a time when I wished the son of a bitch would break;
that the Camaro's engine would simply quit, and I could
leave the damn thing stranded on the track. With the car
sputtering more seriously with each passing lap, I knew I was
going slower, and I felt that urge to explain to each one of
those pasty faces behind the fences that it wasn't me, that
they should blame the car for my troubles. I was depressed. I
felt glued in place, suspended in a container of noise. Donohue went by again. This time he was alone, apparently holding a clear lead. He waved, poking his hand out the window
as he ducked the Javelin in front of me and snubbed its speed
for a hard left-hander. I waved back, feeling a near-manic
gratitude for his having broken my spell of isolation.

Jerry Breon was standing at the pit wall. This time I understood his signal. It said "P-11," followed by a series of dollar signs. Eleventh place? Could that be? After all my puttering around with a sick engine and three stops, could I be in eleventh place? Then came the checkered flag. It was a glorious sight, the kind of thing that required the entire MGM orchestra booming a triumphant Dmitri Tiomkin arrangement in the background to provide a proper mood. Fireworks lacing the sky, and perhaps a rainbow, might also have been approriate. I slowed immediately and cruised toward the pits with a cluster of other cars, a part of the seventeen machines still running at the end. From behind the fences, I noticed extra motion. There, against the gloomy cloud cover and the rising smoke of campfires, thousands of spectators were waving at us. The flagmen and safety workers had joined them, in a kind of universal salute. None of the cars around me was a high finisher, so the crowd wasn't acknowledging any major accomplishments, merely cheering our presence, much as a chorus is accorded part of the encores. Perhaps they understood after all, I thought.

The pits were clogged with people and cars by the time I arrived. Grimy, sweat-soaked men were climbing out of the cockpits, yanking off their helmets, and swilling sweet breaths of air. People were slapping each other on the back and handing around soft drinks and beer. Warren was the first to greet me as I rolled to a stop and killed the engine. He stuck his hand in the window and smiling widely, shook mine. I slumped in my seat. It felt as if sirens had been stuffed inside my head. I got out of the car and my body felt light, as if I'd just stepped off a roller coaster. Somebody handed me a can of Genesee Cream Ale.

"Eleventh place. That ain't all bad," said Warren.

"Maybe we even made some money," I said.

"About $750, we think. That isn't bad for two hours' work."

"I can think of a lot easier ways to earn money," I mumbled.

"Hey, what are you doing to our cars?" Dave Hoselton

yelled through the crowd. I looked at him across the roof of
the Camaro. He was smiling and pointing to a nasty-looking
dent in the roof, a deep gouge in the metal. I looked at the
damage blankly for a moment, then it came to me. Good God,
Swede and his damn exploding engine! "That wasn't my
fault. You'll have to talk to Swede Savage about that one," I
replied.

It was over. My shoulder ached, and my ears still rang, but
deep inside I felt great. Maybe it was the euphoria that medical people say arises with the conclusion of a so-called "risk
exercise," or maybe it was simply pleasure that I'd made it
with a minimum of trouble. Or perhaps simply that I'd made
it. I couldn't pinpoint my pleasure, except that life somehow
felt more real, that for some reason or another, I was operating at a maximum state of aliveness. It even gave me the
strength and patience to try to explain to my sons why Donohue had lapped me so many times.

11

David Pearson, the freewheeling stock-car champion from the deep South, had raced once at Bridgehampton and had hated it. He had stood in the sandy paddock and gazing over the hazy waters of Great Peconic Bay, had complained, "This here is the end of the earth, and that ain't no shit." The Bridgehampton racetrack was hardly on the outer edge of man's geographic perimeter, but it certainly was situated in an unlikely spot. There it sat, carved out of scrub-timbered hillocks, smack in the middle of the socially big-league Hamptons region of eastern Long Island, surrounded by golf clubs, splendid estates, and a few stubborn, truck-farming natives who survived the damp, cold winters thanks to the sturdy, weathered-brown shingle houses that dotted the landscape. A consortium of New York area sports-car enthusiasts had built the Bridgehampton race circuit—an uphill and downhill course that was as difficult and challenging as any in North America. But it was a financial albatross from the beginning.

The track was created without the slightest regard for the
buying public. It was reachable only by one winding, back-
country road devoid of any directional signs. An experienced
guide was practically essential in finding the place. Once
there, all traffic was forced to filter through a single gate
manned by amateur ticket vendors. Spectators were restricted
to a rotting wooden grandstand and a selection of crude
vistas that had been chopped from the surrounding underbrush. To make matters worse, fans from metropolitan New
York were faced with a postrace traffic jam that sometimes
obstructed the entire hundred-mile route to Manhattan.
These difficulties, coupled with a chronic shortage of invest-
ment capital, prevented the Bridgehampton circuit from becoming the major auto-racing facility its founders envisioned;
but it had staggered on, clinging to its existence in the face of
endless financial crises, neighbors' complaints about the
noise, and persistent rumors that the place would be sold for
real-estate development.

During my three years with *Car and Driver*, we had used
Bridgehampton numerous times for car testing, an event
that generally served as an excuse for the staff to flee our
New York offices and spend a day lashing around the track
in somebody else's automobiles. Those cars were generally
provided by company public-relations people who had
learned that the attrition rate was so high with automotive
journalists at the wheel that no collision insurance whatsoever was carried. (During one twelve-month period, *C/D*
wrote off seven cars in a variety of track and traffic mis-
haps.) If the cars crashed, the companies merely towed
them off to junkyards and forgot them. Actually, a *Car and
Driver* test at Bridgehampton was a major event for us.
While other magazines scientifically—and soberly—evaluated their test vehicles on well-equipped California tracks,
the barbarians at *C/D* generally accumulated acceleration
and speed data with the unknowing consent of the American public. David E. Davis, Jr., the editor and publisher
most responsible for boosting *C/D*'s languid circulation from

230,000 to more than half a million in a spectacular thirty-six-month period, often conducted his tests on the East River Drive of Manhattan and on the Brooklyn Bridge, while commuting between his Brooklyn Heights apartment and the office. Steve Smith and I, Dave's coconspirators, were inclined to make our runs on the relatively open vistas of the New Jersey Turnpike. We were the bane of Ziff-Davis, our parent publishing company, by constantly ignoring printing schedules, rupturing budgets, scorning company politics, and worst of all, outraging advertisers. For example, *Car and Driver* stunned the automotive world in 1964 by describing the sacred VW as an unsafe antique. A short time later we infuriated Anglophile car snobs everywhere with the comment that the Rolls Royce Silver Cloud was "... a superb example of what modern manufacturing technology and a spare-no-expense philosophy can do for a 1939 Packard." To make matters worse, we compared automobiles and ranked them according to their good and bad qualities. For the most part, automotive magazines (a majority of *all* enthusiastic-oriented magazines for that matter) were—and still are—shamefully mush-mouthed when it comes to criticizing an advertiser's product, but we at *C/D* felt compelled to *say* something, to somehow attempt to inform our readers about cars, and to hell with the advertisers. For some reason or another, William Ziff, the owner, tolerated our antics, despite constant cancellations from enraged advertisers. He stood by us in the face of multipage losses from such major accounts as Volkswagen and Plymouth, to name two, primarily, I suppose, because circulation was zooming. Or maybe he just liked a few lunatics lurking in his empire.

The comparison tests caused the management and our advertising salesmen the most trouble. When we set out to evaluate one or more cars head-to-head, it was known in advance that one machine would be declared a clear winner, one would be a total loser, and the others would occupy a limbo somewhere in the middle. That meant one thing to our ad peddlers: in a six-car test, there rose the specter of as many as five clients refusing to buy space because they didn't win. It was, therefore, incumbent for all participants to make the best showing possible, which prompted several manufacturers to provide us with test vehicles that were a considerable improvement over what the general public might find in the showroom. Perhaps the most absurd manifestation of a *Car and Driver* comparison test took place in the late autumn of 1965 on the sand-swept desolation of the Bridgehampton race circuit.

Those were the halcyon days of the so-called "super cars"—intermediate-sized American coupes that had been stuffed to the gunwales with oversized, overpowered engines to sate the newly discovered "young market's" thirst for fast automobiles. The trend had been started a year earlier by the legendary Pontiac GTO, in actuality a gussied-up Tempest two-door with a high-performance, triple-carbureted V–8 engine. Boosted into prominence by a razzle-dazzle Pontiac ad man named Jim Wangers, who went so far as to get such forgettable compositions as "Gee-toe Tiger" high on the bubble-gum set's top forty charts, the GTO was a runaway sales success. In no place in the world is imitation a more sincere form of flattery than in Detroit, and within eighteen months, practically everybody was trying to cash in on the "super car" business. As the 1966 models were introduced, we at *C/D* decided to conduct a bonanza, eight-way test of the principal contenders in the field. We would include the Oldsmobile 4–4–2, the GTO, the Mercury Cyclone GT, the Chevrolet Chevelle SS396, the Buick Skylark GS, the Dodge and Plymouth 426 street "Hemis," and the Ford Fairlane GTA. Our test cars were to be provided by the individual manufacturers. While this procedure increased the risk of tampering, it was our only alternative, for two reasons: one, we had no budget to purchase our own cars from showroom stock; and two, the cars were so new (the Chevy was in fact a preproduction prototype) that only the factories would be able to provide properly equipped models that early in the manufacturing cycle. In notifying the various companies, Dave Davis made two specific written references to the fact that we wanted the cars to be in utterly showroom stock condition and warned that we would have an inspection team on hand to detect any cheating. We did, in fact, arrange to have a group of technical specialists from a high-performance equipment manufacturer attend the test to examine the cars. This in no way deterred our friends in Detroit. Dodge and Plymouth flatly refused to participate, claiming that we would be unable to police the cheating. They were perfectly correct, although ironically their cars were so powerful in comparison to the competition they would easily have won in stock trim.

We decided that an impartial expert driver not connected with the magazine would add additional impact to the story. Masten Gregory seemed to be an inspired choice. He was (and is) one of the freest spirits in the racing world and on occasion has shown glimpses of world championship talent behind the wheel. An owlish man who peers at the world from behind thick glasses and talks with a basso twang that rises out of his slight body with improbable force, Masten had grown up in a wealthy, socially prominent Kansas City family with a consuming fascination for fast cars. After he had established himself as a high roller in American amateur racing circles in the midfifties, and caused his family no little consternation, Masten's mother is said to have provided him with a stipend and recommended that he go to Europe for a few months "to get this racing bug out of your system." Fifteen years have passed, and Masten has yet to return to Kansas City. Once located in Paris, Masten proved himself to be a driver of substantial talent on the Grand Prix scene, although his reputation was primarily built around a series of horrendous crashes from which he escaped unscathed. It became Masten's trademark to lose control of a speeding race car, then just before it smashed itself to bits, to sail gracefully out of the cockpit (seat belts were not used in Europe until the middle

1960's), and to land softly in a clump of grass.

During the summer prior to our test, Masten's career had taken a major upswing. He had run the Indianapolis 500 for the first time that May, starting in thirty-first position and slashing through the field in the first 150 miles until he reached sixth place. His car broke at that point, but his performance had been dazzling. Less than a month later, he had won the great twenty-four-hour endurance race at Le Mans, teaming with the late Jochen Rindt, in an aged, clapped-out Ferrari, to thrash soundly the combined factory teams of Ford, Porsche, and Ferrari.

Masten was our man. While he made arrangements to fly over from Paris, word was filtering to us that the manufacturers were preparing cars with more than the desired enthusiasm. Monty Roberts, who was then working in Ford's New York public-relations office, phoned to tell us that the Fairlane GTA was being "tuned" at the Charlotte, North Carolina, stock-car-race shop of Holman & Moody, while the Cyclone GT was getting special treatment at Bud Moore's elaborate competition facility in Spartanburg, South Carolina. "We just want them to make sure all the nuts and bolts are tight," Monty chuckled in reply to our concerned questions about Ford's efforts. The balloon was up. Exactly what we had feared was happening. Some massive cheating was underway. After all, you don't send a passenger car to places like Holman-Moody or Bud Moore's for a grease job and a tune-up. Both organizations had widespread reputations as expert rule-benders in Southern stock-car racing circles—collectively a group of competitors whose cleverness at multiplying the performance of supposedly production-line automobiles was legendary. To make matters worse, we knew that Wangers was notorious for providing magazines with Pontiacs that were outlandishly fast when compared with showroom models. Then Oldsmobile got into the act by announcing that they had delivered their test 4-4-2 to former driver and expert development engineer John Fitch for a little extra "work," in-

cluding a day of testing at Bridgehampton! Only Buick and
Chevrolet didn't appear to be fooling around with their
cars, but who could tell? They might show up with the
biggest cheaters of all!

Smith was convinced the test was headed for total disaster. Dave and I remained hopeful, at least until we left for
Bridgehampton to begin the three-day session. I will never
forget driving along Route 27 on eastern Long Island when
we spotted a red truck parked at a roadside diner. It was a
specially built race-car transporter, complete with custom
tool compartments, winches, tanks for compressed air,
water, etc. It was a complete mobile race shop. On its door
was printed BUD MOORE ENGINEERING, SPARTANBURG, SOUTH
CAROLINA. Chained on the rear ramp was a red Cyclone GT
—our test car! "Jesus Christ, that's beautiful," groaned
Dave. "They've modified the goddamn thing so much it
won't even run on the road. This is going to be a million
laughs."

We arrived at Bridgehampton to find a collection of factory engineers, mechanics, and public-relations men huddled around their collective entries. Wangers had appeared
with *two* dazzling "Tiger Gold" GTOs, both looking mean
and race-ready. The one to be used in the test had been
towed from Detroit by the other—hardly what you would
expect for a "production model." The Fairlane had somehow been driven from Holman-Moody's place on public
roads, but it had well and truly been modified to a point
where it was more a racing machine than a passenger car.
Fitch was shepherding his Oldsmobile, which looked be-
nign enough, but was the subject of suspicion simply because John was too clever and too competitive to have let
the car sit untouched before bringing it to the track. The
Buick and Chevrolet seemed to be legal, but that was a
subjective response. We didn't have the vaguest notion one
way or the other. Our "inspection team" wasn't helping,
either. They stuffed their heads under the hoods of the various entrants, checking displacements, compression ratios,

etc., and came up for air looking completely poker-faced.
They had obviously seen things they knew weren't legal,
but refused to point any accusing fingers, because the company they represented did a thriving accessory business
with the Big Three. They were, we discovered too late,
under firm orders not to rock the boat.

The Cyclone, in the hands of Big Bud Moore himself,
was a travesty. Moore, a burly Southerner with a creased,
friendly face, only smiled when we blustered that his car
wasn't in the spirit of our rules. His associate from Lin-
coln-Mercury, a porky engineer and race expert named Fran
Hernandez, was constantly at his side, arguing vehemently
that the car was perfectly legal—that every component on
the machine was a "factory option." That in itself was true,
but at the time the Ford Motor Company was in the midst
of a multimillion-dollar-per-year racing program and was
producing thousands of quasi-production bits and pieces
for its racing machines that weren't available to the general
public. To begin with, the Cyclone was 1½ inches lower
than normal production models. We knew Bud had modified the suspension for better handling, but we couldn't
pinpoint where he'd done the tampering. The car used the
venerable 390-cubic-inch V–8 that had been in the Ford
lineup of engines for years. It was known as a loyal, affable
workhorse with limited high-performance capability. It
would not rev effectively beyond 5,300–5,500 rpm without
serious modification. A showroom Cyclone GT of the type
we were testing would run the quarter mile in about 14.5
seconds, with a trap speed of 98–99 mph. Our car, thanks
to Bud Moore's genius, traversed the same distance in 13.9
seconds at 103.8 mph—using an rpm limit of 6,500 rpm!
The Holman-Moody Fairlane carried a more stock engine,
but the automatic transmission had been extensively modified to produce crisper, quicker shifts, and the suspension
had been tidied up considerably. Wangers's GTO was a mar-
velous machine, but bore only coincidental resemblance to
a car one might purchase from a Pontiac dealer. It was even

faster in the quarter-mile test than the Cyclone!

The Buick, Chevrolet, and Oldsmobile representatives were aware of the rules-bending and were pressuring Dave, Steve, and me for some kind of disciplinary action. Trying to avoid a showdown, we decided to let Masten drive the cars before making a ruling. Our star arrived at the wheel of the white Toronado with an elegant blonde at his side and began thrashing the cars around Bridgehampton. He seemed to be a perfectly impartial judge, never having driven any of the subject cars before and never having raced at that particular track. The Cyclone was clearly the quickest around the 2.85-mile circuit. At about the time we were resolved to making a decision concerning whether or not the Cyclone was going to be included in the final ranking, it blew up. Masten was thundering along the short back straight when a connecting rod let loose, and Bud Moore's lovingly assembled powerhouse scattered itself all over the Hampton dunes. The Fairlane was next to go. Masten brought it into the pits noting that the engine was about to seize from the strain of the hard running. It was parked. Then the GTO's race-tuned carburetor setup caught fire. Jubilation! Through a clear act of Providence (and Masten's heavy foot), the racers had ceased operating, leaving us justification to disregard them in the final results and judge the other three. Masten loved the Olds. While relatively docile in terms of outright speed, it handled excellently on the bumpy course, and Masten claimed it was the hands-down winner. Between his official evaluations, we drove the cars as well and agreed with the judgment.

We decided to rank the Oldsmobile first, the Chevy second, the Buick third, the GTO fourth, the Fairlane fifth, and the Cyclone last. As we were completing the test in a cold rain, Hernandez was so enraged he could hardly speak to us. Bud Moore, however, having encountered about every adversity imaginable in automotive competition, was more relaxed. As he and his crew loaded the stricken Cyclone back on the transporter for the long trip south, he turned to us and smiled. "You know, you boys is complainin' about us stretchin' the rules, but I'll tell you one thing: that lil' ol' Oldsmobile is the sneakiest one in the place. That thang ain't any more legal than us."

Ol' Bud Moore knew the score. He understood more than we ever would about the uncanny ability of men like John Fitch and Oldsmobile engineer Dale Smith to subtly improve the handling of a production automobile. But he was overstating his case. We learned later that stiffer shock absorbers had been installed on the 4–4–2, which, in company with some harder bushings in the control arms, had made the car much more manageable in the corners. The car was essentially a stock package that had been tuned and tweaked to the limit—a limit probably well beyond the capability of the average car owner. The lesson was clear: none of the test cars, with the possible exception of the Buick, represented "showroom stock" automobiles. We had opened the door for the factories to assist in the preparation, and we had paid the price. As so often happens, our search for truth had only added to the general acrimony and confusion.

Whenever I returned to Bridgehampton, the memory of that hectic session with the "super cars" came to my mind. I had never raced on the track and had, in fact, attended very few major events there. My impression of the place was one of desolation; with a few of us huddled in the pits around a collection of gold GTOs and road-hugging Cyclone, arguing with Fran Hernandez and listening to Masten's basso profundo being swallowed by the cold winds.

The weekend following the Watkins Glen Trans-Am brought with it the opportunity to frolic again at Bridgehampton—once more in company with *Car and Driver*. Only this time I would be racing. The magazine had purchased a Datsun 240Z, of the type I'd used at Bondurant's school, and had modified it to a point where it was nearly raceable. It had many of the competition suspension components, racing wheels, etc., but its engine remained unmodified. Datsun racing expert Bob Sharp—a perennial SCCA champion—had installed the necessary roll bar, shoulder harness, etc., to make it safe and stable, but it was not a pure, out-and-out racing car. If anything, the C/D Datsun was half-racer, half-road-car, heavy and underpowered, but equipped with a sophisticated suspension system. In that configuration it would not be competitive in the SCCA National program, but might work acceptably in the lower-key environs of regional racing. The New York Region of the SCCA had scheduled a race of that nature at Bridgehampton, and we decided to enter the Datsun.

It had been several years since I'd been to the track, but nothing seemed to have changed. It still languished in solitude, unaffected by the bursts of real-estate growth that had been taking place elsewhere on Long Island. Financial problems, exacerbated by a powerful Atlantic storm that had washed out several sections of the track surface, had prompted yet another change of management. Public announcements had been made about the intention to schedule major professional races there, but limited funds had prevented anything of the sort from becoming a reality. It had become isolated in time, a seedy, windswept memorial to the euphoria of the grand amateurs of racing, who believed that their fervor for motor sport would infect the nation like a flu epidemic, forcing the multitudes to places like Bridgehampton in overwhelming numbers. That had never happened, and now the track was slowly returning to the arms of nature. Its scattered buildings, a two-story timing tower, a few public lavatories, and tool sheds, were creaking and paint-shorn from the incessant wind and salt. The track itself was crumbling along the edges, and heaves and ruptures marred its surface.

When we arrived on a clear and warm Saturday morning, a few cars were clustered around the entrance gate. Nearby, a small green hut resembling an aged hot-dog stand was surrounded by a few-score people and parked racing cars on trailers. This was the registration building where the race officials were signing in the entrants, giving out credentials, and collecting the myriad forms and documents necessary to run even a minor regional event. Since Bridgehampton had opened in the fifties, this hut had served as registration headquarters, and many of the best drivers in the world—Gurney, Hill, Surtees, McLaren, Hulme, Hansgen, Donohue, etc.—had at one time or another signed themselves into races at that same rude structure. Perhaps the most colorful men came when the Grand National stock cars ran for several races in the midsixties. It was during one of these events that David Pearson had made his previously noted denouncement of the place, but it was left to a lesser-known driver named Neil "Soapy" Castles to make the final statement on the Southerners' feelings about Bridgehampton and its amateurs.

Most stock-car racing is done on oval tracks (disdainfully called "circle" or "roundy-round" tracks by road racers), and while the oversized, ill-handling, noisy cars put on a spectacular show at road courses like Bridgehampton, such programs never attracted large crowds. To complicate matters, many of the established stock-car drivers and crews lacked enthusiasm for road racing, primarily because it involves unfamiliar driving techniques and special chassis adjustments. On the few occasions they ran at Bridgehampton, the stock-car boys shared the program with a preliminary series of amateur sports-car races—a subject of universal fascination for the Southerners. In the first place, they could not comprehend why anybody would race for tin cups in place of money. Secondly, a firm rule in stock-car circles (generally observed in all oval racing) banned women from the pits, and the free mingling of the sexes permitted in road racing caused them a certain puzzlement. Finally, foreign cars were rare in the rural South, where stock-car racing was the king of all sport, and they viewed "them lil' ol' toy furrin cars" with outright amusement.

"Soapy" Castles was one of those gaunt Scots-Irishmen

who populate the back country of the Piedmont Plateau. Inside their Jack Sprat bodies resides the courage of wolverines. Soapy Castles's ancestors stare at us in equal parts amusement and defiance from Civil War tintypes. While never attaining any real prominence in big-league racing, Soapy had followed the Grand National circuit for years, driving a series of battered machines to sufficiently high finishes to pay the bills. When he was not racing, Soapy was crashing cars. He loved to crash cars. When several low-budget films were produced on stock-car racing, Soapy did much of the stunt driving, including the execution of numerous flips and crashes. At one point a friend of mine hired Soapy to make a special guest appearance at a demonstration derby he was staging at a small North Carolina dirt track. Soapy showed up, enjoying a certain celebrity status with the local folk, at the wheel of a beat-up Lincoln —a leviathan well-suited to battering the opposition in such an event. Soapy easily disposed of his rivals, using his monstrous car to best advantage, until the rest of the entrants had been reduced to junk. It was then that Soapy revealed his flare for showmanship. As the last car running on the track, he lined up at one end of the front straightaway and backed the Lincoln past the crowd, ramming the retaining wall at the far end at full speed. Soapy stepped out of the crash unhurt, leaving the Lincoln glued against the fence, utterly destroyed, with its ruptured gas tank draining fuel across the track. As a final touch, Soapy flipped a lighted match into the gasoline and faced wild cheering as the Lincoln exploded into a thousand pieces!

Such a story would have made little sense to the sports-car racers who were to share the Bridgehampton circuit with Soapy and his cohorts. Because it lies in the heart of the posh Hamptons, the track has always attracted a surfeit of rich boys who parade around the pits in expensive blazers and Oleg Cassini scarves. The cultural gap between them and ol' boys like Soapy Castles is one of planetary dimensions. Add to that swish group the earnest weekend sports-car workers

—junior ad agency and Wall Street types who form the heart and soul of the New York SCCA Region—and any common ground between the "sporty car people" and the "redneck stockers," as the opposing camps referred to each other, disappeared completely.

Into this scene came Neil "Soapy" Castles and his crew. They dragged a semijunk Chrysler stock car up to the little registration shack and sauntered over to sign up for the race. The Chrysler had been in so many smashups that its fenders, doors, and roof had the surface smoothness of a bag of walnuts. Shocked as they were to witness the appearance of this haggard hunk of iron and its crewmen, the amateur registrars did their best to greet Soapy and his boys with goodwill.

"Welcome to Bridgehampton, Mr. Castles," said a pretty, weekending secretary in a racing jacket covered with emblems.

Soapy grunted and began signing the entry forms. Then he looked up, his watery blue eyes squarely engaging her wide, innocent gaze. 'We 'uns gon' to git a chance to race with them sporty car boys?" he asked.

"No, Mr. Castles," the girl replied. "They will race separately in the preliminary events. You'll just be racing with the other stock cars."

"Aw shit, that's too bad," Soapy said, unsmiling. "I was fixin' to kill me a couple of them little gentlemen." He turned and strode away, leaving those in the hut to ponder if he was kidding or not.

Soapy Castles hurt no one that weekend. It was, in fact, an extremely safe race meeting, with the big stock-car event won by a slight, since-departed Southerner named Billy Wade. Billy was in a hot streak at that time, and he was to win four straight races on the Northern tour. However, there was grumbling among his competitors that he was running too large a gas tank and therefore able to outdistance his competition between pit stops. That accusation was never proved. Ironically, the man who owned, prepared, and entered the black and red Mercury that Billy drove was Bud Moore of Spartanburg, South Carolina.

Compelled more by curiosity than nostalgia, Smith showed up for my regional race, his hair considerably longer and more frazzled, but still looking uncannily youthful for his midthirties vintage. Chuck Kreuger, a longtime racing friend and perhaps the most naturally gifted mechanic I'd ever met, came down from upstate with me to keep an eye on the workings of the car.

Bob Brown, the current editor of *Car and Driver*, drove out from Sea Cliff, Long Island, to take part. A bright, easygoing New Jerseyite who'd wandered into automotive journals via a few casual years at Syracuse University and editing a defunct East Coast surfing magazine, Brown looked perpetually harried. His thin, wispy hair and thick beard somehow added to this impression. Like me, he was inept with tools, but he had brought along a stopwatch to add to our meager collection of gear and appointed himself the chief timer for the team.

This was a one-day event. I would get some practice in the morning, then run a single, twenty-minute race later in the afternoon. Bridgehampton was a difficult course to learn, and I was hoping for as much practice as possible. Most American race circuits look as if they'd been designed by highway engineers. Rather than conforming to the natural terrain, which produces informal, exciting courses with corners of uncertain camber and radii, and radical elevation changes, most tracks are built with the bulldozer mentality of a real-estate developer, i.e., scrape everything level and then reorganize things in sterile symmetry. I remember being amazed that Denis Hulme had bettered the lap record at Elkhart Lake, Wisconsin, within *four* laps of his first practice *ever* on the track. This was particularly shocking, because Elkhart Lake, as one of the most beautifully situated and best-run road courses in North America, was also considered to be one of the most challenging to drive. Of course, Hulme was a world-champion driver, but to exceed the record in four laps seemed to border on the superhuman. I asked him about it. "Quite simple," he said. "Except for a short, squiggly bit, all the corners are ninety degrees. It's a shame, really, to spend all this money to build such a beautiful circuit and then make all the corners the same."

Other American tracks have a similar brand of civil engineer's dullness, but Bridgehampton is not so cursed. It is laid out in the rough outline of a squashed horseshoe and features everything from blind hillcrests and fast, sweeping bends to tight, strangely contoured hairpins. It is like riding a roller coaster, in that only a few moments per lap pass when you aren't jerking one way or the other through a corner. There is a constant sensation of speed. On some tracks, Watkins Glen included, there are fast sections and slow sections. At Bridgehampton it seems as if you are going fast, no matter where you are on the course. What's more, one of the most terrifying sections of track in the United States is part of the circuit. At the end of the three-quarter-mile main straight is a blind crest leading into three incredibly fast, oddly angled downhill right-hand bends. Fast cars reach speeds of 175–180 mph on the straight before they plunge over the hill and through this series of turns. In walking the track or driving slowly around the course, they seem practically insignificant and amply separated by straight sections of road. But at 100-plus miles an hour, they appear clumped together in a matter of a few yards. My first exposure to those corners came during a casual ride with Walter Hansgen, who was known to traverse that section faster than any man on earth. He was giving me a tour of Bridgehampton in a 230 SL Mercedes-Benz roadster—hardly a scary, high-speed sports car. Because he was so familiar with the track, he whipped the Mercedes around and around, chatting and driving one-handed. Little did he know that every time he charged over the hillcrest and drifted through the right-handers—sawing casually on the wheel and discoursing on a variety of subjects—I was convinced I was about to die. I had ridden with many professional drivers, including a number of laps in excess of 170 mph around Daytona, while sitting on the floor of Lee Roy Yarbrough's Grand National Dodge Charger, in my street clothes, sans seat belt or crash helmet, but never had I been more petrified than at Bridgehampton with Walter Hansgen.

Prior to my first practice session, I climbed inside the Datsun to adjust the seat belts. Its interior was civilized compared with the barren environs of the Camaro. Most of the passenger amenities remained, including the upholstery, the seats, and even the radio. A roll bar that Sharp had installed behind the seats, a small, thick-rimmed steering wheel, and an ultrawide rearview mirror that significantly reduced windshield visibility were the only clues that the car was intended for anything beside casual boulevard frolicking.

Its mufflers had been replaced by straight exhaust pipes, but they opened beneath the rear bumper and not under the doors, making the engine noise seem positively soothing compared to the Camaro or even the Lancia. The car felt smooth and heavy as I accelerated onto the track. Up ahead lay the Place: that ominous point where the track seemed to disappear. That spot in the road marked the hillcrest I remembered so well, and as I dropped over the lip, running slowly, and began the descent through the corners, the whole thing looked even more terrifying than I could remember. The track was terribly narrow, actually little wider than a rural two-lane highway. Rain-washed stones and gravel littered its surface. There were no guard rails, only rutted shoulders of sand leading to sloping, scrub-covered hills. One thing I did not want to do, I thought, was spin off in this place. Getting sideways on the bordering sand would probably flip the car, which could lead to all kinds of unhappiness. The entire track was rough and unkempt, but its general layout still retained that touch of genius. There was no place to relax, no corners that were easy. If only it had been built where people could reach it, I mused, as I took a couple of easy familiarization laps. Decrepit as it was, it had genuine class.

I picked up speed as I went past the pits and spotted Brown, Kreuger, and Smith standing impassively behind the wall. The first test was coming up. There is one sure sign of trepidation at the hill at Bridgehampton. From the pits it is easy to see who is using his brakes early. If one's brake lights wink on before he plunges over the crest, it means he is running scared—or more correctly, revealing that he is running scared. That I was trying not to do. The hill dropped away under me, and I fought an urge to punch the brakes. I finally succumbed to fear and lifted my foot slightly, then shifted from fifth gear to fourth. The car got light as centrifugal force sent it crabbing across the track toward the outside. I whisked through the last of the three corners and shot onto a short straightaway feeling as if I'd accomplished a major feat of driving. With each ensuing lap, I gained confidence, finally translating my braking, shifting, and cornering into a smooth, integrated series of movements, so the bends seemed to flow together in a single line. By the time I stopped and Kreuger made a few small adjustments on the engine, I felt I was beginning to reach competitive speeds.

"About two minutes, Yates," said Brown, referring to his stopwatch. That lap time was about twelve seconds slower than Sharp's lap time in his full-race Datsun—a car perhaps 300–400 pounds lighter and producing 50–75 hp more than ours. But our time was adequate for a regional, especially when only one other car seemed to be entered in our class, C-Production. This particular category in National racing is extremely competitive. Yet at Bridgehampton that weekend we faced a single Lotus Elan. The car looked well-equipped and properly maintained, but we knew nothing of its potential. Regional racing is virtually unpredictable. Rank novices and incompetents often show up in excellent cars. Superb drivers might be found in junk cars. And occasionally a fine, experienced driver will bring a high-quality car to a regional merely to test some new components or to partake in an afternoon of low-key competition. Therefore, we had no idea whether the man in the green Lotus Elan would be fast or slow. While he was the only direct competition, there were plenty of cars to race. As we lined up on the grid, there were seven cars in front of me, ranging from a hot Camaro Trans-Am car to several Corvettes. Directly in front of me was a custom-built sports racer. Gridded beside me was a new Volvo sedan owned and driven by a Washington-area dentist. He was known to have spent substantial sums of money to make the car competitive in the under 2.5-liter Trans-Am class, but simply couldn't find the horsepower or handling to enter the same league with the factory-backed Datsuns and Alfas. I figured I could beat him. As at the Glen Regional, I was underestimating the Volvo.

It was a motley collection of automobiles. Beside the Volvo and the Corvettes and the assorted sports racers, my rearview mirror revealed a few Mustangs, another Volvo sedan, a couple of slower Corvettes, some Triumphs, etc., strung out behind me on the starting grid. This was the final race of the afternoon and included a hodgepodge of the faster cars. My only rival, the Lotus, was directly in back, indicating our qualifying speeds were roughly equal. I thought I could beat him, but I was distracted by the notion of finishing as high as possible in the overall standings. We took a pace lap, then made a flying start on the long straight leading to the hill. The dentist in the red Volvo was my yardstick. After all, Volvos were not highly regarded in any serious racing (for the simple reason that the factory had no interest in spending the money to develop competition equipment), and if I couldn't beat at least him, there wouldn't be much to crow about.

I couldn't. The red Volvo was faster. I hung with him for a few laps, but the result was inevitable. His superior acceleration would add a few feet to his lead on each corner, until it was extended to yards and finally furlongs. After a while, he was out of sight. But a bonus had come during the pursuit. Flinging the Datsun around as best I knew how had brought me up on the sports racer that had started immediately in front of me. It was a low, slab-sided machine, painted red and white. Called a Royale, it was one of a multitude of custom racers imported from England for club racing. Theoretically, it was very fast—perhaps as fast as the Camaro and Corvette, which were leading the race—and certainly seven to eight seconds per lap faster than my car. But then nothing follows form in regional racing. I had no idea who the driver was. His lower face was wrapped in a Nomex scarf, making him anonymous. I was not competing against a "him" anyway, but rather an "it": a conglomerate man/machine whose personality was more mechanical than human. After all, the driver's visible form was like more than a plastic globe protruding out of the bodywork. An abstraction.

It braked early going into a curvy section with high sand banks called "echo valley," and I passed. The chase was joined by a TVR coupe, a stubby English sports car that snubbed in behind the Royale, and the three of us made several laps as if we were chained together. The green Lotus had fallen back and was out of sight. We slowed briefly for a waving yellow flag. A Triumph had flipped. We went past the crash at reduced speed, giving me a glimpse of the wreck. It was upside down against a gravel hillside with its wheels pointing awkwardly toward the sky. Its driver, a youth with a prominent nose and heavy brows, was holding his helmet in one hand and rubbing his head with the other. He seemed unhurt, although, to be honest, it didn't really matter to me. I was so immersed in my own struggle that I viewed the crash with total dispassion, as if I were looking at photos in a magazine.

With a bit more straightaway speed, the Royale challenged as we headed for the hill. It came alongside, and I knew a showdown was coming. Somebody was going to have to brake first. A game of chicken. In a situation like that, a driver must marshal all his poise in order to drive slightly beyond his limit without losing control of himself or his car. I lost my poise somewhere near the crest of the hill. I had been carrying over the crest about 115 mph in fifth gear, touching the brakes, downshifting to fourth, and running the bends about 90 mph. But with the Royale beside me, trying to probe its nose inside my right front fender, I forgot to downshift! I poked the brakes, then powered through the section faster than I'd ever run before—in fifth gear. Each of the three downhill curves got progressively tighter, and suddenly I found the last one looming up at a terrifying rate. I rammed on the brakes hard and caught fourth gear at the last moment. The Datsun yipped in protest, then scrambled through the corner. As I sailed onto the short straight, my outside wheels skidded off the edge of the pavement and tossed a thick cloud of sand and stones onto the track. I looked back to see that the Royale had fallen well behind, no doubt presuming that the Datsun driver had gone starkers.

Whether the Royale was being driven by a novice trying to learn his machine, or whether his pace was being slowed by mechanical troubles, I could not tell, but he seemed to show moments of great speed, interrupted by periods of lethargy. He clung behind me for several more laps, then used his extra speed on the straight to scurry past. I was helpless, and I chuckled about the perpetual race driver's excuse, "I caught him in the corners, but he passed me on the straights." But thanks to my accidental discovery about using fifth gear on the hill, he never managed to get far ahead. We'd bustle over the crest with him holding a four-or-five-car-length lead, and I'd gobble it up with savage glee. On several occasions, I nearly whacked him in the tail as we drifted through. That sensation of swooping down on him produced in me a kind of primitive delight that I suppose hides in the dark dens of every man's brain, dating from the eons in which our entire consciousness centered on the destruction of prey.

Then it was over, and I cruised into the pits to find a

collection of marshals waving me toward the starting line. The starter was holding out a large checkered flag for me to grasp. Good Lord, I was a winner! I was being given a victory lap. I had beaten one other car in C-Production and had finished perhaps sixth overall. Hardly a feat worthy of a victory parade, but I was willing to serve tradition. Chuck Kreuger jumped into the passenger seat, and we went off on a lap of the track, with me trying to support the waving banner in the windstream and steer at the same time. At each flag station, the workers—the communications men, the emergency crews, and the flaggers—were waving at us. Some were clapping. For a moment I was staggered. They were cheering me, for God's sake, and I tried to acknowledge them as best I could by flapping the checkered flag in a crude semaphore of thanks. It was a sweet moment of triumph, and I loved it.

We parked the Datsun in the pits and went off to the combination beer party and trophy presentation being held in a small private pavilion overlooking the pits. We drank a few drafts, compared notes with some of the competition, and got another silver-plate serving tray. René Dreyfus, the great 1930's Grand Prix driver who ran a New York restaurant, came over and told me I'd done a good job. He was a thin, sad-eyed man whose porcelain complexion indicated he didn't get outside his beloved Le Chanteclair on East Forty-ninth Street in Manhattan very often. His place was a kind of racers' refuge in the city. Its walls were tiered with photos of the sport's celebrities: racing's reply to Sardi's. Our conversation at Bridgehampton had been our first in perhaps five years. It was good to see him again. He was a gentleman driver of the old school, when most of the myths and legends about international racing were realities; when pretty ladies swooned on the pit counters and noblemen in silk scarves and linen helmets raced over cobbled roads and celebrated their victories with magnums of champagne. René Dreyfus, the star driver of the unforgettable Bugatti team, represented those days, as did, in a sense, the crumbling track at Bridgehampton. If the driver naïveté that they embodied was swallowed up, replaced by icy technology, the sport would surely die.

We drove away from Bridgehampton savoring our limited victory, but somehow sobered by the fear that modern times were catching up. A facility like that could not survive with the periodic appearance of a few amateur weekend racers. Elaborate, professional events attracting the great stars and multitudes of spectators were its key to salvation. Otherwise the developers and their bulldozers would arrive one day, and Bridgehampton would become "Spyglass Hill Acres" or some such real-estate magnate's contribution to prepackaged suburban paradise. If that happened, the monstrous iron blades ripping into the old track might get us all—Soapy Castles and René Dreyfus included.

12

▪▪▪▪▪▪▪▪▪▪

The green Galaxie leaped across Michigan International Speedway's paddock, coming straight at me. At the last minute it veered aside and jerked to a stop with its smiling driver at my elbow. It was Follmer, looking loose and relaxed. "Watch it, boy," he said in a mock-Southern accent, "or I'll lay a little metal on you." I hadn't seen him since the race at the Glen two weeks earlier, where he had finished second to Donohue, caused in part by a brief excursion off the track. "Some of the same goddamn brain fade," he said, his face turning sour. I suggested that his chances might be better at Michigan, what with Mark not arriving until race morning because of the "California 500" Indianapolis car race at Ontario. "Yeah, maybe, but Mark's got that car so sorted out he won't need more than a few laps to get competitive. We'll thrash around here for the next couple of days, and he'll blow in here a few hours before the race and be tougher than hell, you wait and see."

We chatted for a while in the welter of activity around us.

Trans-Am cars rumbled past, pulverizing our voices with their exhausts and leaving us helplessly shaping words like deaf mutes. "Maybe turbines are the answer. At least you could carry on a normal conversation in the pits," I said.

"You been around the track?" George asked.

"Yeah, very slowly. My car is all screwed up. The same fuel starvation problem is there like it was at the Glen, and it won't handle, especially on the twisty part on the back of the course."

"This is a sorry-ass excuse for a racetrack," George said. "Mickey Mouse. Jesus Christ, is it *Mickey Mouse!*" He was using the standard racer's jargon for tight, slow, uninspired racetracks. No one was sure of the term's origins, but it predated Michigan International Speedway by many years. This vast, multimillion-dollar track, set in rolling farmland near Jackson and several hours from Detroit, was primarily designed as a superspeedway for Indianapolis and Grand National cars. Its road course appeared to have been added as an afterthought. To Follmer and me it looked like a hodgepodge of twisty pavement that spread over an expanse of open fields behind the big oval. It began on the banked stretch of the main straightaway directly in front of the grandstands, then ran across the infield to a point where it crossed the back stretch of the superspeedway at right angles. After wandering around the countryside in a jumble of turns, it recrossed the speedway at another 90-degree junction. It was this pair of intersections that caused the trouble. Because the speedway was slightly banked, even on the straights, a level crossing was impossible. Hitting the intersection at full speed on the road course would send a car flying through the air like a refugee from Joie Chitwood's thrill show. In an attempt to prevent this, the management had installed hay-bale chicanes at both points. A low wall of bales narrowed the track to a tight, left-right jog, forcing the cars to slow from 90–100 mph to perhaps 60 mph when crossing the speedway. It was a jury-rig at best, simply because the cars kept gnawing at the bales until straw had been spread all over the track and the narrow gate had been breached. The back section was ludicrously tight, as if the designers had decided that any straight stretches of road implied a dereliction of their duty. It was also dangerous. The last time the Trans-Am cars had run there, one had skidded on the rain-slick track and sailed through a flimsy wire fence, killing two spectators. To make matters worse, the constricted nature of the layout made it difficult to pass, except on the front straight past the grandstands. It was indeed Mickey Mouse.

The multitude of turns only complicated my problems. In the intervening two weeks since the Watkins Glen Trans-Am, Agor's crew had modified my front suspension by lowering it and changing the sway-bar adjustments. A Trans-Am car, essentially a passenger machine unintended for racing, is a cranky beast at best, requiring extensive modifications to its suspension before it will stay on the track at all. Bruce Johnson and Agor maintained that my car was now identical to Warren's and registered blank stares when I complained about its handling. The car was treacherous. It felt as if it were running on soft tires. Additionally, the fuel starvation that had developed at the Glen had not been corrected, convincing Rich Dilcher and Mike Fitzgerald that the trouble lay in the fuel pumps or in the gas pickup at the bottom of the fuel cell. I spent much of the first day trundling in and out of the pits, trying to get the two vexing problems sorted out. Once again Dave Hoselton was planning to run in the amateur race preceding the Trans-Am, and he was encountering the same problems. He wasn't as vocal in his complaints, but the deepening scowl on his face and the fact that he remained several seconds slower than I tended to counter any notions on the part of the crew that the troubles were in my head. In fact, he had spun off the track at one point but had not damaged the car.

The Labor Day weekend was beginning with a nasty chill sweeping over Michigan. I climbed into the Camaro to try the car after the crew had fiddled once more with the fuel system and Bruce had made some tentative suspension adjustments.

A dingy bank of clouds was rising over the track. The immense grandstand, with its color-keyed, orange and ocher bleacher seats, was nearly empty. Aside from a few cars out for practice, most of the competitors were clustered in the pair of low, open-sided, steel buildings that served as garages. The Camaro's seat was a familiar place by now, and I found that the starting procedure, the clumsy feel of the clutch and gearshift, etc., had become second nature. I accelerated down the long pit lane and took one lap. As I completed the circuit and sailed down off the speedway's banking, where the suspension bottomed and the machine tried to lash sideways, I noticed another orange machine accelerating out of the pits. Warren!

He merged onto the track behind me, perhaps a dozen car lengths back. His practice times were something like ten seconds a lap faster than mine, and he'd made it clear on a couple of occasions that if I'd drive a little harder, that margin would be reduced. My protests about the cranky handling had only caused him to force his jaw a little farther into the wind, to smile disdainfully, and to recommend that a "little white knuckle" driving would cure everything. I wasn't going to let him pass. I started to race his Camaro as it chased me with its blank black headlight holes looking like flaring nostrils in my rearview mirror. It was an evil-looking thing. I crested a low hummock and slid through a tight left-hander well off the apex. Driving as hard as I could, my car kept sliding off line, at first trying to nose off the outside of the track, then trying to whip its tail around and spin off rear end first. Agor was snubbed against my rear bumper. I could see him back there, sitting well back from the steering wheel, chin out, and his face utterly passive. He was racing, too. I could tell from the way he was using all of the road, sliding wide coming off the corners and kicking up little clots of dust.

I refused to slow down and wave him on, as a responsible junior teammate should have done. At the very least, I intended to deny him passage until after we got through the twisty back part, where his presumably faster machine could operate at an advantage. Ahead lay another small hilltop with fast, right-left esses. The opening right-hander had to be taken with precision, otherwise you would find yourself out of position for the left. It was a classic example of a warning Bondurant had given me: "You don't pay the penalty for taking a corner improperly until you reach the next one." I sailed into the left-hander too wide, and I stayed too wide— right up to the point the tail jerked off line and I found myself spinning off the course. It happened so quickly I had no chance to do anything, other than to let the laws of kinetic energy play themselves out. The car crabbed sideways and began a great arcing loop toward the inside of the track. It seemed to take a sizable amount of time, that spin did. I made a futile twist of the wheel in an attempt to correct it, but it was hopeless. I sat there while my adrenal glands pumped themselves to near bursting in preparation for the impact. There is a moment of serene agony that overcomes one in a high-speed spin. The mind and physical organs momentarily seek equilibrium where there is none, and then, realizing a major trauma may be imminent, seem to stabilize in order to marshal full strength. Nothing happens in slow motion, your life does not pass before you, your sensory perceptions don't seem to accelerate in any way. I suppose it is a great deal like falling a long distance: it is not the trip but the sudden stop at the end that causes all the excitement. Getting there is not half the fun. Nothing was happening in my head. Some interviewer, seeking to plumb the thought process during such a situation, had once asked Indianapolis star Lloyd Ruby what he had been thinking during a spin and crash he had experienced during the 500. Ruby, a taciturn Texan, thought for a minute, then replied, "I thought, 'Oh, shit!'" That was the perfect answer.

The car came around to a point where it was traveling at right angles to the track and plunged into a mire of deep sand. There was no screeching of tires, simply because modern racing tires don't make that kind of noise. In fact, it was forebodingly silent. The engine stalled almost as soon as the car looped around, and the entire slide, which probably consumed two hundred feet, was undertaken with no more fuss than some loud scrubbing sounds from the tires and some metallic rattles and rumbles from the suspension. The Camaro entered the sand nose first and jerked to a stop within a matter of inches. Nothing hurt. I knew I was all right.

Warren had slipped past, and I quickly tried to resume the chase. I flipped the starter switch and the engine whirred over. It had undoubtedly flooded. I kept my foot off the throttle, the carburetor throats finally cleared themselves, and the engine fired up. I clanked the transmission into reverse and tried to back onto the track. The wheels spun in the sand. I tried to go ahead. More spinning. It was useless. The car was axle-deep in the sand, and there was no getting out. I would have to wait until the practice session ended and a tow truck came out from the pits to extract the car. I unbuckled my harness and got out. More machines howled past, very close. Back up the track, I could see a group of flagmen waving a yellow banner and pointing in my direction.

I circled the car once, trying to assess the damage. There seemed to be none, except that the clear-plastic "cowcatcher" spoiler under the nose had been bent back. It could have been a great deal worse. At speed, it is very difficult to scout the landscape surrounding the track. That is probably just as well. If I had known what kind of hazards lay around me at the point of the spin, I might have had a cardiac arrest out of sheer fright. The Camaro's front wheels had stopped no more than a yard from a ten-foot drop-off that angled down to a thicket of scrub trees. I had stopped just beyond the sheerest part of the drop, where a culvert coursed under the circuit. I had missed the steel guardrail that separated the course from the creek by no more than fifteen feet. If I had been unlucky enough to soar over the incline and land in the bottom of the gully, I would have been far away from the safety crews. If there had been a fire . . .

An emergency worker appeared on the other side of the

track. He spread his arms in a body-language query—did I
need help? I waved back in an attempt to signal my good
health, then tried to give him a pantomime indication that
my car would have to be towed out of the sand. He wig-
wagged a hazy acknowledgment and sprinted back to his station. Warren thundered past, looking sternly out of his
window at the crippled car. I tried to pass him an O.K. sign
that the machine was undamaged, but he accelerated away
before it could be transmitted. Christ, the cars seem as if they
are going fast, I thought to myself. The machines appeared so
noisy, so rapid, so angry, that it seemed difficult to believe
that a few minutes earlier I had actually been driving one of
them. Paul Nichter charged past, accelerating away from the
left-hander with the wheels of his Camaro cocked to correct a
power slide. He caught a glimpse of my parked machine,
twisted his head to get a better look, and nearly lost control.
He scrambled out of sight behind some trees with the tail of
his car yawing wildly. Through it all, Paul hadn't lifted his
foot. I laughed. Poor old Nichter had nearly sailed off into the
ravine with me, and I was laughing! I recalled an incident a
long time ago at Indianapolis, during a tire test A. J. Foyt was
running for Goodyear. Foyt had been driving his roadster—a
heavy, cumbersome front-engine-type car that had dominated
the 500 for years—when Parnelli Jones appeared at the
Speedway as a casual spectator. He and a group of friends
wandered down to the apron of turn one, where a lone tree
serves as an observation post. It is part of the complicated
Indy litany that everyone goes down to the tree in turn one
during practice to see how the competition is negotiating the
corner. In those days, a kind of good-natured macho contest
was being carried on between Foyt and Jones—a kind of
"anything you can do, I can do better" rivalry on and off the
racetrack. Foyt had been driving hard, lapping the Speedway
at near-record speeds, when Parnelli had arrived. "Watch
this," Parnelli said. "I'm going to wave at Foyt. I'll bet you
anything he'll wave back." Foyt wave back? Was Parnelli out
of his mind? There he was, slashing through one of the most

difficult corners in the world at maybe 145 mph, and he was going to take the time to wave at Parnelli? Come on now! Parnelli walked to the edge of the track and waved wildly as Foyt came by. Suddenly a red-gloved hand darted above the cowling in a cursory answer to Parnelli. The car slid briefly, but A. J. corrected and blasted onward as Parnelli dissolved in gales of laughter. A. J. had answered. Next challenge, please. That's the kind of thing that happens to your sense of values when you drive race cars.

It was starting to spit rain. The sky had darkened, and the track was glistening with moisture. I realized that if I had spun where I did, another car could certainly do the same thing. Rejecting an intemperate thought about climbing back into the cockpit to get out of the shower, I scuttled down the bank and walked to the edge of the brush. The cars were running above me now, and I could see only the upper half of their bodies as they sped by. I imagined one of them hurdling the steel fence and cartwheeling down on top of me, squashing me like a cow flop. I moved back farther and stood there in the low bushes with the rain falling on me, feeling isolated, helpless, and a trifle stupid. Another car spun at the entrance of the left-hander, but managed to stay on the track. It was Tony DeLorenzo, whose father was a General Motors vice president. He was a cocky, slightly rotund guy in his middle twenties, who wore round, undersized glasses that made him resemble a Japanese POW-camp commandant. He had run a team of Camaros and Corvettes for a number of seasons with middling success. This year, however, his pipeline to the Chevrolet sub-rosa supply of racing bits and pieces had apparently dried up, and he had bought a brace of year-old Mustangs from Bud Moore. Nobody seemed to care one way or the other that the son of a General Motors vice president was racing Ford products. His spin had not been as serious as mine (or perhaps he had corrected it with more skill), because he restarted and continued to practice until the end of the session.

The rain had stopped by the time they sent a tow truck to

drag me out. Somebody appeared with a small van and decided the job was too big. Then an El Camino pickup showed up with a length of rope, but after breaking it twice, we decided to wait until the larger, more powerful unit arrived. Finally, a husky Dodge came by, and its thick cable extracted me in a matter of seconds. I restarted the Camaro and idled off toward the pits, leaving the flagmen to sweep my litter of sand from the pavement. I wondered what Warren and the crew would say.

Not very much, as it turned out. As a group, they were hardly loquacious, even in moments of great joy. When one of their cars had just spun off the track, they turned downright dour. Even Dilcher, who bordered on being outspoken, fell into silence as the crew checked for damage. I didn't hesitate to voice my complaints.

"Listen, Warren, that goddamn thing is uncontrollable."

"You were way wide in the corners. You didn't hit any of the apexes," he replied loftily.

"I couldn't keep the thing on line. First it tries to understeer, and then the front end pushes. When you get off the throttle, it oversteers, and the ass end tries to come around. I'm not kidding. I realize I may not be the world's fastest driver, but dammit, I'm not *twenty* seconds slow. Some of that has got to be the car."

"We've been all over the thing. It's set up just like mine," he said.

"What about the fuel starvation? That isn't fixed."

"No, but that didn't cause you to spin."

"I admit that, and I'll admit I got into those curves too hot. I was trying to keep up with you and got a little overeager."

"I could tell you were in over your head," Warren said. "I was just cruising back there. Not even trying, wondering if you were going to make a mistake."

Warren's barb had hit its mark. His implication was clear: I had been running so slow that he had been able to loaf along behind me as a kind of detached observer. That made me furious. To begin with, I was convinced he had been chasing me as hard as he could, based on the way his car had been using up all the road in little skids and slides. Secondly, I believed that Warren was the kind of competitor who would never "cruise" behind anybody. He was trying to pass me anywhere he could (and undoubtedly would have if I hadn't spun), but to report that he had been chugging along at half speed was a jab at my driving that I took very personally. It was a subjective reaction, based purely on the classic ego-wrestling that typifies racing, but I was extremely irritated. I went off to find Sally, who I knew would be worried. I found her as she returned from the infield, where she had gone to see if she could locate me. Wives never know what the hell is going on at a racetrack. They tend only to watch for their husbands, and their brains work as stopwatches, recording to the exact second the moment their husbands' cars should appear for the next lap. If that arrival is not on schedule, panic often sets in. Sally is a patient, rather stoic lady, and she didn't come unglued at my absence. She did, however, grab a car and drive into the infield spectator area to see if she could spot where I'd gotten off the track. From her vantage point, she could make out what appeared to be an orange car askew on the edge of the course (since the fatal spectator crash, no one other than course workers had been allowed on the twisty section at the back of the circuit). Someone let her stand on top of their camper and lent her a pair of binoculars, which she had used to identify my car and to determine that I was the seemingly healthy figure standing near it. "Next time, please go off somewhere where I can see you," she said, half smiling, when we met.

"Unless something gets fixed on that son of a bitch, I can guarantee you one thing: there *will be* a next time," I grumbled.

Bruce Johnson, the team's chassis expert, was concerned. He tended to accept my and Dave's complaints about the handling and spent considerable time puzzling over the problem. He moved around the two Camaros with a kind of somber precision. He was quiet and exacting and seemed to understand a great deal about the mysterious art of chassis tuning. He had learned much about the craft from his friend Mark Donohue. "We've changed the shock settings," he said, "and that may help. You can try your first qualifying session with the car set up that way. If that doesn't work, I think I'll take some of the preload out of the front sway bar before Dave runs his race this afternoon."

"Preload in the front sway bar? What the hell is that?" I asked. I knew next to nothing about suspensions, and every time somebody like Johnson explained one of its aspects, it tended to whisk through my brain without making the slightest impression. I knew from the moment Bruce began his explanation that I would forget the entire thing within the hour.

"Preload is when the sway bars are twisted in a static position. Ideally, you set up a race car on a perfectly level surface —in fact, guys like Donohue use a precision steel platform called a surface plate, where they make sure the springs and sway bars are perfectly set in terms of the amount of weight on each wheel, so the weight is distributed properly on each corner of the car. That's a tough thing to do. I usually spend three or four hours before every race on both cars. If there's any twist or preload in the sway bars, it'll affect the handling by transferring weight in the suspension where you don't want it to be. It'll be just like getting a stronger spring rate on one wheel than on another, which means you'll get more roll in, say, a left-hand turn than in a right-hander. The bars have to be set at zero if you want the car to roll equally in both directions. So what you do is adjust the vertical links between the Heim joints..."

He had me. Bruce was a bright, earnest guy, with a clarity of expression and an authentic desire to help, but the conversation was drifting away from me. That's the way it always was with suspension talk. It is the heart and soul of racing. While much of the glamour in race-car mechanics lies with engines and the power they produce, it is handling—in terms of suspension and tires—that produces winners. Many races have been won by underpowered, well-handling cars;

practically none have been won by overpowering, ill-handling cars. It is an extremely complicated subject, using applications of physics and advanced geometry and trigonometry. The vast powers of computer technology have been brought to bear on chassis design and development, and even Bruce Johnson had availed himself of lengthy computer data relating to Warren's car and its sway bar and spring rates, etc. But talking about it is like trying to foot-race a jet fighter. You can hang in there for the first few steps, then all that power comes into play, and no matter how hard the pilot tries to throttle back his engines to keep you in sight, he just rockets ahead, opening the gap at quantum rates. That was the way it was with Bruce Johnson, who was carefully and conscientiously telling me about how preloading the sway bars affected the handling. I tried hard for a few minutes, then he began to accelerate away. My brain was humping along behind, but the gap was widening. "Jounce" and "rebound," "bump steer," "toe-in," "toe-out," "caster," "camber," filtered into the one-sided discourse, and I knew I was finished. My eyes must have glazed over when he got to hard-core suspension engineer's verbs like "crunch" and "dangle," because the flow of mysterious jargon slowed and finally stopped entirely. Bruce smiled knowingly and said, "The subject gets pretty complicated, but I think we can fix the trouble on your car."

"I sure hope so, because it's damn frustrating that I can't translate all that information to you. If I was any good at this, I'd be able to take a few laps, come in, and tell you, 'Hey, the damn sway bars are preloaded' or something."

"That's possible, but you'd be surprised how many drivers can't do it. Even Warren, who's pretty good with a chassis, can't communicate very well with me about how the car is behaving on the track. That's why Mark is so unbelievably good. He can read what a suspension is doing probably better than any driver in history. Then he comes in and makes the changes himself," Bruce answered.

"I really feel helpless when I just stand there and bitch and say things like, 'The tires feel soft,' for Chrissakes."

"Actually, that's the way a loaded sway bar might feel," he said. "When the weight transfers from one wheel to another, one might feel light, then heavy, then light again. The car feels like it's running on two wheels—only the wheels keep changing. Yeah, sort of like the tires are soft and the sidewalks keep collapsing," he said, smiling.

"I think some of the guys on the crew think I'm just bellyaching and not driving the car hard enough. But believe me, that thing handles like a pig right now, and I just flat can't drive it any faster. I'll guarantee you, if we don't find the trouble, I'm headed for another trip into the weeds."

Bruce chuckled. "Don't worry about that. I remember I asked Mark about that once, and he said, 'You shouldn't be concerned with going off the road. Everybody goes off the road. After all, how can you know your limits if you never reach them?"

"I'm sure he's right, except for one thing: when Donohue gets off the road, he still has a much higher percentage of control over the car than the average man. He still has control when things are out of control. With me, when that son of a bitch lets go, it's in the lap of God."

The necessary suspension adjustments couldn't be made until later in the day, when Bruce had the time available. It was decided that I should take my first qualifying attempt although the car was not right. There would be another session tomorrow, prior to the race, so I would get a chance to improve my time. I rolled the Camaro to the pit lane and lined it up with four other machines. I was in the first group —the slowest cars. I tried hard to psych myself. Sitting alone in the cockpit, I tried to remember all of Bill Shaw's hard, firm talk about smoothness and precision; about my tendency to slip off the apex in corners and run them too wide. I went over and over his points about "squeezing" on the power and brakes. By the time I accelerated out of the pits, I was consumed with thoughts about élan behind the wheel. No more rushing into the corner and trying to wrestle the car through. No more trying to race Warren Agor.

I almost spun again in the same place. Once more I got too wide entering the left-hander and found the tail end swerving out of line. This time I saved it, with a series of jerky, sawing motions on the steering wheel, and the Camaro stayed on the track. The remaining three laps were better. Smooth and slow. Jerry was along the pit wall, giving me signals. His signs said "2.08." That was about the way I'd been running in practice. No improvement whatsoever. I remained eighteen to twenty seconds slower than Follmer and ten seconds slower than Warren. I was terribly embarrassed. Very little was said back at the garage. The crew was sullen, partly because of the troubles with my car's suspension and fuel system that had had to be repaired, and partly because of the fact that Warren was also running slower than expected. Dave slumped in a corner of the building, looking sullen, his large eyes scanning the increasing throngs of paddock wanderers who elbowed their way around the machines, peering into the cockpits and gaping over the mechanics' shoulders. Underneath my car, the feet of Bruce Johnson were visible. Around them was a litter of tools, to be used in the exacting process of resetting the sway bars. The first man to test the new setup would be Dave Hoselton.

The SCCA National event would serve as a yardstick for the team's chances in the Trans-Am. If Warren could win against the amateurs—some of whom were contenders in the pro race as well, his outlook for tomorrow would surely improve. And if Dave found the handling and fuel starvation corrected, my gloomy situation might rectify itself. As race time approached, the crew fell into almost total silence, pushing the two machines out into the midafternoon sunlight with hardly a word being spoken. Even the disappearance of the cloud cover and the arrival of warm temperatures did nothing to dispel the sobriety. The atmosphere in the motor home, where Coralei Hoselton was sitting with a group of

crewmen's girlfriends and wives, was no different. I entered
to change out of my driving suit and found the women tight-
lipped, idly stirring coffee and fingering ragged newspapers
and race programs. Only Lynn Wilson, Warren's fiancée,
cracked an impish smile as I entered the home. Coralei eyed
me coldly, and I was sure she was wondering if I recalled her
warning from Watkins Glen.

The National race launched our hopes for tomorrow. Dave
instantly improved his lap times and stabilized at 2.02, about
ten seconds faster than he had been running. Sally and I
drove out near the back part of the course to watch the race.
Warren and a rich young Michigan driver named Marshall
Robbins were contesting for the lead. Dave was running
fourth, then moved into third when another Camaro dropped
out. I could hear his engine sputtering at the same places on
the course that bothered me, and I knew the fuel starvation
problem had not been solved. But the handling looked fine.
All the celebration was directed at Warren when we got back
to the garage. He had, after all, passed Robbins on the final
lap to win. But I was more concerned about Dave. He was
drinking a Coke from a paper cup when I walked up. A satis-
fied smile was on his face. It was hard for Dave to look anything other than stony, and I knew that his evidence of
happiness was the equivalent of positive giddiness. "It's a
whole new car. It handles so much better, it's hard to remember how bad it was. It'll be better for you tomorrow, too.
Only thing is the damn fuel problem is still there. But Rich is
going to change the filters in the fuel pumps and remount the
pickups tonight. He thinks that will cure it. Hell, we've
changed everything else; that's got to be it."

I went up to Bruce Johnson, who was standing near Warren. "Dave says you fixed it," I said.

"I was pretty sure it was the preload, but you never know.
If that hadn't been it, we'd have been in a heap of trouble."

"Warren looked good," I said.

"Yeah, he's feeling supergood. Marshall's car is brand-new,
and he's spent a bundle on it. He's tested on this track a lot,

too. Really knows his way around here. If we get a decent break tomorrow, we might do real well."

"Anybody hear what's going on at Ontario?" I asked. The California 500 was being run, and I was sure that news of the event was filtering along the paddock grapevine.

"I heard Foyt was leading," Bruce answered.

"What about Mark?"

"He's out. Somebody said he ran out of fuel. They said he had to push the car a mile and a half to the pits."

"*Ran out of fuel?*" I asked incredulously. "How can that be? The Penske crew hasn't screwed up like that in years. I can't even imagine them screwing up like that." Mark and the Penske-McLaren had been favorites to win the big Ontario event. They had been decisively faster at Indianapolis and had led the early stages of the race by a wide margin before the rear end had broken. At Pocono, the second stop in the so-called Triple Crown for Indianapolis-type cars, Mark had led practically the entire five hundred miles and had won easily. But at Ontario, things had not been so simple. He had crashed his car during a practice session earlier in the month. Now the news indicated he had lost the race on a foolish error. "The poor bastard. Now he's got to get on a damn plane and fly here for the thing tomorrow," I said.

"Don't worry, Penske'll just pack him aboard the Lear and have him here in a few hours," Bruce replied.

"Either way, he's got two major races in two days, at opposite ends of the country. That's got to take it out of you especially if you've got a thing like running out of gas, while leading the second-richest race in the world, praying on your mind."

"Like they say, man, that's motor racing," Bruce said jauntily.

A crowd of racers had accumulated at the pool of the Jackson Holiday Inn by the time Sally and I got back to our room and wriggled into our bathing suits. A few were thrashing through the tepid water, while others lounged on the plastic beach furniture that littered the patio. I recognized a large man with pale skin leaning back on a lawn chair, his hands clasped innocently on his substantial belly. It was Bud Moore. Seated near him was a lean, tanned man in his middle forties, with chiseled features and a small, straight nose. He was Maurice Carter, a wealthy Canadian car dealer who was one of the best independent drivers on the Trans-Am circuit. Mo, a man of substantial bearing and manner, asked us to join them. We ambled through a few conversational preliminaries, during which I skirted specifying my slow qualifying time but dwelled on my rising hopes for tomorrow. We talked of Ontario and Donohue's bad luck. It might hamper his chances of winning at Michigan, we agreed.

Bud Moore's broad, friendly face opened with a smile. "Nuthin' I'd rather do than win here tomorrow, 'cause that'd force Penske and Donohue to run in California. It'd raise hell with their plans, but it sure would be good for the series."

Bud was referring to the open secret that had been drifting through the sport for weeks. If Penske and Donohue could clinch the Trans-Am Championship for American Motors at Michigan International, they planned to turn the car over to another driver and then enter a McLaren Formula One car for Mark in the Canadian and United States Grand Prix races. However, if they didn't win at Michigan, the Mustang, in the able hands of Bud Moore and George Follmer, still had a numerical chance of overtaking them in the championship points race. This would in turn force them to run the last two races at Kent, Washington, and Riverside, California. It would also benefit Bud Moore. It was no secret that Bud, without Ford's open checkbook as in the past, was in a financial bind. Peter Gregg, a competent Florida driver with substantial funds, had injected money into the operation in return for the opportunity to drive the second-team Mustang, but it had hardly replaced Ford's six-figure donation of past seasons. Parnelli Jones had originally announced his intention of defending the Trans-Am Championship he had won for Moore, but had reportedly stipulated that each promoter would have to fork over $5,000 in "appearance money" before he would grace their starting grids. While this is standard practice in European competition, wherein big stars generally make a lion's share of their income *before* the race, most domestic competition operates on a more conventional incentive system, with prizes being distributed on the basis of finishing position. None of the Trans-Am promoters was willing to spend five grand for Parnelli, so Bud had run the entire schedule with Follmer and Gregg. He did, however, need extra money from the West Coast operators. If the title was undecided and the crowd-pleasing struggle between the Mustangs and the Javelin could be guaranteed, then the Riverside and Kent promoters might be willing to give Moore a little extra aid to transport his team west. But if the title was won at Michigan and Donohue dropped out of the series, a great deal of Bud's financial leverage on the West Coast would disappear. Therefore, there was something more than his boyish zest for competition that motivated Bud's wish for Donohue to appear at Riverside and Kent.

"I'll tell you this," Bud said, shading his eyes against the sun that slanted over the roof of the inn, catching him full in the eyes, "it's gonna cost me a boatload of money to haul two cars out there, no matter how we do here. Transporting those cars costs me about sixty cents a mile each, and when you figure in my eight-man crew, getting time and a half on the weekends, you're talking about a lot of dough. And experienced racing mechanics don't come cheap. Hell, one of my boys is makin' more money a year than Follmer! But I gotta say this about the Trans-Am; at least it's cheaper than running Grand National in the South."

"Why is that?" I asked. "The cars are about the same in terms of construction time, modifications, etc., why would it cost so much more to build a car for stock-car racing?"

"Cheatin'!" barked Bud, jerking forward in the chair. "You gotta cheat so damn much just to be competitive down there. Hell, their damn rules are so hazy you *gotta* cheat, just to stay even. And you know what? Cheatin' is expensive. Hell, when you get through cuttin' down and whittlin' away at a damn

stock-car body, there ain't a production piece that'll fit it.
When we were running the factory team for Mercury, it used
to cost us three hundred bucks to modify a front fender so
it'd work. Three hundred bucks for a *stock* fender. Then
you'd get to the race and you wouldn't know who the
powers-who-be had decided to favor that week. Sometimes
they'd let you through inspection with hardly a second
glance, with a car they knew was a damn cheater. The other
times they'd go over your car with a fine-tooth comb. It all
depended on which manufacturer was in favor with the management and which was on the outs. It was the damnedest
thing you ever saw," said Bud, laughing heartily as he
slumped back in the lounge.

Then he surged forward again, shading his eyes once
more. "You'd get in the damn race, and if anybody got too big
a lead, they'd put out the yellow flag and let everybody else
catch up. 'Debris on the track,' they'd announce. Damnedest
bunch a' shit you ever saw. It was more like being in a damn
dance class than a race. You couldn't get a lead and hold it,
before the yellow'd come out and they'd tell the crowd they
found some 'oil' or 'debris' on the track, and all the rest of the
cars would catch up. That don't happen in the Trans-Am."
He smiled again. "I don't know whether that's because these
boys is too stupid or too honest." He laughed again as he fell
back into the chair. After twenty years of big-time racing
competition, Bud Moore had seen it all. Something triggered
in him an urge to talk about the old days, and he began a long
discourse on the black magic of cheating: about how in the
early fifties, when stock-car-racing rules required production
camshafts, a sleight-of-hand trick was perfected whereby a
modified, high-performance cam could be slipped into the
engine right before the inspector's eyes; how all the major
Detroit manufacturers managed to plant extravagantly modified "production" cars for such sanctimoniously regimented
tests as the Mobil Economy Run and the Pure Oil Performance trials. Bud liked that, and he recalled the game with
relish. "Them things was real fun. They had these rules, see,

that they'd go out and pick the cars at random from dealer showrooms. Now that sounded good to the public: after all, how in hell could Detroit plant cheaters in every showroom in America? Easy. The rules also said that the manufacturer could specify which model would be used in the tests. So we'd go ahead and prepare some strange versions—like some damn coupe with a little two-barrel engine and three-speed manual transmission and a real high axle ratio. Hell, nobody in the damn world would actually buy a car like that. So we'd build a dozen or so of 'em, stickin' in things like over-size floats in the carburetors that'd give about two extra miles to the gallon and then plant 'em around the country. Some guys were putting secret gas tanks in the glove compartments; all kinda things like that. Pretty soon those poor suckers runnin' the economy runs would find out where these models were through our dealer grapevine and go buy 'em. They'd be smug as hell, thinkin' they outsmarted the boys in Detroit, when in fact they'd picked the *exact* cars we'd rigged up to win their tests. I tell you this, *every* manufacturer who ever participated in those tests did that at one time or another. You can see why they canceled both those tests. It was all a buncha shit. But it was kinda fun trying to outsmart the inspectors."

It was all a beautiful game with Bud Moore. He was a terribly bright and crafty man, whose easy manner covered a fierce desire to compete. It seemed that the game of racing was a test of intellect for him: that it challenged him like a vast puzzle demanding to be solved. The rules were hazy, and within that absence of definition he was prepared to drive his advantage to the limit.

He was shading his eyes again, squinting as he scanned the small audience that had clustered around him. "Those inspectors were the same as you find anywhere. There's a way of dealing with them. In the old days we used to show up at a race with two or three flagrant violations. I mean, they were just stickin' out there for everybody to see. Then the guys running the inspection would come up and say, 'You got to change those things. They're illegal. If they ain't changed, you don't race. Then we'd holler like hell. Raise the damn roof! Of course we'd be planning to change 'em all the while, because we knew that by concentrating on those really conspicuous violations, the inspectors would be sure to let us through with the stuff we'd cheated on that was really important!" Loud laughter.

"Dammit, Bud, now all that crap we went through with you at Bridgehampton makes sense. You remember the infamous Car and Driver super-car test, don't you?" I asked.

"Hell, yes," Bud answered easily. "Everybody was going in circles on that one. Ol' Fran Hernandez was about to have a damn heart attack, he was so mad."

"That Cyclone you guys brought up was the worst cheater I'd ever seen," I said.

"Hell, that thing was about stock." Bud chuckled.

"Bullshit, it was stock! That thing was the fastest 'stock' Cyclone ever built," I retorted.

"Well, we did a couple of things. But we used all stock parts, just like your rules said."

"Sure you did. Then how come that boat anchor of an engine would rev a thousand rpm's higher than any other three-ninety?"

"Well, we"—Bud was laughing hard "we did do a little trick to the pushrods. We modified 'em slightly, so that the hydraulic lifters actually worked like solid lifters. But you just couldn't tell without tearing down the engine, and we figured you boys weren't going to try anything like that."

"Masten did that for us, only not quite the way you figured," I said, referring to the Cyclone's engine's, blowing up.

"She went like hell before that happened," Bud said with a detectable edge of pride in his voice.

"While we're being candid about that whole thing, how come your Cyclone was so much lower than regular ones? Did you do that with 'stock' parts, too?" I asked.

"Well, we did happen to slip some little aluminum blocks into the spring mountings, but like with the pushrods, you'd have to have ripped the whole suspension apart to find them. But I'll tell you something, compared to some of the stuff that has been done for tests like that, our Cyclone was pretty damn stock. There were some other guys there who were worse than us."

"We thought the little inspection thing we had would cut down on the cheating, but that was a joke," I said. "Those guys with the P & G meter were supposed to scare everybody into being legal."

"Let me tell you something," Bud said seriously, "I've got five ways of making a P & G meter read any displacement you want. You name a number, and I'll have it come up on the gauge. Four of the ways everybody in the business knows about; the other one is my secret." Bud leaned back to let that revelation sink in.

Mo Carter shook his head in bafflement and said, half in awe, half in jest, "Good God, how can we ever expect to win in the face of *that?*"

Bud Moore said nothing, but his face was covered with a broad self-satisfied smile.

The talk with Bud had reestablished in my mind that my troubles were minuscule compared to those of a Moore, a Donohue, or a Follmer, who had entire careers riding on their showings. The single thing that would count after the season was complete was who had won the championship. Even individual race victories would be forgotten, and surely the placings of competitors like myself would not even serve as footnote material. That thought tended to loosen me: to convince me that I carried no one's burden but my own, and beyond personal demands for self-satisfaction, little permanent notice would be forthcoming from tomorrow's race. That was for me an acceptable rationale, but I had to wonder how it fit into the aspirations of other back-markers in the field— men who had made long-range commitments to racing, yet knew secretly that they would never reach the big time.

My first glimpse of race morning came through the door of my room at the Holiday Inn. I opened it to find the sky mottled with fragments of cumulus clouds and the parking lot puddled with water. It had been raining for much of the night, although it looked as if the showers might be passing. The radio said no; scattered squalls were predicted for the rest of the day. The crew was bustling around the cars by the time I arrived at the track. Rich and Mike told me they had worked late in order to fix the fuel pickup, and by modifying the fuel cell, they believed that had been accomplished. As usual, there was little casual conversation to be found around the Agor group, and because they seemed to be operating effectively without me, I wandered off through the pit area in search of distracting conversation. I would be qualifying with the first session, and additional thoughts about that would only lead to more brooding about the possibility of being unable to improve my time. I found Mark Donohue standing near the shimmering Penske truck, which in turn stood guard, like a cow elephant, over his Javelin race car. He was surrounded by a collection of autograph hunters—a standard mixture of small boys, wide-eyed women, and men with drugstore cameras looped over their shoulders. I walked up to him, and he seemed pleased to see me, as if I served as an excuse to break out of the trap. He looked awful. His eyes were red-rimmed from exhaustion, and his head was tilted to one side, as if in pain.

"C'mon, let's go talk," he said, handing a slip of paper and a ballpoint pen to a man in a straw hat layered with frazzled pit passes. I fell in beside him as we strode off toward an unknown destination. He was walking at an angle, his back arched and his shoulders dipped. "Hey, man, what's your problem, you're walking like you're all busted up," I said.

"Ontario. That crash. I hit the wall a ton. My back. It's really bruised."

"I didn't realize that. I thought you just spun out and brushed the wall; you know, nothing serious."

"It was pretty rough. I never hit anything that hard in my entire life, like I was going maybe one hundred and fifty when I caught the wall."

"Jesus, that's got to smart," I said, trying for levity.

Mark looked dead serious. Then a kind of dull, half smile crossed his face. "You don't want to try something like that too often." He was veering through the crowd, looking straight ahead, brushing away the scraps of paper being thrust in front of him. He walked as fast as he could, sped along by his physical discomfort and the urge to get out of the crowds. We arrived at a motor home belonging to another race team. It was parked in tandem with an immense tractor trailer that served as a rolling machine shop and race-car trailer transporter. We climbed into the cabin of the motor home, which was occupied by a half dozen people drinking coffee and chatting. They seemed delighted to see Mark, although they appeared uncertain about how to receive such a celebrity. Several of the women leaped toward the refrigerator and tried to ply him with refreshments. The men engaged him in polite small talk about the Ontario race, until it became clear that all he sought was a place to sit and a modicum of privacy. We squeezed through the gathering and into the back of the motor home, where a small compartment was lined with a pair of bunks on opposite walls. Mark eased himself onto one of the bunks with the wooden motions of a man whose vertebrae don't want to bend and rolled on his side in a modified prenatal position. After carefully lodging a pair of pillows against his back, he released a chestful of air and sagged visibly, as if he had been holding his breath against the pain.

"Are you sure you want to race today?" I asked.

"We really don't have much choice. We've got to win this thing—the Trans-Am Championship, I mean—or else it's going to screw up our plans something fierce. See, we've got a deal with McLaren to run a Formula One car in the United States and Canadian GPs, but we can't do it if we don't win the Trans-Am—our contract with American Motors naturally requires that we make a best effort to take the championship. But if we can win it here, we feel it's ethical to turn the Javelin over to somebody else for the two West Coast Trans-Ams."

"Who've you got in mind to take your place?" I asked.

"Swede," he answered firmly.

"Sounds like a good thing for Swede. But that puts a lot of pressure on you today. If you lose, you've got to at least race at Kent, and possibly Riverside."

"Either way it shoots down the Formula One program. We're behind on developing the car as it is, and unless I can start on it first thing in the morning, we just won't have time to get it ready for the Canadian GP in two weeks."

"In the morning?" I asked. "You mean you ran Ontario yesterday and this thing today, and you're going to go back home and start work in the shop tomorrow?"

Mark tried to smile, but managed only to look more exhausted. "That's the racing business. You get only so many days during the season, and you've got to take advantage of them. I'm about ready to drop on my feet, and this sore back isn't helping anything, but we don't have any choice. I'll tell you something else: if I hadn't screwed up so bad at Ontario, I'd be a lot more enthusiastic about working." Looking pained, both from his back and the memories of yesterday's race, Mark manfully accepted blame for the error that caused him to run out of fuel while leading. He claimed that he was so intent on trying to lap Gary Bettenhausen—a feisty sprint car champion—that he had missed three consecutive signals calling him into the pits. He viewed that as an unforgivable error on his part. While many drivers would have found a multitude of reasons to absolve themselves of blame, Donohue huddled there on the bunk of the motor home and candidly admitted guilt for losing a major race. A race he was supposed to win. "It's been a bad couple of weeks. First I crashed the Formula One car in a test at Mosport—not too bad, but it delayed the development program to a point where we've got to work like hell to get ready for Canada. Two days later I hit the wall at Ontario. Then yesterday. Man, I'll tell you, this whole thing isn't the dream world some people think it is."

There was Mark Donohue, seeking rest for his bruised and

battered body and solace from the voracious crowds outside, facing another day of racing, and I thought to myself about the people who would tell you he had the world by the ears: fame, a six-figure annual income, a glamorous life of travel and adventure. They didn't understand the rest of it: the oppressive pressure to win (to his sponsors and business associates, no loss was completely justifiable), the endless motel rooms, the ruptured family life, the constant seven-day workweeks, and the long, omnipresent shadow of death or crippling injury. At that point his body was miraculously unscarred, but Mark was too much the pragmatist not to know that you only go to the Gates just so many times before they open. Few of the other great drivers of the day had avoided hospital beds as successfully as he, and he understood that the next encounter with Ontario's retaining wall could mean the end. Yet he refused to stop, forced onward by the temptations of success: championships as yet unwon, honors not received. If he was to turn away from it now and retire with his bulging bank account, there would be those who would say he had lost his nerve. So he was forced to continue, dodging hazards that the law of averages placed in his path with increasing frequency, driving his mind and body to the very precipice of destruction. He had only two feasible exits from the sport: to run the entire gauntlet, winning things like the Indianapolis 500 and the World's Championship on the way, or be felled in combat and carried from the field in pain and honor. Such is the penalty of success in racing.

I left Donohue to rest and reentered the noise and confusion of the paddock. Around me were dozens of race drivers who knew perfectly well the kind of difficulties that awaited men at the top of the sport. Yet only a handful of them would have hesitated to trade everything—their families, their jobs, their savings, their security, their health, yes, perhaps even their lives—for a share of that exquisite torment.

It was time to take another shot at qualifying. The crew had pushed the car onto the pit lane, and I walked up to

Warren and Bruce. "You feel better about running today?"
Warren asked.

"The way Dave ran, I figure the car's got to be better," I
said. Birdie Martin came by, wearing another outlandish outfit. He was carrying a clipboard and looked a trifle frazzled
around the edges. As the tempo of the weekend accelerated
toward the start of the race, everyone, officials and participants alike, looked increasingly harried. "You guys ready to
go?" he asked no one in particular.

"Yeah, I'm scheduled to qualify in the first session," I answered.

"That's, let's see here... about nine-thirty..." Birdie was
thumbing through the sheaf of papers on his clipboard, looking for the official schedule. "Yeah, here it is, yep, you go at
nine-thirty," he said helpfully.

"Er, Birdie, it's nine twenty-nine right now," Warren said
quietly.

"What? Holy Christ, it is! Where in hell is this day going
to?" He rushed off to get qualifying started while I climbed
into the Camaro for one last try at improving my starting position. The next few moments were spent in the now-familiar
routine of harness-tightening, helmet-buckling, glove-don-
ning, and engine-starting. I was waved away with the familiar
thunder of the Bartz punishing my ears. The track was dry
since the morning rain, but I took an easy warm-up lap, trying to reestablish rapport with the car. It felt decidedly better.
It ran the corners truer, without the wobbly, tail-wagging action that had cursed its earlier behavior. The green flag,
waved from a high platform that hung out over the track from
the immense grandstand, signaled the start of my trial time.
Running as hard as I could, I knew instantly that Bruce had
fixed the chassis. The car felt great. I rumbled along the front
straight, where the crew had stationed themselves with a signal board. It read, "2.01." *Seven seconds faster! I felt great.*
On the second lap of the trial, the left-front brake grabbed
slightly as I slowed for the hay-baled chicane recrossing the
speedway, but my time was still faster: two minutes flat.

Beautiful! I had chopped eight seconds off that embarrassing number of the day before and now was less than *two* seconds slower than Warren. My confidence building, I flung the Camaro into the final qualifying lap, convinced another couple of seconds could be clipped off.

Feeling like a champion, I charged into the second chicane, getting set for the quick left-right flick of the steering wheel that would send me, like a slalom skier, through the narrow gap in the bales. I hit the brake. The left front grabbed harder this time, yanking me several feet to the left of the proper line. In an instant I decided I was running too fast and too wide to get the car through the narrow gap in the hay bales. Ahead was a flat, grassy expanse. By driving straight across the grass I might be able to parallel the chicane, then reenter farther down the track without losing too much time. In the particle of a second that I had to make the decision, that seemed like the most feasible alternative. My only other choice was to blast through the bales, which might have damaged the car. Wrong again. In an instant I was on the grass, as slick as an ice rink from the all-night rain. My fat racing tires had about as much adhesion as a whale's belly on that surface, and in a sickening instant the Camaro snap-spun and began skidding across the grass *backward*. The engine stalled, leaving me skating along, accompanied by no more sound than a soft, liquid, hissing noise from the tires on the grass. Once it hit the lawn, the car seemed to accelerate. Had I been given the time, I would have been terrified. While I couldn't register specific thoughts, every nerve in my body was transmitting *in extremis* alarms. This is much worse than yesterday's spin, they were screaming. I looked over my shoulder. Not that I could do anything about it, but I was moved with a curiosity to see where I was going. I caught a glimpse of a towering chain-link fence coming up at a furious rate. Oh, shit, that's really going to bust up the back of the car, I thought. *Oh, no, it's not, Yates, there's a ditch in front of it!* There it was, a great, yawning chasm in the earth, so deep I couldn't see the bottom. I punched the brakes. As expected, nothing happened. I ducked in the seat, bracing myself for the inevitable impact. The car sailed off the edge of the ditch and for the slightest particle of a second was fully airborne. WHUMP! The Camaro slammed against the far wall of the ditch as if it had been dropped into a sand dune. With the shock came a splashing sound of water, a cloud of steam, then silence.

I sat there in a momentary limbo, trying to orient myself. I felt no particular pain, but I was temporarily skeptical that my body could have absorbed such a jolt without fracturing something. I shut off the ignition switches and slumped in my seat, letting my brain digest what had happened. The Camaro had come to rest on the sloping bank of the ditch, which was perhaps eight feet deep and thirty feet across. It was pointed downward at a steep angle, with the nose of the car buried in several feet of gummy-green swamp water. I had sailed almost the full distance of the ditch in midair before landing on the opposite bank, pointing backward at the track. Bullrushes dotted the opaque surface. The cockpit floor was awash with slimy algae and seaweed, and my nostrils filled with the sour odor of decayed vegetation, overlayed with the suggestion of sewage.

"Are you all right?" a voice called. I looked up to see a course worker, dressed in the inevitable white shirt and pants, peering down at me from the far bank. I nodded my head through the mud-spattered windshield, then unbuckled myself and climbed out.

"Wow, you really took a ride," he called.

"Yeah, goddamnit, a real ride. That last lap was a quick one, that's what pisses me off." I was overcome with a sharp jab of frustration. I suddenly realized that my chances to qualify were ended, that my brief hope of clipping another few seconds off my time, and therefore redeeming myself, was over. I wanted another chance. That was impossible.

"Nobody ever went in there before. That's a first as far as I know, going in the drainage ditch like that," the worker said.

"The damn grass. That's what finished me. As soon as I hit that wet grass, I was history."

"Yeah, we saw your brake grab on the lap before and were worried. Then this time it *really* locked up the wheel."

Other workers had appeared and were gaping at the wreck. I was trying to determine the amount of damage to the Camaro. I was convinced that its rear section had been mashed into small pieces by the crash. It was hard to tell, simply because the wheels were buried in the soft mud, but there seemed to be no way the car could have survived without serious breakage.

"You're going to need a tow truck," somebody pronounced.

I nodded an acknowledgment. For the second day in a row, I had the dubious honor of having a two truck drag me out of the boondocks. "Phone the stewards and tell them I'm off the track and not hurt, so they can continue qualifying," I said. I recalled Donohue, who had not yet had a chance to qualify, and Follmer and the other contenders, who were itching for one final crack at bettering their times. Surely they could carry on while my wreck was being extracted from the ditch.

A worker came up after sprinting from the nearby phone station. "They're sending out a tow truck, but qualifying will be held up until they get your car out."

"Christ, that'll take hours," I said, envisioning thirty-odd Trans-Am crews cursing me in the pits because I was delaying qualifying.

I heard my name drifting on the wind. The public address system. An electronic voice was floating across the vast infield from the grandstand. It was Errol Kaufman, a jaunty New Yorker and sometime press agent, team manager, and general promoter who was announcing the race. "Looks as if ol' Brock has buried himself in the ditch over there." Errol was chuckling. "We have an unconfirmed report that he spun while trying to take notes in chicane."

Beautiful. I turned to look at the stand, towering in the

distance over the flat landscape and sprinkled with a substantial crowd of people. I imagined that every pair of eyes in
the place was aimed at me and my mud-soaked machine.
Kaufman was chattering on, flinging out easy jokes about me
and my plight. I wanted him to quit, to redirect the audience's attention to something else. It was going to take considerable time to remove the car, and the more he dwelled on
the subject, the more everybody was going to blame me for
screwing up the entire freaking program. Oh, shut up, Kaufman, for God's sake, I thought. But Errol kept the gags coming, and I stood there, down in the slime of the ditch, waiting
for what seemed to be several hours before the tow truck appeared. Actually about ten minutes passed before the arrival
of the same crew and truck that had dragged me out the day
before.

"Hey, man, this is getting to be a bad habit." The driver
laughed, a rotund man in a heavy twill work shirt and pants.

"Yeah, we can't go on meeting like this," I said, making an
unsuccessful attempt at humor.

The car would have to be winched out, they decided. I did
not want them to drag it back across the ditch in the direction
from which I had entered because that would mean immers-
ing the entire car in the swamp. Pulling it out tail first was
complicated by the chain-link fence, but a plan was devised
where it would be winched a few feet backward, then the
cable would be attached to the nose of the car, and it could be
yanked out without sinking it in the bog. It would take more
time, but damage to the machine would be minimized. The
thick cable shimmied out from the back of the truck, and
within a few minutes its ponderously powerful mechanical
advantage had pulled the Camaro clear of the water. I then
took the cable around to the front of the car and began to
attach it to a strong point on the chassis. I flipped open the
hood to find the engine covered with algae and dripping with
foul gray water. A flash of motion caught my eye near the
carburetor. A frog! "Hey, there's a goddamn frog in my engine," I yelled. Startled by my voice, the poor creature cata-

pulted off the engine and plopped out of sight into the mire beneath the car. There I was, stuck in a swamp, delaying the entire race program for perhaps an hour, and a frog shows up in my motor to add a final touch of absurdity to the situation. Thank God, Kaufman doesn't know about that, I thought.

The car would actually roll. The wheels turned, the steering worked, and aside from looking as if it had been lifted out of harbor silt like the *Vasa*, a blasted automotive salvage job, covered with slime and seaweed, nothing seemed to be seriously damaged. I didn't try to start the engine, figuring it could be plugged with everything from lily pads to tadpoles, and therefore bore up under the ignominy of being towed back to the pits. There I rolled, at the end of the cable, down the long pit road, in full view of the grandstand, with Kaufman yakking it up on the PA system. Building to the climax, Errol called for a round of applause for the returning hero. Clapping rattled across the track from the stands. I wanted to hide.

Warren and the crew were waiting at the paddock gate. Wonder of wonders, they were smiling! Just when I'd expected them to come at me like a gang of rabid longshoremen, they greeted me with wide grins and a babble of wisecracks. Maybe it had been Kaufman. Maybe all his hacking around on the loudspeaker had loosened them up. At any rate, we all shoved the car into the garage in a lusty display of camaraderie. It was perhaps the attention I had accidentally brought to them. Sports enthusiasm feeds on novelty. The delay of qualifying caused by some idiot sinking his car in a drainage ditch had brought a certain temporary notoriety to the Agor team, thanks to Errol's embellishment, and it may have been a response to this spurt of attention that had improved their tempers. In any case, part of the crew pitched into the cleanup, while Bruce, Rich, and Mike probed underneath to evaluate the damage. Seaweed was everywhere: in the air intakes, the brake ducts, under the seat, even in the trunk. After an hour of hosing and scrubbing, the car begun to look normal. "Aside from some dents in the rear and a busted brake light, I don't think you hurt a thing," reported Bruce. It seemed hard to believe that I could have hit something that hard without damage, I said. "Don't forget, these things, with all the extra bracing, are really tough. Also, you hit the bank on an angle, partly with the rear wheels, which helped to absorb energy. So did the mud. Once we get it cleaned up, I think we can make the race."

A squall had rolled in from the southwest and was pelting the track with rain. People in the pits scurried for cover, while the crowd in the open grandstand tried to protect themselves with newspapers, unfolded programs, blankets, and sheets of plastic. My neck was hurting. It had begun with a dull pain and had increased in intensity, until I decided it might be good to get it checked. I left the garage and jogged across the rain-swept paddock to the infield infirmary, a pre-fab steel building surrounded by a Cyclone fence. At many tracks, the infirmary fence is shrouded on race day with tarpaulins to stifle morbid curiosity in case a seriously injured driver is brought into the compound. I shut the door against the wind and the rain to find a large, nearly empty room. Two nurses and a track official were lounging against a row of low cabinets, drinking coffee. The walls were bare, save for an eye chart and an engineering blueprint of the track. I told one of the nurses, a tall sturdy woman in her early forties with a mound of burnished black hair and heavily made-up eyes, that my neck was sore. Putting down her coffee, she led me into an adjacent room. It was another barren space, except for six hospital cots and a few storage cabinets. There was a military starkness about the infirmary that seemed to be emphasized by the rain pounding on the roof and the harsh fluorescent lights. She told me to sit on the edge of the bed while she probed around the back of my neck with her firm, confident fingers. "I think you're all right. Maybe you strained a muscle slightly, but it's nothing serious."

"Too bad. I figured I had a case of whiplash," I said in jest.

"Better call off the lawyers," she said, stepping back to let me put on my jacket.

"I guess you're right. I suppose I'd have a helluva time collecting anyway." I thanked her for the checkup and stepped outside. The rain had stopped. By the time I got back to the pits, the final qualifying order had been posted. Mark had won the pole. He'd done exactly as George Follmer had predicted by arriving the morning of the race and quickly setting the best time. Five minutes after his run, the rain had started, preventing George from trying to improve his speed. I thought of my crash and how much time it had consumed. Perhaps George would have had a chance to try again if that hadn't happened. My official qualifying was listed at 2.00.3, good for twentieth place on the starting grid. That put me exactly in the middle of the forty-car field. More satisfying to me was the fact that I was only 1.9 seconds slower than Warren, who was starting fourteenth. I entertained a brief fantasy about how that final qualifying lap might have been sufficiently faster to put me ahead of him on the grid. But that was not to be, and I was left to be thankful for the big improvement in time that had come before the crash and sustained by the ego-massaging conviction that my final, uncompleted lap would have been significantly faster.

The track was practically dry and the grandstand cluttered with people when we lined up for the start. Parked beside me on the starting grid was Ed Hinchcliff, a burly Ford engineer who was campaigning his own Mustang. A bright, rather serious guy who'd been running Trans-Am on his own for several seasons, he was typical of the men who occupied the middle of the grid. Hardly wealthy, unsupported by major corporations, unrecognized as a major driving talent, he plodded through the seasons, rupturing his budget and consuming every waking hour in the service of his Mustang, all for the simple pleasure of competition. His chances for high finishes were almost solely dependent on widespread bad luck among the leaders, but he persisted anyway, lured forward by the same siren song that caused me to be convinced that *if* I'd completed that last qualifying lap...

Jerry Breon helped me buckle up my harness. "This thing

smells like a fish wharf," I mused as I settled into the seat. "That won't bother me a bit," Jerry said as he smiled and shook hands with me. "Luck," he mumbled.

"There are some guys I know who give their driver one instruction before the race," I said, chattering in the face of my rising nervousness. "They tell him, 'Keep it on the *black* part.'"

"Yeah," Jerry agreed, then added, "and remember, both the weeds and the water are green."

I was alone in the car. I looked up at the grandstands and felt that same silly titillation that kids get when they peek through the curtain at the audience prior to their first school play. I was part of it. For better or for worse, I was doing it, not watching it. I'd rather be a second-rate participant than a first-rate spectator, I thought to myself. A kind of giddiness rose in me, based partly on childhood dreams of someday running powerful race cars on big-time speedways, partly on the natural exhibitionism that lives in any man who would climb into a brightly colored automobile and do stunts in front of a live audience.

Les Richter, the ex–Los Angeles Rams linebacker and highly respected racing executive who headed the management team that ran Michigan International, was introduced on the public-address system. He was going to formally start the race with the traditional words from the Indianapolis Motor Speedway. I instantly recognized his high, thick voice, doubtlessly caused by his cartilage-blocked nasal passages from the football wars, shouting, "Gentlemen, start your engines!" Noise—hammering, deafening noise—billowed around me, vibrating my helmet and my fingertips. The earth seemed to be tremoring with the guttural blaring of the cars. My ears hurt.

We took the green flag on the banked curve in front of the grandstand. I mashed down on the throttle, but the Camaro didn't respond with its customary crispness. Perhaps the plugs were slightly fouled from the pace lap, I thought as I followed the field down off the banking and onto the infield course. Suddenly water was splattering on my windshield and brake lights were winking. Crash! Several cars ahead were lashing sideways on the grass next to the track. I spotted DeLorenzo's black and white Mustang parked awkwardly at the track side, its grille crushed flat and a large kink in its bumper. The pileup must have happened among the fourth- and fifth-row cars, but aside from De Lorenzo's dents, nothing serious seemed to have happened. I rushed on, chasing Hinchcliff, who was opening a big lead on me. Through the twisty back part, the car felt squirrelly again, just as it had before Bruce had made the sway-bar adjustment. I looked in the mirror to find a strange collection of cars on my rear bumper. What the hell were they doing there? I was supposed to be faster. Why wasn't I going faster? I bore down as hard as I could, rushing through the corners with the kind of urgency that I had promised myself I wouldn't use in the early, crowded stages of the race. A number of cars slipped past me on the main straight. Was it me or the car? Had the crash inhibited my driving, or had the ditch done more damage to the Camaro than anybody realized? A red Camaro nosed past me just before entering the nasty right-left esses that had been the scene of my first spin. But he got too wide, much as I had done, and began a long, lazy slide that carried him sideways off the track and down into a clump of tangled underbrush. I enjoyed it. I watched him spinning, out of control within a few feet of my front fender, and I liked what I saw. He was in serious trouble, perhaps heading for a terrible accident, but bolted inside that machine of mine, surrounded by the fury of the race, I enjoyed watching the poor devil skidding out of the park! I am sure the same sensation overtook the other drivers who witnessed the spin. Yet an ironic contradiction gripped us as well. All of us would have done anything in our power to help him had he been hurt. There are countless instances of drivers racing each other without mercy until one crashes, at which point his rival stops his car on the track to come to his assistance. The competitive juices course through mysterious rivers in the brain, and even the most

perceptive psychologist would probably have to participate
in an emotional and dangerous contest like racing before an
appreciation of this state of mind could even begin to clarify
itself. It may involve the bright, brutal core of the ego, which,
after it is laid bare in intense competition, deludes itself with
the myth of invulnerability. Perhaps all of us had sublimated
simple fear to a point where the idea that the driver in the red
Camaro could actually hurt himself was inconceivable.
Strange and perhaps primeval things were happening inside
our heads, and glib cocktail-party treacle about "death
wishes" or the neurotic fear of death as explanations about
why men race automobiles crumbles in the presence of this
substantial mystery. As Andretti had observed, "Before the
race, we all talk good sense. Then we go out and do foolish
things." Perhaps that is true for all mankind.

Jerry's pit board told me I was in twenty-sixth place. Good
God, I'd lost six places to slower cars. I struggled onward,
becoming convinced that the handling was at fault. Finally,
with a collection of even slower machines making up ground,
I decided to stop. Mike and Bruce were waiting as I hollered
over the engine. "Handling! It's squirrelly as hell!" They
dashed off to look at the tires, to scramble underneath the car
to see if anything had fallen loose, and to bounce the suspension to determine if a shock absorber had failed. They returned, looking baffled. "Everything is O.K.," Bruce yelled.
"Keep going!"

I accelerated out of the pits and took a few more laps. More
people passed me. The handling was beginning to prey on
my mind. I was losing heart and thereby perhaps rationalizing that the machine was worse than it actually was. I
stopped again, shut off the engine, and got out. "The damn
thing is unmanageable," I grumbled, pulling off my helmet.
Bruce looked irritated. Mike and Rich eyed me, stone-faced.
Bruce got some tools and crawled under the car. The rest of
the crew was watching Warren, who roared past, apparently
running well. Mark seemed to have established a solid lead
in the race, with George perhaps fifteen seconds behind.

Bruce lifted himself out from beneath the car and came over to me. "I can't find anything that's really the matter. Why don't you take it out and just see if you can finish?" I started to protest. The twisty section out back was so tight and so narrow that a car cruising along at reduced speed would seriously hinder the fast guys. The last thing I wanted to do was to get in one of the leaders' way. A lot was at stake, as at Watkins Glen, and I had been trying very hard not to block anybody or force one of the quick cars off line. But it was too noisy and too frantic a situation to try to make that sort of rationale clear to Bruce. So I got back in.

Two laps later, the left front brake grabbed again at the end of the main straight. Running perhaps 130 mph, the car jerked to the left, nearly sending me against the stout concrete retaining wall. "Screw this for a row of soldiers," I said to myself, slowing down. I drove straight to the pits and parked the Camaro. "That thing is fucked up. I don't care what anybody says. Something is wonky in the chassis, and I'll be goddamned if I'm going to risk my ass or the other guys out there with that shit-box!" I shouted at the crew. They looked at me as if I were jumping ship in the middle of battle. I yanked off my helmet and climbed over the pit wall, leaving the Camaro sitting abandoned. Bruce and Mike lowered their eyes and sullenly returned to the cluster of orange-shirted crewmen in Warren's pit. I leaned against a trash receptacle, feeling awful. Sally came over and patted my arm with wifely understanding. She smiled but said nothing. Then Dave Hoselton came up, wearing his driver's suit. "Do you mind if I drive it?" I was dumbstruck. What was this, some kind of gesture to discredit my complaints? I reacted with overblown defensiveness.

"I'm telling you, man, the car is fucked up! How many times do I have to say that? The suspension is just as squirrelly as it was, and the brakes are grabbing. I'm not kidding; somebody is going to get hurt in that thing!"

Dave looked at me with a trace of a smile on his face. He didn't seem to have heard a thing I said. "It may be my only chance to ever drive in a Trans-Am. I'd like to try it for a few laps."

"Do as you like, it's your car," I said angrily.

He climbed into the Camaro and drove off.

"I hope the son of a bitch spins out," I said to Sally. "On second thought, I hope he doesn't. They're going to think that's me out there. Everybody in the goddamn place is going to wonder why in hell they let me and that shit-box, wobbling all over the track, keep getting in everybody's way. Goddamnit, this is the worst thing that could have happened." It suddenly came to me: what if Dave sailed around with quick lap times? What if it had all been in my head? What if the car was perfectly all right? The stopwatch on my wrist chronometer was broken, so I borrowed one from a spectator to clock Dave. Relief. He was going very slowly, between 2.12 and 2.15. But on the other hand, at that pace, everybody in the place was passing him. And no doubt everybody in the place thought he was me. What's more, Dave didn't have permission from the stewards to run the car. He didn't even have the proper license. If he crashed, they would think it was me. Either way I was screwed. If he did badly, I looked bad to the crowd and the other drivers. If he went quickly, the crew would call me a crybaby and a quitter. Slumping alone and humiliated, praying for the damn race to end, I watched Warren make a pit stop. It was perfectly choreographed. Every man in the crew moved with authority and precision, filling his gas tank and checking his tires with professional quickness. Warren was running a perfect race—a solid eighth. Robbins, the man he had beaten the day before, was ahead of him. What the hell does that mean? I thought. There is poor old Warren, driving his ass off, with the car working perfectly, and he's stuck in eighth place. How long can you sustain a career on finishes like that?

Mercifully, it ended. Mark Donohue won easily, having opened a half-minute lead on Follmer by the end. Dave had cut his lap times just before the finish to 2.03–2.04. Warren rolled to a stop and climbed out, bathed in perspiration. He looked exhausted and not particularly happy. "What happened to you?" he asked abruptly.

"The handling went all to hell. I parked it before I hurt somebody. Then Dave wanted to take it out. He was driving it at the end."

"I wondered what had happened. The car was sitting on the edge of the track out back, and the guy standing next to it looked like Dave. I couldn't figure out where you went."

"You mean he spun out?"

"Yeah, why?"

"Nothing. I just figured it would happen sooner or later."

They broke out some Genesee Cream Ale while they loaded the cars. Maybe they forgot, but nobody offered me one. I made a few perfunctory good-byes and left. I never wanted to see the Michigan International Speedway again.

13

■.■.■.■.■.■.■.■.

The unpleasantness at Michigan
bothered me much longer than it should have. I reported to
friends more about the frog under the hood than the actual
race, and as the days passed, I began to wonder if I had done
the right thing by parking the car. After all, Dave Hoselton
had managed to keep the Camaro running, despite its handicaps. Had I quit too soon? It is not uncommon in racing for a
driver to drop out of a race when his car is operating below
par, but the crew obviously felt that I had lost heart; that it
was me, not the car, that wasn't performing. Could that have
been true? Could the spin into the ditch have psyched me
into a skittishness during the race? The more I grappled with
the problem, the more I rationalized the fact that the car *was*
squirrelly. Yes, it had to be the car. After all, it had darted
toward the retaining wall under braking, it had been unstable
in the corners. Yet, if it was all in my head...

The phone rang. It was Warren. We had not spoken since
Michigan, and I wasn't sure how he had reacted to my trou-

bles. We had parted without any explanation on my part, and I was sure that he felt like the rest of the crew. Yet he seemed affable enough on the other end of the wire, and we wandered through a period of preliminary banter without broaching the subject. Perhaps I was trying to avoid the issue when I asked, "You all set for next year, Warren?"

"I hope so. We're buying another car—the one Marshall Robbins had this season, and we've sold the one you drove. We got a pretty good price for the thing, but money's going to be tight."

"What's the matter, isn't Dave selling enough Chevys?" I asked, half kidding.

"No, he's in good shape, but he wants the team to operate on a more pay-as-you-go basis. Especially now that he's quit driving himself."

"What do you mean, he's quit driving?"

"He's through," said Warren flatly. "He said he's tried it, and he's proved his point. That's the end. Dave's a funny guy that way."

"You mean his last time in a race car was at Michigan? Maybe that's why he was so determined to drive in my place at the end of the race. He must have figured it would be his only chance to try a Trans-Am," I said.

"I'll tell you something. Dave will never race again. When he makes up his mind, that's it. He's got the discipline to make it stick. Dave is a very tough guy. By the way, I forgot to tell you, we found out what was the matter with your car at MIS."

"Oh, yeah?" I asked, a trifle defensively.

"The shims in the left-front suspension. They were gone. That's what made it handle so strange. It probably happened when you went into the ditch."

"That's good to know. I've been trying to figure out if it was me or the car. I was afraid the whole thing was in my head. It's a relief to know it wasn't."

The shims . . . whatever they were. It didn't matter, the important thing to me was the knowledge that it hadn't all been a figment of my imagination. A great relief came over me, and suddenly, as Warren chatted on, it seemed silly that I had fretted for so long over the Michigan thing; that I had let such a minor incident fester in my mind. Nearly a week had passed since the race, and all of the racers, Donohue, Agor, Follmer, etc., had moved on to other problems. They had shoved Michigan out of their thinking, regardless of how they had done there. They seemed to possess a buoyancy that was not mine—at least in the context of racing. They looked only to the future. They refused to look back, as if those vistas might shake their resolve. The life force of all racers is ego-centered optimism, the unshakable conviction that tomorrow will be better because *they* will make it better. In the meantime, I had been looking over my shoulder, fretting about mistakes and letting my confidence be shaken.

"Are you going to Riverside?" I asked Warren.

"Can't afford it. It's just too far to travel. Only a few of the guys are going from the East Coast. Just the rich ones. It won't be much of a race."

"I think I'll go out anyway," I said. "It's the end of the season and a couple of guys from Atlanta are entering a new Challenger. Dick Brooks, the stock-car driver, is going to run it, and I've got a chance to help out on the crew. I guess I'd like to see the last Trans-Am. And maybe it'll help me forget all that trouble at Michigan."

"You can't let that bother you. Everybody is going to take a shit once in a while. You've just got to forget the bad stuff," Warren said firmly. "Like myself. We had some bad luck this season. I know we could have done better if we'd gotten some breaks, but I can't let that worry me. Next season with the new car, I know I'll do better. I just know it."

And then he was gone. I hung up feeling guilty about how I had been irritated at him during the Michigan episode. He was a good man, self-centered to be sure, but that was an asset in his chosen profession. I hoped that his future would be brighter. He wanted so badly to be a top professional driver and had committed everything in his life to that goal.

He was convinced that it would come to him in good time. Tomorrow would be his. Unfortunately, others had laid claim to it as well. In the end, tomorrow would belong to no one.

Riverside Raceway sprawled across the California desert moonscape like an aborted housing development. Save for a collection of grandstands that towered over the far turn, there was little to set it apart from the surrounding desolation except for the twisting network of asphalt that composed its track. The weather was hot and dusty. Back East, the frosty slopes of Watkins Glen were vibrating with the nasty shriek of Formula One cars contesting for the United States Grand Prix. The Indianapolis cars and drivers were set to run on the New Jersey Fairgrounds track at Trenton. This meant that a number of the Trans-Am stars, Donohue, Revson, Savage, Elford, etc., would be racing elsewhere. What's more, poor old Bud Moore had not been able to persuade the Riverside promoters to give him financial aid in transporting his Mustangs to the West Coast, and he, too, would be absent. The field would be thin. George Follmer had switched to one of the Roy Woods Javelins when Moore had failed to enter.

"In the corners this thing is like sitting in a bucket of shit," Dick Brooks grumbled as he untangled himself from behind the wheel of the Challenger after a few laps of practice. Brooks was trained for duty on the banked superspeedways of the South and was not totally at ease on the treacherous contours of the Riverside road course. His complaints about the Challenger were directed at Jim Ruggles, a tall, laconic man in a short-sleeved sports shirt. Ruggles was a master racing mechanic, a man with long and impressive credentials ranging from Indianapolis to Daytona. He listened to Brooks's criticism of the Challenger's handling and turned to regard the low orange beast, sitting inert in the shadows of the Riverside garage area. "It's the rear suspension. I figured it'd be too loose. We've got to stiffen the thing up. Only thing is, I didn't bring along any spare leaves." Ruggles was thinking. His quick mind was clicking over in search of a quick source for Dodge leaf springs. His face brightened. "Brooks! Get that U-wreck-em over here. We'll just borrow a few springs from that."

Brooks left to extract the team's rented Dodge Monaco from the paddock parking lot while the Challenger's owners strode up. They had been in the pits during Brooks's practice run and had not understood why their driver had returned their car to the garage. A pair of young Atlanta junior executives—Dick Rawlings was a towering, powerfully built sales manager for the Marriott Hotel management, and Karl Day was a Southern Airways supervisor whose soft face and vulnerable eyes belied his rugged credentials as an ex-major in the Green Berets—this was their first experience in owning a big-time racing car, which they had hired Ruggles to build and maintain for the Riverside Trans-Am. They were neophytes in the racing business and were understandably curious about every move that Ruggles and Brooks were making with their precious automobile. It was a solid machine, having been fabricated with the kind of fussy attention to detail that only a professional like Ruggles could bring to the job, but racing cars seldom work properly right out of the box, and suspension adjustments of the type Ruggles was about to administer were normal—although scavenging springs from rental cars was a trifle out of the ordinary.

"What's the trouble?" Day asked seriously.

"Nuthin' really. Brooks says the thing won't handle. Rear end's too loose. I'm going to add another leaf to the springs."

"Have we got any spares on the truck?" asked Rawlings.

"Nope, we're going to borrow a couple off the U-wreck-em," Ruggles said matter-of-factly.

"What? You're going to *steal* the springs off our rental car?" Day questioned in disbelief.

Ruggles was the total pragmatist. "No choice, really, you leave the suspension the way it is and Brooks will likely crash and bend your racer all to hell. We haven't got any spare springs of our own, so we've got to use the only source. It won't make any difference, anyway. The next guy who drives that renter might experience a little understeer, but otherwise nobody'll know the difference."

Rawlings chuckled at the prospect, but Day was not pleased. His mind marched along in orderly, military fashion, and this was obviously against regulations. "Are you sure?"

Ruggles interrupted. "Listen, if you want the son of a bitch to run, this is your only choice. Otherwise, let's load it up and tow it home. Now, let's get this car up on the jack stands and start taking off the springs so that we'll be ready to make the change.

Day shruggled and went off in the direction of the big toolbox that sat on the bench in front of the Challenger. Rawlings laughed some more and said in his deep Georgia drawl, "Goddamnit, Jim, you're too damn much."

Ruggles was placing a hydraulic jack under the frame of the Challenger. He pumped away until the left side of the racing car slanted off the ground, but as soon as it reached the proper altitude, a low hissing sound emitted from the jack's innards and the car slowly dipped back to earth. "Oh, shit, we've got us a French jack," said Ruggles.

"What?"

"A French jack. We've got us a fuckin' French jack."

"What the hell is a French jack?" asked Rawlings, getting ready to laugh.

"One that keeps going down on you, for Chrissake," snickered Ruggles as he pumped away on the handle in an attempt to raise the Challenger back off the ground.

Brooks came up, looking despondent.

"Whatsa matter? Where's the Monaco?" asked Ruggles.

"Still over in the lot. I can't get the thing started. I left the keys on the dashboard and they dropped down the defroster vent."

"Oh, shit, that's beautiful," said Ruggles in mock disgust. "Yates, you go over and help Brooks get the keys out and we'll finish getting the springs unhooked off the Challenger." Brooks and I collected a bundle of screwdrivers and pliers, then marched across the stone-covered paddock toward the

Monaco. Practice was still underway, and the rumble of the
nearby exhausts made speech difficult. We set to the chore of
finding the keys in the defroster. Cursing the heat, lying on
our backs under the Dodge's instrument panel, we began ripping away at the labyrinth of wires, ducts, pipes, tubes, and
switches packed against the firewall. Soon the ground was
covered with pieces we'd yanked clear of the car. Furiously
jabbing at the heater duct that barred my way, I thought, how
typical this is of the malice racers everywhere harbor for
rental cars. The stories of destruction to the rolling stock of
Hertz and Avis are as much a part of the sport's inside legends as any conventional feats of driving on the racetrack. No
one has truly been initiated into motor racing's inner sanctums until he has smashed, spun, or abused a "rent-a-racer."

But doesn't the standard litany about race drivers claim
they have this *thing* about machines? That they have some
weird hang-up with cars—a deep psychic reverence that
could keep your average psychology doctoral candidate writing for months on end? Hardly. A machine to the racing
driver—a *real* racing driver, as opposed to a hobby racer or
dilettante—is essentially something to be dominated, ruled,
overcome, tamed. There is little sentimentality associated
with an automobile for a real racer. Authentic car freaks, like
classic-car collectors or customizers or people who belong to
organizations like the Porsche Club of America worship machines, and in so doing subordinate themselves to the automobile. Automobile journalists, for the most part, devote
their efforts to fiendishly detailed documentation of the automobiles and their arcane components, at the expense of the
men who build and drive them. In their frame of reference, a
racing car is a source of fathomless mystery and fascination.
Not so with the professional competitor, who relates to his
machine primarily as a tool—perhaps even a weapon—that
will permit him to beat somebody else. For example, when
Bill Vukovich, one of the most talented, most resolute, most
courageous drivers of all time, first saw the car that would
provide him with his rookie ride at Indianapolis, he was

hardly moved to rhapsodizing about its beautiful lines or expressing gratitude that it might transport him to fame and riches. "I can drive that pig," he said defiantly, expressing in succinct fashion the sentiment of every great race driver, anywhere, anytime. It is said that the late Marquis de Portago, the extraordinary Spanish nobleman who was such a standout driver for Scuderia Ferrari in the mid fifties (before dying in a spectacular crash in the Mille Miglia—a 1,000-mile open road race around Italy), had so little regard for the masterfully crafted Ferraris he drove that he had to scratch marks on the dash in order to identify his car in the presence of the other team drivers' automobiles.

Brooks and I gave up. The keys to the Monaco were swallowed somewhere in the heating tract, and there seemed to be no way of finding them, short of dismantling the entire instrument panel.

We reported our failure to Ruggles, who shook his head in despair and left to do the job himself. By this time, Mike Bailey had arrived on the scene and was probing through a cluttered briefcase that he had perched on the hood of the Challenger. Bailey, a curly-haired Canadian, was a member of a unique subculture in motor sport. He made deals. There is no firm financial basis for building and campaigning a racing car. Few individuals can afford to foot the bill to enter Indianapolis, for example, which might cost upward of $300,000 for a single, well-equipped car, spares, crew, and front-line driver. A minimum budget of $75,000 per season would be necessary in any type of major-league racing, which means that outside sponsorship from private concerns interested in the promotional benefits of the sport must be found. Therefore, men like Mike Bailey hover around the edges of many racing operations, using their considerable sales talents to promote funds. They work on a percentage of the total expenditure, forever aiming at Big Casino, which might come from luring a major corporation into a multimillion-dollar deal, but generally settling for modest arrangements with minor automotive-accessory manufacturers. Deal men are

eternal optimists; resilient, tough-skinned, and endlessly loquacious. They live out of briefcases, their heads glued to
telephones, forever snuffling away at the coattails of the
money vendors in important businesses and advertising
agencies.

Mike Bailey was scrambling. He'd been working for years
trying to get Coca-Cola to swing for one of his ideas and had,
in fact, sold them on a few projects. His efforts with the Challenger at Riverside had been critical. He'd put the owners,
Day and Rawlings, in contact with Ruggles and Brooks, had
made a deal with Chrysler for some indirect aid in obtaining
a powerful, specially built 305 engine from the California
shop of Keith Black, had arranged with Goodyear for tires,
had worked out a deal with the Riverside management to assist in defraying Brooks's expenses, and had nailed together a
small patchwork of sponsorships to help pay the bills. It
being the first time out for the Challenger, little chance existed that it would contest with the leaders, but if Bailey's
plans reached fruition, the car would return the following
season as the spearhead of a full-blown, properly bankrolled
racing effort. That goal provided the life force for Mike Bailey.

Karl Day found Bailey hard to take. Mike's soaring flights
of optimism, his hyperbole, his lack of organization, were
anathema to an orderly man like Karl, and as the days at
Riverside passed, they found even the briefest exchanges of
civil conversation difficult to maintain. A check was overdue
from one of the sponsors, money from a major corporation
that Bailey had been assured was in the mail. Suspicious because a number of Bailey's other "sure things" had failed to
materialize, Day was on the verge of pulling the car out of the
race unless the money arrived.

We headed for the hour of the race with acrimony growing
between Bailey and Day—a typical situation in racing, where
strong egos perpetually clash. Beyond that, the Challenger
was simply too new to be competitive. Brooks managed to
maintain his good nature, slouching around the garage area,
squinting in mock malice with a cigarette dangling from his

mouth. Ruggles had returned with the Dodge's lost keys almost immediately. "You son of a bitch!" exclaimed Brooks. "How in hell did you find those keys so fast?"

"I ain't saying, but you dumb shits ought to be ashamed of yourselves," Ruggles said, smiling.

He went back to work on the Challenger, his marvelously dexterous hands flicking over the engine in an effort to make a series of last-minute adjustments. "This car is sickeningly legal," he mused in reference to his years among the rule-benders in the South. Then he started the engine. It had an awesome exhaust note, multileveled, with sharp darts of sound mixed with the heavy, deafening thuds of detonation. He leaned into the engine compartment and began fiddling with the timing. The car's great bellowing brought a cluster of spectators. They seemed mesmerized by the raw noise. Similar engines had been running in the garage all day, but there was a special cutting edge on the Dodge's racket. So they stood there, that group of a dozen or so, getting their tympanic cavities whipped to jelly, watching in deadpan, semi-hypnotic states while Ruggles coolly stood over the throbbing iron container of 450 horses and probed for maximum power. When he stopped and the Challenger fell silent once again, they drifted away, ears ringing and faint smiles playing at the edges of their mouths.

"We've got a little leak in the transmission, the starter is bad, and we haven't even thought about practicing a pit stop," said Ruggles, wiping his hands. "I guess you could call this an exploratory operation."

The exploratory operation lasted for eighteen laps. Then something broke deep inside that rasping engine, and Brooks was out. It was over, another afternoon of racing, another collection of euphoric hopes and fantasies shattered. The car was a DNF, the official code for "did not finish." Day and Rawlings looked stunned, not only at the rapidity with which their entry had left the race, but at the prospect of repairing the broken engine. Brooks and Ruggles, the longtime professionals, were calm. They had failed to finish a multitude of

races, and one more made no difference. Bailey disappeared
to make a phone call, working on another deal. I stood there
in the relative silence of the garage, listening to the machines
rumble by outside. Follmer was far in the lead, headed for an
easy, deserved victory. My mind was idling about the general
futility of racing and why men keep coming back for more in
the face of insuperable odds. The race was about over. The
season was gearing down. But somehow I knew that all of us,
broke, spirits ruptured, friendships strained, would be back
again. Ruggles summed it up when he looked at the Challenger, injured but hardly dead, and smiled whimsically over
the collective disappointment. He said, "That, sports fans, is
motor racing. Ain't it a bitch?"

14

Mad enterprises seldom have cogent beginnings, and therefore I can't recall with any clarity why the idea for the Cannonball Baker Sea-to-Shining-Sea Memorial Trophy Dash roiled up in my brain in the first place. It came to me in the offices of *Car and Driver*, that much I remember, and it was met with general apathy, punctuated with isolated reactions of hostility. Nevertheless, I was delighted with the plan: a free-form competition from New York to Los Angeles, à la the old open road races of the early days of motoring. It was ironic that within three months a Hollywood group announced plans to produce a film about a two-car race from Los Angeles to Washington, D.C., to be called *Two-Lane Blacktop*. Hearing the news, I joked with a friend that because our event would primarily be run on interstates, any resulting film would have to be titled *Four-Lane Cement*. In an age when every facet of our lives was being organized and codified, it seemed that a balls-out run from coast to coast might act as an appropriate protest in behalf of adventure and enterprise. Unlike other motor races, which operate within a thicket of rules that would rival the postal service, the Cannonball Baker would be undertaken with a minimum of regulations. In fact, I imagined that its purposes could be articulated in a matter of a few words, i.e.: "Entrants must drive a land-based vehicle of any configuration, with any size crew, over any route they choose, at any speed they deem practical, between New York and Los Angeles. The car covering the distance between the start and finish in the briefest time will be the winner. There are no other rules."

Naming the event after Cannonball Baker seemed appropriate. Cannonball was a great cross-country record setter in the early days and established numerous nonstop records that still stand. Perhaps his greatest feat was crossing the United States from Los Angeles to New York in sixty hours in the late 1920's. Driving a Franklin, Cannonball made the trip alone, on a network of two-lane highways that penetrated every city and town along the way. A remarkable accomplishment under any circumstances, but to pull it off within the relatively primitive travel environment of the Roaring Twenties placed Cannonball's trip in the realm of the miraculous. While the old gentleman had long since passed on, it seemed to me that he would have been amused to find another effort at cross-country record-setting being undertaken in his memory.

Because of the tightening noose of traffic laws, flat-out travel on the public roads in the United States (except Nevada) is a sub-rosa, antisocial endeavor, much like cock fighting and crapshooting. Ironically, it is legal in most European nations, where speed laws are much more liberal (and in the minds of most good drivers, more enlightened). In fact, nobody had made any serious attempt to set a coast-to-coast record in years, although several automotive journalists, public-relations men, etc., laid informal claim to having made the trip in the neighborhood of forty-four hours. With the ever-expanding interstate system, we knew this time could be reduced sharply through some serious, nonstop running. While a number of my friends reacted with predictions that the participants would spend the rest of their days rotting in an Oklahoma jail, a substantial quantity of lunatics within the sport rose up to say they would like to take part. It suddenly became a serious idea. Why the hell not do it? I thought. In addition to the obvious challenge of driving, tactics, route choice, type of vehicle to be used, etc., it seemed that the Cannonball Baker offered an opportunity to make some interesting symbolic statements about the general state of driving in the United States. The simplistic, ineffective, profit-oriented, speed-law-enforcement establishment certainly deserved opposition, and if a group of good drivers could run coast to coast in really brisk time, it might serve notice that our laws needed radical updating in the face of modern realities. Additionally, if one could drive between New York and Los Angeles in the range of forty hours, it seemed a worthwhile basis for arguing that excesses of superhighway construction had reached absurd limits and should be stopped immediately. After all, how many more four-lane roads do we need?

Arguments immediately arose as to what kind of vehicle would be best suited to the job. Many favored high-speed grand touring cars of the Ferrari-Maserati-Corvette genre. Others said a specially equipped sedan like a Cadillac would be ideal. Vans with enough auxiliary fuel tanks to make the trip nonstop were mentioned, while others advocated small imported coupes with moderately high-speed potential and long cruising ranges. At the height of our fancy came ideas for ploys such as black-monster limousines with official flags, liveried chauffeurs, and diplomatic license plates; bogus hearses or ambulances (with such outlandish gear as fake coffins or iron lungs operating as additional gasoline storage)—anything, in fact, that would delude the various state police into thinking the cars were on a serious mission of some sort.

Steve Smith was my most enthusiastic supporter. We decided to run the first Cannonball in early May, before the summer racing season got started, and before the roads became clogged with summer vacationers. Others promised their participation, so Smith and I began serious efforts to prepare our vehicle. We would use a powerful Dodge Sportsman van that Moon Mullins, a longtime friend and public-relations man for Chrysler Corporation, had provided for test by *Car and Driver*. It was an imposing machine, powered by a 360-cubic-inch engine, with air conditioning, disc brakes, heavy-duty suspension, etc. Smith and I added to its potential by installing a set of special, German-built driving seats, a battery of quartz-iodine driving lights, mag wheels with high-performance, low-profile tires, a small refrigerator, a radar detector, and an outlandish racing spoiler mounted high on the rear roof section. It was the toughest, fastest Dodge car extant, we thought, and we named it Moon Trash in honor of our friend Mullins.

Jim Williams, a young, bearded associate editor on *Car and Driver* and my fourteen-year-old son, Brock, Jr., were added to the crew, and lengthy plans were made about the route, the gasoline stop procedures (which would be critical, since all time lost at the roadside would nibble away at the average speed), and other details that had to be figured into the equation of how you drive nearly three thousand miles on public roads at the fastest possible speed. In the meantime, half a dozen other crews claimed to be preparing for the race, but that turned out to be a hollow expectation. As the hour of the event approached, a steady string of calls brought news that people were declining. Apparently the thought of thrashing across this immense nation in an exhausting, expensive, risky burst was reaching full impact. After all, there was nothing tangible to be gained: no money, and precious little glory, while the opportunities for censure, lengthy sessions with local traffic magistrates, and substantial fines seemed plentiful indeed. By the afternoon of the day prior to the departure, the last team dropped out, leaving Moon Trash the only official entrant in the first Cannonball Baker Sea-to-Shining-Sea Memorial Trophy Dash.

Crabbing about the flabby resolve of our fellow racers, Smith, Williams, my son, and I vowed to go anyway, if for no other reason than to set a new cross-country record and perhaps establish a bench mark for what we were sure would be future Cannonball Baker events. We left midtown Manhattan on a midnight in May, having determined that such a departure would permit us to leave the New York metropolitan area with a minimum of traffic and hopefully, to arrive in Los Angeles sometime at midday when the freeways might not be jammed. Having loaded our refrigerator with provisions and buckled ourselves into our seats, we rushed into the night, across the foggy New Jersey flats and the black hills of Pennsylvania. The morning came with a gray rain falling across Indiana, but with Williams driving, we averaged over 80 mph on a stretch of Interstate 70. I was driving in western Illinois when Moon Trash swallowed its last ounce of gas while passing a line of trucks on a two-lane road. I managed to skid to a halt at the roadside, where we leaped out and dumped two gallons of high test into the tank from our auxiliary jerry can. Running smoothly again, we plunged into the darkness in central Oklahoma. With our powerful headlights probing into the night, we zoomed along in utter isolation, racing ourselves across the continental United States. A bad choice of routes slowed our pace in California, delaying our arrival at the Portofino Inn, a small but excellent hotel on the edge of the Pacific Ocean in Redondo Beach. Staggering out of Moon Trash, filthy and exhausted, we computed out total travel time at forty hours and fifty-one minutes—a span that we were convinced was the outright record for cars between New York and Los Angeles.

My subsequent story in *Car and Driver* brought a flood
of mail, letters by the hundreds, some critical of such an
insane gesture, but a vast majority were favorable, and
dozens of correspondents wanted to participate in the next
race—an event I had assured them would take place at
some hazy point in the future. But once the initial burst of
excitement about the run subsided, the Cannonball began to
give way to other distractions. The racing season was beginning to move ahead at full speed, and I was concentrating on the upcoming drivers' school, Glen race, Trans-Ams,
etc., when a telegram brought the Cannonball back to the
forefront of my thinking. It was from the Polish Racing
Drivers of America, a tongue-in-cheek collection of car
freaks that had been formed by Brad Niemcek, a New York
public-relations man, and Oscar Koveleski, a well-known
amateur sportscar racer and auto-accessory seller. The telegram read, THIS CONSTITUTES FORMAL ENTRY BY THE POLISH
RACING DRIVERS OF AMERICA IN THE NEXT OFFICIAL CANNONBALL
BAKER SEA-TO-SHINING-SEA MEMORIAL TROPHY DASH. THE
DRIVERS ARE OSCAR KOVELESKI, BRAD NIEMCEK, AND TONY ADA-
MOWICZ. IF WE CAN FIND CALIFORNIA, WE'LL BEAT YOU FAIR AND
SQUARE.

That was it. We had a challenge. And a race. While they
refused to take anything with complete seriousness, the
PRDA weren't fooling about the Cannonball. Their third
driver, Tony Adamowicz, was one of the best young professional prospects in the nation and with Mario Andretti, was
the only American to be graded by the FIA (thanks to a
high finish at Le Mans, Tony had qualified for such an obscure, complicated international rating). What's more, a fol-
low-up phone call by Niemcek indicated that they were
building a specially modified Chevy van with enough auxiliary gas tanks to make the trip *nonstop!* We had made
fifteen stops for fuel, which had kept Moon Trash sidelined
for a total of one hour and fifteen minutes, and their plan
to go the distance made sense. Except for one factor: Brad
told me their van would carry 298 gallons of gasoline,

which he felt would be adequate to make the trip. I knew
that Moon Trash, a much lighter vehicle (considering the
PRDA would start with nearly a ton of extra gas on board),
had consumed 314 gallons—a fact I neglected to share with
Brad.

We decided to go on November 15, after the racing season had ended and the roads had cleared of vacation traffic. After returning from Riverside, I began to prepare for
the Cannonball in earnest. The first order seemed to involve getting a faster car. While Moon Trash was a fine
machine, its limited top speed—perhaps 105 mph—and
stock fuel tank presented severe handicaps in the face of
the PRDA challenge. Kirk White offered a solution. Within
his stable was a 4.4-liter Ferrari Daytona, a slippery,
ground-hugging coupe with a V–12, four-cam engine and
five forward speeds, considered to be the fastest road automobile built. Its top speed was in the neighborhood of 175
mph, and with a large gasoline tank, cruising ranges of
300-350 miles could be expected. It was handicapped in
that only two men could fit into its small cockpit, which
meant greater fatigue, but I accepted Kirk's deal anyway.
Now my only problem was finding a codriver. Smith and
Williams could not participate owing to the pressures of
their jobs. Why not get a real, honest-to-God racer, someone
suggested. The idea made sense. I called Dan Gurney. He
loved the plan. I could hear him chuckling on the other
end of the transcontinental connection as I explained the
Cannonball to him. He accepted. Jubilation. Then he called
back a day later to decline. He mumbled about pressures
from sponsors and how a man in his position shouldn't be
out roaring around on the public highways. I understood. I
called Phil Hill. A perfect choice, I thought. After all, Phil
was America's only World Champion, a title he had won at
the wheel of a Ferrari, and I had heard that he was an
excellent highway driver. What's more, Phil was a terribly
bright and engaging man whose company would not wear
thin after a day and a half of steady association. Phil said it

sounded like fun, but he was simply too busy to go.

"What are you going to do about the cops?" he asked.

"What about the cops? I figure we'll have to treat them just like other road hazards: like ice, rain, snow," I said.

"Yeah, but if you get caught..."

"You know, Phil, your reaction is typical. Every guy I talk to about the Cannonball asks right away, 'What about the cops?' like they're the most fearsome thing on earth. Look at yourself. You spent half your life risking your ass in a race car, and yet if you're like the rest of us so-called racers, the thought of getting a traffic ticket sounds worse than a 200-mph crash at Le Mans."

"That's madness, isn't it?" he said reflectively. "I suppose we've been so preconditioned that it's a reflex action. Good God, I'm terrified about losing my driver's license. How screwed up can our priorities get?"

With Phil and Dan unavailable, I decided to call Don "Big Daddy" Garlits, the drag-racing champion. He was a good friend, a fine highway driver, and was possessed of the kind of iconoclastic, problem-solving mind that would be fascinated with the challenge of racing nonstop across the United States. Like Gurney, Garlits accepted, then had to refuse a day later when several critical business appointments could not be rescheduled. With less than a week to go, I was without a driving partner, although Mo Campbell, an associate of Kirk's, was prepared to run if I was unable to find a serious pro.

As the word of the Cannonball spread through the underground of the sport, more and more entries began to surface. Unlike the first time, these appeared to be serious competitors. Suddenly one afternoon, a pair of bearded young men appeared at the offices of *Car and Driver*. They announced themselves as Tom Marbut and Randy Waters and said that they had driven from their home in Little Rock, Arkansas, nonstop to test their new van for the Cannonball. Finding their story hard to believe, Jim Williams followed them down to the curbside of Park Avenue, where he found a brightly painted Dodge van, similar to Moon Trash but rigged with a special, 200-gallon fueling system. They planned to run across the country with one stop, they said.

My phone began to jangle constantly. As the originator, or Dr. Frankenstein, of the Cannonball, I was the recipient of unending calls from people who wanted to enter; who had entered and were dropping out; who would enter if I could find them a suitable car; who thought the whole thing was childish madness, etc. Bill Broderick, the racing public-relations director for Union 76 Oil Company called to say that he and a crew of four friends were entering the event in a rented Travco motor home. The chief pilot would be Joe Frasson, a NASCAR Grand National stock-car driver. "We don't expect to beat all you fast guys, but we'll set a record for motor homes, I'll guarantee you that," announced Bill.

Larry Opert, a Cambridge, Massachusetts, lawyer and sometime SCCA club racer, entered with a pair of friends, but said, "Unfortunately, we don't have a satisfactory car, but we'll have that problem solved by race time." He wouldn't elaborate on his plan.

Robert Perlow, a rotund graduate student from Hofstra University on Long Island, said he was prepared to compete with his MGB-GT coupe, but was having trouble finding a riding partner. Acting as a matchmaker, I rooted through the lists of interested people who had called and teamed Perlow up with Wes Dawn, a California television technician and club racer who wanted to use the Cannonball as a high-speed hitchhike to the West Coast.

Moon Trash was back in the program, despite some misadventures. Poor Williams had crunched the front end (including all those expensive quartz-iodine driving lights) in a chain collision on Manhattan's East River Drive, and Jim Stickford, Chrysler's area public-relations director, had worked long and hard to arrange for a quick repair. Its crew would be Kim Chapin, a regular contributor to *Sports Illustrated,* and Steve Behr, a competent young race driver who, among other accomplishments, shared the distinction of being the highest-placed (twelfth) American finisher in the history of the famed Monte Carlo Rally. In phoning to announce that Moon Trash would also carry Holly Morin, a particularly game TWA stewardess as a nondriving member of the crew, Behr commented, "In the Cannonball, we'll be sneaking along, trying to avoid the police. In the Monte Carlo, they stand on the side of the road and flag you through the tough spots. That says something about our philosophy of law and order, I think."

The last and eighth team to enter the Cannonball roared across the country just in time to make the start. Ed Bruerton, a supermarket manager in Oakland, California, and his younger brother, a pharmacy student at Cal, planned to leave their home a few days before the Cannonball, drive south to the Portofino, and run across the country in reverse as a sort of reconnaissance. Their car would be a tired AMX sport coupe with 90,000 miles on the odometer. They had already made numerous endurance trips with the old car, including a rocky ride the entire length of the Baja, California, peninsula.

Everybody was ready except me. While I knew and liked Mo Campbell, I had virtually no knowledge of his skill as a driver, and it seemed a shame that the lofty performance of the Ferrari might not be used to its full potential. That might be possible with Mo, but I knew it would have been assured if an experienced veteran like Gurney or Hill could have been persuaded to go. The evening before we were to gather in Manhattan for the start of the race, Sally and I were having dinner with friends when the telephone rang. It was Gurney. We exchanged a few niceties, then I asked him why he had called. After all, we had known each other for years, had liked each other, but our friendship was not so strong that we exchanged phone calls to engage in innocent chatter. He paused for a moment, then said, "I'm ready to go on the Cannonball."

"Are you drunk, or have you lost your mind?" I asked.

"I don't know, maybe a little of both," he said, laughing. "But I've had a change of mind about the whole thing. Something I read. I'll tell you about it when I get there. I've decided we just can't sit on our asses anymore. Everybody's terrified of offending somebody, and I almost got caught in that trap. Anyway, we'll talk about it later. I'm jumping on the red-eye out of Los Angeles right now. I'll catch a few hours' sleep in a motel near Kennedy and meet you just before the start."

Beautiful. I hung up the phone knowing that the Ferrari would be used the way ol' Enzo had intended it to be.

Steve Smith's apartment on Thirty-fifth Street was to be the rendezvous point for the racers. The actual start would be at the Red Ball Garage, a typically grubby Manhattan commercial parking establishment on Thirty-first Street, between Third Avenue and Lexington. It had been chosen because it was near midtown and because as the regular parking area for *Car and Driver*, its staff would be calm in the face of almost any lunacy involving automobiles. Since everybody had intended to start about midnight, we had scheduled a driver's meeting at Smith's place for ten-thirty P.M. Slowly the apartment began to fill up, not only with entrants, but with a vast collection of friends, *Car and Driver* staff members, photographers, etc., all milling around in the relatively cramped confines of Smith's one-bedroom lodgings. The Bruerton brothers staggered in, unshaved and exhausted. They had just completed a forty-four hour, nonstop run from California and announced that they were going to sleep for eight hours before starting.

Larry Opert burst in, smiling. With him were his two friends, Ron Herisko, a law partner, and Nate Pritzker, an engineer. They had a car, they announced, thanks to *The New York Times* and the unconscious generosity of a

wealthy Long Island man. It seemed that the trio, determined to find a car to race in the Cannonball, had looked
in the *Times* classified in search of a "driveway" deal—an
arrangement where one will drive another's car to a destination for nominal expenses. This is a common tactic used
to transport personal cars by people who don't like to drive
long distances. The Long Island gentleman wanted his new
Cadillac Sedan deVille driven to California. Opert and
Company obliged, nodding hazily at his firm orders that his
prized machine not be driven after eight o'clock at night,
not before nine-o'clock in the morning, and not run faster
than 75 miles an hour. All the regulations would be vio-
lated before they left Manhattan!

The Polish Racing Drivers arrived, decked out in full
Nomex driving suits. Niemcek, always the PR man, had arranged for one of the team's sponsors, a Pennsylvania Kis-
kie manufacturer, to host an afternoon, prerace reception at
the Autopub, a chromy, car-oriented saloon situated, appropriately enough, in the basement of the General Motors
building. "They'll need more than fireproof uniforms if
those goddamn gas tanks in that thing explode," mused
Smith. "If those three hundred gallons let go, it'll make
Amchitka look like a wet match!" The room was full of
good-natured banter, as if nobody were thinking of the
three thousand miles that spread out before us. I kidded
Niemcek about their spectacular uniforms and how they
must have mystified the Sunday-afternoon pedestrians
along Fifth Avenue. "That was a lot of fun, but now we get
serious," Brad said, still smiling.

"Yeah, like they say, 'When the green flag drops, the bullshit stops,'" added Tony Adamowicz, who was standing
nearby.

"The Detroit street racers—the guys who drag-race up and
down Woodward Avenue for money—have a saying: 'Money
talks and bullshit walks,'" I added. "The only trouble is, we
haven't got a cent riding on this thing. Goddamn, when was

the last time guys like Adamowicz and Gurney raced for nothing?"

"And three thousand miles yet," said Tony. "Good God, I must be crazy."

The doorbell rang over the din and there was Gurney. It was that familiar chiseled face, revealing half the age of its forty years, with its firm mouth set in a crooked, little-boy grin. Dan Gurney is a big man—six foot two and perhaps two hundred pounds, so big, in fact, that he spent much of his career on the Grand Prix circuit wedged into tiny cockpits that had been intended for smaller men, racing sort of sideways, with one buttock perched on the seat. He was wearing a tweed sport coat, a navy blue Lacoste pullover, and a pair of khaki pants. He carried only a shaving kit. Dan obviously intended to get the trip over with in a hurry.

The drivers' meeting was brief. I outlined the Rules once again, noting that we would start from the Red Ball in one-minute intervals, with the PRDA going first. They had, after all, requested the "pole" position. The team arriving at the Portofino Inn in Redondo Beach in the briefest elapsed time—to be documented by the electronic time clocks at the Red Ball and at the Portofino's registration desk— would be the winner. Beyond that, everybody was on his own.

The cars had been parked on the main floor of the Red Ball, lined up under the light of the bare ceiling bulbs. There was the Little Rock van, with its spectacular red, white, and blue paint work; the red and white PRDA van, with its flanks covered with sponsors' decals and large type proclaiming, THE POLISH DRIVERS OF AMERICA GO COAST-TO-COAST NONSTOP! By contrast, Moon Trash had been painted, from bumper to bumper, in a murky coat of flat black. Crouching beside it was our Ferrari Daytona, its mirror-polished, royal blue paint glinting in the raw light. Its elegant finish was highlighted by a masterful network of yellow pinstriping, and its fenders were amply covered with decals from sponsors that Kirk White's staff had attracted to help defray expenses. Gurney's and my name were displayed in neat lettering under the windows. It had been the first time I'd seen the car up close, and its appearance was a trifle stunning. "Holy Christ, it's been cunningly disguised as a racing car!" I gasped.

Wind was kicking up litter on Thirty-first Street as the midnight starting time approached. While the first four cars departed, Gurney and I went off to gather up some provisions at an all-night delicatessen. We bought a few large blocks of Swiss cheese, a batch of gum, some chocolate bars, peanuts, and some cans of soft drink and Gatorade. Smith provided us with a large thermos bottle of hot coffee and a jar of chewable vitamin C tablets—a most useful remedy for the dryness in the mouth and nasal passages that seems to trouble long-distance travelers.

We rolled the Ferrari out of the Red Ball and into the dark street. As a cluster of friends stood by, Gurney and I fitted our gear around the seats; the food, maps, flashlight, watches, average speed computer, etc., and wound ourselves into the elaborate seat belts and shoulder harnesses. We were set. Already the PRDA, the Cadillac, the MG, and the Little Rock van were on the road, Moon Trash would leave half an hour after us, while Broderick's motor home and the Bruerton brothers would depart later in the day.

Dan would drive the first leg. He cranked over the engine, and a potent, whirring rumble rose out of the Ferrari's long hood. He flipped on the headlights, and the black leather cockpit glowed with the soft green luster of the large instrument panel. A friend stamped our ticket on the Red Ball time clock—our official record of departure—and amid a tiny chorus of windswept cheers, we accelerated away-roaring down Thirty-first Street toward the Lincoln Tunnel and California. We went about two hundred feet. The stoplight at the corner of Thirty-first and Lexington winked red as we approached, and we sat there through its full cycle. Every crosstown light then conspired to stop us, and we were immobilized at seven intersections before reaching the tunnel.

Our route was to be different from the others'. While most planned to cut directly westward to the Pennsylvania Turnpike, I'd decided that a more northern route across Interstate 80, with a subsequent cut south to Columbus, Ohio, was fastest. It was a trifle longer, but I-80 had less traffic and patrols than the turnpike and appeared to permit higher cruising speeds. It had to be reached via a series of two-lane roads in New Jersey, which were thick with tractor-trailers in the daytime. However, in the deep of night, and with Dan driving with relish, we traversed the slow section with an average speed that approached 60 mph.

In the process of trying to reach various road maps, lights, and other paraphernalia, I found my movements restricted by the safety harness. I unsnapped the latch and let the belts fall free. "That's better, at least I can move around," I said.

"These damn things," complained Gurney. "I'm taking mine off, too. They drive me nuts." So off we went on a headlong rush to California, with our life-saving seat belts crumpled on the floor of the Ferrari. We knew about the benefits of seat belts and had both advocated their use from various public platforms, but somehow, cocooned inside that uncanny car, which purred along with the precision and control of a big cat, they seemed superfluous. At first I felt like a naughty boy smoking corn silk behind the barn, but within a few miles the belts were forgotten.

Gurney began to hit his stride as we reached the broad expanses of Interstate 80. He was cruising the Ferrari at 95 mph—a virtual canter. At that speed, it was so positively in contact with the road that Gurney complained that it was boring to drive. To understand the excellence of a machine like the Ferrari, one has to have driven a thoroughbred sports car. There is no other way. Otherwise, the statement that such a car is cantering at 95 mph seems ludicrous. But the fact remains that some machines—such as the Ferrari, Maserati,

Porsche, BMW, Mercedes-Benz, Jaguar, etc.—have a poise and élan at high speeds that is virtually beyond the realm of comprehension for the average American driver. The absence of speed limits in Europe has helped to stimulate advances in suspensions, brakes, steering, etc., that are simply unavailable on domestic cars.

Lights appeared behind us. Thinking it might be the highway patrol, we backed off slightly and let the car overtake us. It was a Camaro with a man in his early twenties at the wheel. He was cruising at about 100 mph. Gurney watched him sail past, then accelerated to keep pace. I knew he wouldn't let the Camaro stay ahead. He opened the throttle plates on the Ferrari's twelve carburetor throats, and the big car clawed ahead, gobbling up the distance between it and the Camaro. We rocketed past. The engine noise increased slightly, but hardly to objectionable levels. The Camaro's headlights dwindled in the distance. "That's one hundred and fifty, just as steady as you please," said Gurney. Then he laughed.

Dan eased back to an indicated 120 mph, and we cruised down the deserted road, cutting over the humpbacked Allegheny Mountains of central Pennsylvania without effort. Gurney was driving with one hand and drinking coffee with the other when we sighted a dim pair of taillights far ahead. Again, it could be the police, so he slowed to about 100 and approached cautiously. I have 20-20 vision. I see well at night. Yet I was still trying to get some rough identification of the vehicle ahead when Gurney announced, "It's O.K., it's only a Volkswagen," and got back on the throttle. Sure enough, it was a Volkswagen lumping along there in the dark, and I silently pondered the power of Gurney's eyesight. It is said that most great drivers possess uncanny eyes, but I had never taken that seriously. Now I was a believer.

I napped sporadically while Dan sailed onward, running for an hour in excess of 100 mph and increasing our trip average to 81 mph. That was exceptional time, but neither of us expected it to hold up across the country. Three hundred miles from Manhattan, we stopped for gas. I had leaped out and stuffed the pump nozzle into the tank before the sleepy attendant had gotten out of his chair. Dan, in the meantime, had lifted the hood and was making a routine check of the oil. This pit stop procedure would be repeated for most of the trip, with me concluding the stop by stuffing a wad of dollar bills (brought specifically for that purpose) into the startled attendant's hand, leaping into the Ferrari, and spurting back onto the highway. In this manner we were able to keep most of our stops under five minutes.

It started to rain in western Pennsylvania, and the windshield wipers wouldn't work. Dan drove on for a while, letting the air stream blow the glass clear, but finally cut into a rest area to make repairs. We jumped out into the cold, predawn air and raised the hood. We checked the fuses, the switches, the linkage. Everything seemed in order. With time ticking away, I angrily gave the wipers a jerk, which freed them from the mysterious obstruction and caused them to begin cycling routinely across the windshield. Back on the road, Dan said, "You any idea what was wrong?"

"Hell, no, I just jerked on them, and they started working. Typical Italian car. They all have personalities of their own. I suppose this one is reminding us that it's in command and we're just along for the ride."

Again Gurney's miraculous eyes identified another pair of taillights. This time it was a Pennsylvania Highway Patrol Plymouth, and we slowed accordingly, falling obediently into his wake at 65 mph. It felt like we were walking. We reached Columbus in six and a half hours. We were one hour ahead of the time I'd run with Moon Trash and averaging 81 mph. We presumed we were far ahead of the rest of the entrants. The sun was bringing a bright, warm morning to the Midwest, and we felt great. Purring along Interstate 70 in western Ohio, Dan began honking the powerful air horns at the herds of cows and porkers that lined the fences. Not one animal even raised his nose at the sight and sound of the blue Ferrari Daytona whistling past at 100 mph.

Dan had been at the wheel nearly twelve hours when we reached St. Louis. He claimed he felt fine, and I believed him. After years of being around automobiles, one can sense a change in the reactions and movements of a driver —his very cadence with the car alters—when he becomes fatigued. Gurney was in excellent shape. As the traffic got slightly heavier west of St. Louis, we backed off our speed to about 85 mph, keeping a steady eye open for the law. We passed three pimply youths in a GTO, and they tried to race us. Gurney, racer to the end, responded. The Ferrari shot ahead, and witnessing that awesome burst of acceleration, the boys gave up.

Slouching back in his seat, driving with his left hand and nibbling a hunk of Swiss Cheese with his right, Dan began to chat. It was our first really steady communication since leaving. The deep concentration necessary to drive quickly on the highway required the full attention of us both—Gurney driving and me navigating, computing fuel stops, average speed, etc. (For example, the radio was never turned on the entire trip. Too distracting.) But now the big cat was merely loafing, and we began to talk; inevitably about racing. We discussed the separation of Swede Savage from Gurney's team. A simple cutback in finances was forcing Gurney to campaign a single Indianapolis car next season. It would be for Bobby Unser, an established star. Swede, the junior of the team, was released. It was not something Gurney had done with enthusiasm; he had after all brought Swede into the big time and had wanted very badly for him, as his protégé, to become a champion. But reality intervened. Money was tight, and one driver would have to go. That would have to be Swede.

"You told me you were going to explain why you changed your mind and came on this nutball trip," I said, shifting the subject.

Gurney paused for a second, gathering his thoughts. He

was inclined to do that, to fall silent, his jaw set, his eyes glazed in a faraway look, while he carefully composed a reply. He was a complicated man—infinitely deeper than his public image as an affable, all American nice guy. While he was engaging and easy to reach in public, he was essentially a private person, subject to dark moods and a mercurial temper. Most experts believe him to be among the very best race drivers who ever lived. I remember Max Muhleman telling me of an incident at the funeral of the great Jim Clark, a man usually mentioned with Tazio Nuvolari and Juan Manuel Fangio as perhaps the best ever. As Dan and Max were leaving the Clark family home near Duns, Scotland, Jim's father escorted them to the door. The old gentleman, still stunned at the loss of his son, took Gurney's hand and said, "You know, Dan. Jim often told me that of all the men he ever raced against, he felt that you were his strongest competitor." At that, Dan Gurney broke into tears. It was the only time Max Muhleman had ever seen him lose his composure. For the most part, he used his good looks and easy smile as a shield, letting them serve as representatives of the real Gurney. Even at that, there was a powerful aura of decency and integrity about the man that transcended the perpetual smile and the airy chatter that inevitably rose out of his public interviews. Of the elite of world-ranked drivers, probably none is better liked, and less understood, than Dan Gurney.

"This race, it was kind of a turning point for me," he said thoughtfully. "When you first called, it sounded like a great idea, a real lark. Then I began to think about my sponsors, about their reaction to my doing such a thing. I was letting concern for myself get in the way of my real feelings. What in the bleeding hell is that worth? Anyway, somebody had given me an essay by Ayn Rand. I'll show it to you when we get to California. It's called a 'Moratorium on Brains,' and it deals with the rising power of the federal government and the loss of individual freedoms. Now I'm no great Ayn Rand nut, but this particular thing hit home.

There I was, sitting around worrying about my image, when I thought the Cannonball could be an act of protest, a kind of personal adventure that could prove that we still know how to handle ourselves without a cop stationed every fifty feet on the highway. So I said, 'To hell with it, and I decided to come."

When was the last time Ayn Rand sent somebody on a cross-country motor race? I asked myself. Dan's reaction to her protests about a mindless, shapeless system overwhelming individuals and stifling any desires in behalf of any self-fulfillment made a certain amount of sense. In any case, he hadn't embarked on the enterprise with a simpleton "hunger for thrills" and a "lust for speed," which are rote reasons given by the hacks of the world for driving quickly. I wondered if Miss Rand would consider driving down a superhighway at 100 mph as a healthy objectivist outlet.

I took the wheel for the first time in mid-Missouri. Dan had driven fourteen hours and thirty-five minutes. A long time, to be sure, but with the near-mystical ease with which the Ferrari gobbles distance, the time becomes less amazing. "This thing is a whole new dimension in driving," I said as I accelerated onto the deserted Interstate. "If you told some Joe Doak who'd spent his life lumping around in a Pontiac or something that a guy could drive a car at speeds over 80 mph for fourteen hours straight in utter safety, he'd probably call you a lying Commie weirdo. And the beautiful part about the whole thing is that if the bureaucrats have their way, thoroughbred machines like this will be illegal, run off the road by herds of dumb Detroit iron."

Racing drivers make notoriously bad passengers. They generally trust no one but themselves, and some refuse to ride with anyone at all. Therefore, I tried my very best to put Gurney at ease. With the Ferrari on my side, the chore was simplified. After an hour of watching me like a mother hen, I saw his body relax and slide back in the form-fitting leather passenger's seat. "You drive well. Very smooth. Most people make me nervous. You don't. I think I'll catch some rest." He slouched in the corner of the car, resting his head against the window. I drove on, as proud as if I'd just taken the checkered flag at Indianapolis.

The sun dropped behind a thick bank of clouds in the west, luring us into our first full night on the road. I drove for eight hours before Dan took over. We were maintaining our average at 83.5 mph. As we reached the New Mexico border, a nasty thunderstorm lit the sky with orange fireballs and sent sheets of rain pelting against the windshield. It turned to sleet, and thickets of fog lurked in the dips of the highway. But I slept. With a man like Dan Gurney at the wheel, I think I could have rested if we'd been traversing the South Col of Mt. Everest.

We reached Albuquerque in the twenty-fourth hour of our trip, convinced that not one of our competitors was within three states of us. As we stopped at Gallup, New Mexico, we spotted several approaching cars with their grillework smudged with snow. We had just crested the Continental Divide and were heading for the high country of eastern Arizona. If we were to encounter ice, it would be in this dark and desolate stretch. I called the Highway Patrol from a gas station, while the attendant leisurely filled the tank and Gurney sipped a can of hot soup from a vending machine. We were getting cocky, and the urgency of our earlier gas stops had given way to a kind of relaxed elegance reserved for big winners. The phone operator at the Highway Patrol was vague: some snow squalls, some fog, perhaps a little ice, but nothing alarming. With the temperature sitting somewhere in the low thirties I took the wheel and headed for the mountains, knowing that conditions were perfect for hellish weather.

I might as well have talked to the Highway Patrol in Honolulu. The lights of Gallup still winked in the valley below when the highway became sheathed in a thick layer of slush, punctuated by long stretches of hard ice. First came the fog, then fat lumps of wet snow that flung themselves into our headlights, cutting visibility to zero. The Ferrari was slewing all over the road. It was nearly uncontrollable, and we couldn't understand why our wonderful machine had become so inept in the face of this nasty but hardly unusual squall. Dan figured it out. He recalled that the Kirk White crew had increased the tire pressure to forty pounds for added safety and efficiency in the high-speed, dry stretches. Surely they hadn't anticipated snow. The tires, of course! As we were debating whether or not to stop and cut the pressure to perhaps twenty-six pounds—which would mean a double penalty with more time lost when we hit the desert to reinflate—a quartet of headlights blazed in my mirrors. A car was overtaking us at high speed, seemingly navigating the ice without difficulty. It disappeared in a patch of fog, then surged alongside and swept past. It was a cream-colored Cadillac. Gurney and I paid it little attention, still engrossed in strategy talk about what to do with our slipping tires.

"Jesus Christ, wait a minute!" I yelled as Dan was in midsentence. "That Cadillac. That thing had New York plates! That couldn't be those three guys from Boston!" Or could it? Stunned, even horrified that any other competitor could be that close, we pressed on, trying to narrow the distance between us and the fleeing Sedan deVille. "If those guys are with us, where are the PRDA and some of the others that left earlier?" Gurney wondered. "In the lead, hell, we may be dead last!" I said bitterly.

The lights of the agricultural inspection station on the New Mexico-Arizona border loomed out of the fog and snow. A car was stopped under the canopy. Its trunk was up. A smiling man with a heavy shock of black hair was standing beside the machine—a cream-colored Cadillac with New York plates—while a uniformed official probed through the luggage.

"Oh, shit, that's Larry Opert," I moaned. "Those are the guys, and they're blowing our doors off!" They squirted away into the night as we stopped for our inspection. Real-

izing there was precious little room for any dangerous
quantities of wormy peaches or infected chickens to be
stowed on board the Ferrari, the officer let us pass after a
few routine questions. Our cockiness of a few miles back
had given way to shocked despair. Our only comfort lay in
the knowledge that the Caddy had started about twenty
minutes earlier and was, therefore, still behind us on
elapsed time. But what about the others? Surely *somebody*
was in front of the Caddy. "Us cruising across half the
damn country figuring we were hundreds of miles ahead,
what a bad joke that was," I mumbled as I rushed through
the black, fog-shrouded night. Fortunately, the roads were
improving, and while they remained wet, the ice was dis-
appearing. The fog lifted for a minute, and we saw their
taillights, perhaps a mile in front. As the road and visibility
cleared, we began to gnaw at their advantage, although the
Cadillac seemed to be running in the neighborhood of 100
mph on the straight stretches. Mile after mile we traveled,
losing them for long periods in the gloom, then catching
tantalizing glints of red up ahead. We had them in sight by
the time the outskirts of Winslow, Arizona, were breached.
They pulled into a gas station. As they leaped out under
the brightly lit canopy, I gave them a blast of the Ferrari's
air horns. They waved wildly as we accelerated past, no
doubt figuring we would have to stop soon ourselves. We
had chased them for over one hundred miles in a frantic
period that seemed to have been condensed into minutes.
Most of the road between Winslow and Flagstaff, fifty-eight
miles away, was deserted, dry Interstate, and I kept the Ferrari humming along at a steady 125 mph—a speed that
could not be exceeded without overrunning the range of
our headlights.

We were fully awake now, vibrating with the idea of the
newfound competition. We had not sought it out; in fact we
would have been perfectly contented to putter on toward
California at a leisurely pace. But now that the Cadillac
was surely thundering down the road behind us, its gas

tank topped off and set to run for hours, we readied ourselves to play our trump cards. That meant Dan would take
over at Flagstaff, in preparation for a run down our secret
shortcut—a pair of moves that might put us back into the
lead. My earlier run with Moon Trash had revealed that by
taking Arizona Route 89 south to Prescott, then cutting toward the desert and Interstate 10, we could trim at least
half an hour off the trip. To our knowledge, everyone else
would take the conventional old Route 66–Interstate 40
network that was slightly shorter but more congested. Ad-
mittedly, our route was more dangerous. It involved negotiating the endless switchbacks on the fifteen-mile stretch
of Route 89 through the Prescott National Forest and the
murderous plunge down a mountainside south of Yarnell,
where the road featured minimal guard-rails and thousand-
foot drop-offs.

Our stop for gas in Flagstaff was slow, simply because
the pumps of that particular station moved fuel into our
tank at a rather slow rate. By the time we got underway
again, with Dan driving, the Cadillac had caught up. We
immediately passed it after returning to the interstate.
Opert and Co. were running the big crock at its maximum,
perhaps 115 mph, and it was easy to see how they had not
lost any time with their stop. Their tank was smaller, and
therefore more quickly filled, and their top speed at night
was only a few miles per hour less than ours. Ergo, they
were back in contention.

Gurney was opening gobs of distance on the Caddy as we
rushed down the winding, pine-bordered four-lane. It was a
lovely stretch of road, made even more beautiful by the thick
layer of snow that had fallen on the trees earlier in the night.
But the highway surface seemed clear, and Dan was running
125 mph when we sailed onto a bridge that was part of a
long, downhill bend to the left. It was covered with a glaze of
ice. Suddenly Gurney was jabbering, and his hands began a
series of blinding twists of the wheel, "This is glare ice! Glare

ice! This is *bleeding glare ice!*" he repeated with increasing volume as he slashed at the steering wheel. I had been in the middle of a statement about something (I cannot recall the exact subject), and I remember that I kept on blathering throughout the trip across the bridge, as if my brain had decided that if I did not acknowledge Gurney's alarm, perhaps the ice would go away. Thanks to the talents of Gurney, we traversed the bridge with merely a slight twitch of the Ferrari's tail. Because he so skillfully maintained control of the car, only he will ever know how far beyond the ragged edge we had traveled.

"That's enough of that shit," said Gurney firmly as he slowed down. "Race or no race, we aren't going to wipe ourselves out on ice like that. Man, that was scary, and I don't mind telling you I didn't like it one bit!"

"God, I wonder about the Cadillac. I sure hope those guys get across that stretch all right," I said. We cruised onward, our speed reduced to a modest 70 mph. I was relieved to see the Caddy's lights pop up behind us. They had slowed, indicating they, too, had encountered a few thrills on the bridge.

"That would have been a helluva crash," I mused. "And just think, not a soul within miles to see it. Most of your crashes took place in front of thousands of people. What a switch this would have been." I was talking rather aimlessly, trying to get our minds off the recent adventure. "That crash business. I get so tired of telling people who don't understand motor racing that fans don't go to races to see smashups."

"That's crap," Dan said edgily.

"Huh?"

"That's crap about people not wanting to see crashes. *Of course* they want to see crashes. They want to be where the action is. That's a natural thing. If you were in a rowboat in the middle of the ocean, which would you rather see sail past, the Queen Mary or the *Titanic?*"

"I get your point. But I still don't think people actually *like* to see death and destruction," I said.

"I agree. Very few people at races want to see anybody get killed. Wild crashes are all right, but they don't ask for blood. But I'll tell you this: *if* it was going to happen anyway, you'd be surprised how many of them would rather see it than not," said Dan.

"I guess I'm double happy that we didn't crash on that bridge," I said.

"Why?"

"Because if you're right, think of all the folks we'd have deprived of a little healthy entertainment."

A tactical problem was arising. With the Cadillac cruising behind us, it was possible that they would trail after us on our shortcut. The turn to Route 89 was only a few miles ahead at Ash Fork, and we somehow had to get the Caddy out of sight before then. Outrunning them was impossible, considering the treacherous roads. Our only choice was to let them pass, then drop back and make our turn as they sped ahead.

"Hey, slow down and pull over on the shoulder," I told Dan. "Maybe they'll just drive past and we'll let em' get out of sight before restarting."

Gurney stopped the Ferrari on the roadside. The Cadillac pulled over, too, drawing alongside as it came to a halt. We switched off our engines and sat there in the still, clear mountain night. The three men in the Cadillac looked haggard and hollow-eyed, obviously fatigued from the run.

"How'd you guys like that icy bridge?" Dan asked through his open window.

"Bad shit. We thought we'd had it," said a voice from inside the Caddy.

We chatted for a few minutes about the various adventures we had encountered. They reported that so far they'd been stopped by the police four times. Gurney started the Ferrari's engine, preparing to leave. The Cadillac hesitated, as if to follow us onto the road in the original order. "Go ahead. You guys go first," said Dan casually. "After all, we've got a twenty-minute lead on you." Taking the bait, the Cadillac scurried away and rushed down the road. We followed at a discreet distance, letting them get half a mile ahead. By the time we reached the Route 89 turnoff, they were out of sight.

Thanks to the lower altitude, the road to Prescott was bare, clear of ice or any evidence of precipitation. It was a wide, level stretch of two-lane, virtually deserted, and Gurney ran the entire fifty-one miles with the speedometer needle glued on 130 mph. Whisking through Prescott and not seeing a soul on its streets, we plunged into the national forest. Mile after mile of tight mountainside switchbacks whispered underneath us. The masterful timing and discipline of Gurney became more apparent with each passing yard. I sat there in admiration, watching him run quickly and easily through the nasty turns, never squealing a tire, never wasting a motion on the steering wheel. Each corner was negotiated with a precision of line that seemed to place the car in perfect position for the next, until we hurried onto the open road again with me wondering why I had thought the Prescott National Forest was so difficult in the first place. I had witnessed a virtuoso playing with a fine instrument, and it came to me that this had to be the peak of excellence that every driver must aspire to. Surely all men cannot be Gurneys, nor all cars Ferraris, but such lofty goals still must remain, as opposed to the current egalitarianism that presumes all drivers are helpless dolts who must be packaged in mediocre, crash-proof capsules, lest they hurt themselves. The same mentality would determine that because a Van Cliburn appears only in every few million piano students, all piano lessons must be restricted to the teaching of "Chopsticks."

The nasty cut beyond Yarnell was traveled with similar ease, and suddenly we were on the desert floor. Flat, open road lay between us and Los Angeles. Dawn lit the way, and Gurney upped the pace to 140 mph across the desolation. Not even a stray jackrabbit or a tumbleweed was moving in the morning stillness; only the rounded, bullet-shaped Ferrari shrieking southward toward Interstate 10 and possible victory.

He caught us on a back street in Quartzsite, Arizona. I'd spotted his car, a mud-brown Dodge Highway Patrol sedan, parked in front of a run-down café at the roadside. The car had been empty, indicating that he'd been having his morning coffee when we'd ripped past, doubtlessly rattling the windows in the little place. I'd told Gurney about the car, then kept my eyes focused on the café, watching for movement. I saw headlights flick on. "He's coming. He's chasing us."

"He'll never catch us," Dan said firmly.

"He's gaining. He must be running one hundred and forty miles an hour!" I reported.

We sat there, speeding along in limbo, trying to figure out what to do. There was no sense trying to elude him on a side road. There were no side roads. Outrunning him was out of the question. A short distance ahead was the Arizona-California border on the Colorado River. He could easily radio ahead and stop us at the agricultural inspection station. We drove onward, as if in a trance, letting him close the gap.

"We'll turn off in Quartzsite and get some gas. Maybe he'll miss us," said Gurney. He sailed onto an off-ramp and scuttled down a back street. Sighting an empty self-service gas station, he braked the Ferrari to a stop. Perhaps our pursuer in the mud-brown Dodge hadn't seen us get off the interstate.

Perhaps he had. In fact, we had barely shut off the Ferrari's engine when the boxy form of the Dodge, its twin gumball roof light flashing crazily, skidded to a halt in the gravel beside us. A tall patrolman in a starched khaki uniform leaped out. He was wearing a crash helmet. His glands still pulsing from the pursuit, his feathers ruffled in a kind of cock-rooster triumph, he marched over to Gurney and curtly demanded his license and registration. Little more was said as he strode back to his car and removed a pad and pencil. We stood there, the silence broken only by the furry, electronic jabbering from his radio and the hushed background rumble of an occasional passing truck. He obviously recognized Gurney, and for a few minutes hope rose in us that he might issue a stern warning and send us on our way. But he kept on writing. A summons was being issued, and a hardness crept across Dan's face.

Ripping the ticket off the pad and handing it to Gurney, the highway patrolman, as if to signal the end of official business, turned to regard the Ferrari for a moment, then asked rather affably, "Just how fast *will* that thing go?"

"C'mon out on the freeway, and we'll let you find out," Gurney snapped.

Fortunately, the officer chose to take Dan's crack as an attempt at humor and let us go. Although he had spared us the agony of being dragged off to a justice of the peace, which would have consumed perhaps an hour, the incident had used up at least ten minutes. "That does it, we've probably lost for sure," I said dejectedly as we pulled back on the interstate. "What really kills me about a deal like that is the whole absurd logic of high-speed pursuit. If we are being unsafe at one hundred twenty miles per hour, isn't he at least *doubling* the hazard by driving even faster to catch us?"

"It's simple enough," said Gurney. "Those guys are just like you and me; they like to drive fast. Imagine having a license to go flat-out anytime you wanted. Just look at this bleeding highway, for example." Ahead lay a black asphalt expanse of four-lane that stretched to the horizon. It was deserted. "And the speed limit is sixty-five miles per hour. No wonder people crash out here. They die of boredom."

An evil smile spread across Gurney's face. "He was wondering how fast this thing will go. Let's find out." The Ferrari began to gain speed, whisking easily to 150 mph. The car felt smooth and steady. There was not much wind noise, considering the velocity. "There's one hundred seventy!" said Gurney. The needle pushed its way around the big dial, then stabilized at 172 mph. Gurney laughed. "This son of a bitch *really* runs," he said in amazement. "And it's rock steady." He took his left hand off the wheel, and we powered along toward Los Angeles, the Ferrari rushing through the desert morning at 172 mph.

"You think we ought to turn back and answer the cop's question?" I asked. But our amusement from the 172-mph run was only temporary. As we slipped back to a more normal cruising speed, we both decided that the delay from the arrest had ended our chances of winning the Cannonball. "Those other guys have to be miles ahead by now," I grumbled. We stopped for gasoline in Indio, California, where our general discouragement led to more torpor and lost time. Once on the road again, with the end in sight, we managed to perk up, drawing on our final reservoirs of energy. "Listen, at least we ought to try to make the trip in under thirty-six hours. If we can do that, we can't shame ourselves too badly," said Gurney.

We were back in it again, running hard. To reach our goal, we had a little over two hours to run about 130 miles —practically all of it over heavily patrolled Los Angeles freeways. "You watch out the back for the Highway Patrol, and I'll run as fast as I can," said Dan. I turned in my seat, scanning the off-ramps and the passing traffic for the familiar black-and-white California Highway Patrol cruisers. Gurney drove through the building traffic with incredible smoothness, seldom braking and never making severe lane changes. We took the Riverside Freeway to the Newport, up the Garden Grove to the San Diego. Traffic was heavy, but we still had a chance. We turned off at the Western Avenue exit and bustled through three miles of heavy urban congestion, heading for Redondo Beach and the Portofino Inn. The masts and spars of the yachts moored in the Redondo Beach marina appeared, and Dan accelerated the Ferrari the last few yards into the inn's parking lot. I was out of the car before it stopped moving and sprinted into the lobby, where a pair of mildly shocked bellhops looked up to see an unshaven, grubby form rush up to the desk. The clerk punched our ticket.

Our elapsed time was thirty-five hours and fifty-four minutes. What's more, no one else had arrived. We were the first car to finish. Unless Moon Trash or the Bruerton brothers bettered our time, we were the winners. A couple of photographers appeared, a reporter from the Torrance *Daily Breeze* showed up, and a representative of the local Chamber of Commerce brought along the bikini-clad "Miss Redondo Beach" to peck our cheeks for the cameras. Groggy and filthy, we staggered upstairs to a room to shower and shave. Suddenly we felt great. The tiredness drained out of our bones as the impact of what we'd managed became clear. We'd crossed the nation, a matter of nearly 2,900 miles, in less than a day and a half.

With the Pacific Ocean puffing a soft breeze into the balcony window, Dan ran a comb through his hair and turned serious. "You know," he said, "the best thing about this whole deal is the fact that we came the entire bleeding distance without bothering *anybody*. Nobody else even knew we were on the road."

"Except that cop," I mused.

"I don't count him. I'm talking about the average guys out there with their families. We did it all without them having the slightest idea of what was going on. As long as you can do something without endangering anybody or inconveniencing them, how can you say that something like the Cannonball Baker is wrong?"

Leaving that question unanswered, we went back to the lobby to find that the PRDA had arrived. As I expected, they had been forced to make a fuel stop in Albuquerque. They had also engaged in a two-hundred-mile duel with the Cadillac, running with them from Needles, California, to a point where they had snuck away on a shortcut in Los Angeles. Their time was thirty-six hours and forty-seven minutes, and they hadn't been bothered by the police. Seven minutes later the Cadillac thundered in. They'd been arrested once more in Needles, giving them a grand total of five speeding tickets for the journey. How had they gone so quickly? By running the car flatout between stops, they reported. The Cadillac had survived the trip without difficulty, save for consuming a quart of oil and evidencing some prematurely worn tires. They faced only one more problem: the owner wasn't expecting delivery of his car for four more days!

Then came the Little Rock van and Moon Trash, both of which had encountered minor mechanical problems that had slowed their pace. Word was received that the MG had blown its clutch in Columbus, Ohio, and had limped back to New York. As the hours passed, it became obvious that no one was going to beat our time. For whatever it meant, we had won the Cannonball Baker Sea-to-Shining-Sea Memorial Trophy Dash. The *Los Angeles Times* mentioned the race briefly, noting our time and quoting Dan as testifying that "we never exceeded one hundred and seventy-five miles per hour." They no doubt thought he was kidding around when he said that.

I slept a night on the edge of the Pacific and headed home, alone. Dan was back at work in his race shop, preparing a new Eagle that he was convinced would be the fastest Indianapolis racing car in history. It was the Ferrari and I. Sympatico. I took a southern route, heading for Texas, to avoid the mountain squalls. It was warm and sunny, and the big car was as strong and supple as ever. I felt great. I felt like a winner. I stopped in a music store and bought some 8-track stereo tapes for the car's tape deck. We hadn't used it on the trip, but at a more leisurely pace on the way home, they would provide pleasant company. Country-and-western seemed appropriate. Cruising across New Mexico, with the guys high in the cabs of the giant Kenworth and Peterbilt semi-tractors tossing friendly waves, I pondered what the whole thing had meant: begin-

ning with those uncertain gropings at the wheel of Bob
Bondurant's Datsun, Watkins Glen, Bridgehampton, Michigan International, and on to the Cannonball. I was a good
driver, I had learned that much. But I would never be a
true racer. I seemed to lack the power of concentration, the
final hunger to sacrifice everything for victory. A lot, but
not everything.

A yellow 4-4-2 Oldsmobile Cutlass appeared in the rearview mirror. It was running fast, coming up on me at an impressive rate. Two guys were on board, and I sensed that they
were looking for a race. They drew even, and we ran along for
a way nose to nose. I looked over to catch eager grins on their
faces. I smiled back and slipped the Ferrari from fifth to
fourth gear. We were running a steady 100 mph when the
Olds leaped ahead. I let him have a car-length lead before
opening the Ferrari's tap. The big cat burst forward, its pipes
whooping that lovely siren song, and shot past the startled
pair in the Oldsmobile. I glanced over at them to see their
faces covered with amazement. Like most of the populace,
they had no comprehension of an automobile that would accelerate from 100 mph that quickly. The Ferrari yowled up to
150 mph without effort, leaving the Olds a minuscule speck
of yellow in the mirror.

I slowed and turned up the volume on the stereo. Buck
Owens and his Buckaroos were singing "I've Got a Tiger by
the Tail."

"Yates, you are a silly son of a bitch," I said out loud. And I
laughed all the way to Las Cruces.